The Changing Position
of Philanthropy in
the American Economy

FRANK G. DICKINSON

WITH AN INTRODUCTION

BY SOLOMON FABRICANT

Occasional Paper 110

National Bureau of Economic Research
New York 1970
Distributed by Columbia University Press
New York and London

Relation of the Directors to the Work and Publications
of the National Bureau of Economic Research

1. The object of the National Bureau of Economic Research is to ascertain and to present to the public important economic facts and their interpretation in a scientific and impartial manner. The Board of Directors is charged with the responsibility of ensuring that the work of the National Bureau is carried on in strict conformity with this object.

2. The President of the National Bureau shall submit to the Board of Directors, or to its Executive Committee, for their formal adoption all specific proposals for research to be instituted.

3. No research report shall be published until the President shall have submitted to each member of the Board the manuscript proposed for publication, and such information as will, in his opinion and in the opinion of the author, serve to determine the suitability of the report for publication in accordance with the principles of the National Bureau. Each manuscript shall contain a summary drawing attention to the nature and treatment of the problem studied, the character of the data and their utilization in the report, and the main conclusions reached.

4. For each manuscript so submitted, a special committee of the Board shall be appointed by majority agreement of the President and Vice Presidents (or by the Executive Committee in case of inability to decide on the part of the President and Vice Presidents), consisting of three directors selected as nearly as may be one from each general division of the Board. The names of the special manuscript committee shall be stated to each Director when the manuscript is submitted to him. It shall be the duty of each member of the special manuscript committee to read the manuscript. If each member of the manuscript committee signifies his approval within thirty days of the transmittal of the manuscript, the report may be published. If at the end of that period any member of the manuscript committee withholds his approval, the President shall then notify each member of the Board, requesting approval or disapproval of publication, and thirty days additional shall be granted for this purpose. The manuscript shall then not be published unless at least a majority of the entire Board who shall have voted on the proposal within the time fixed for the receipt of votes shall have approved.

5. No manuscript may be published, though approved by each member of the special manuscript committee, until forty-five days have elapsed from the transmittal of the report in manuscript form. The interval is allowed for the receipt of any memorandum of dissent or reservation, together with a brief statement of his reasons, that any member may wish to express; and such memorandum of dissent or reservation shall be published with the manuscript if he so desires. Publication does not, however, imply that each member of the Board has read the manuscript, or that either members of the Board in general or the special committee have passed on its validity in every detail.

6. Publications of the National Bureau issued for informational purposes concerning the work of the Bureau and its staff, or issued to inform the public of activities of Bureau staff, and volumes issued as a result of various conferences involving the National Bureau shall contain a specific disclaimer noting that such publication has not passed through the normal review procedures required in this resolution. The Executive Committee of the Board is charged with review of all such publications from time to time to ensure that they do not take on the character of formal research reports of the National Bureau, requiring formal Board approval.

7. Unless otherwise determined by the Board or exempted by the terms of paragraph 6, a copy of this resolution shall be printed in each National Bureau publication.

(Resolution adopted October 25, 1926, and revised February 6, 1933,
February 24, 1941, and April 20, 1968)

Contents

Tables

Note

Frank Dickinson worked on the final stages of his study of "The Changing Position of Philanthropy in the American Economy" while suffering from what proved to be a mortal illness. He managed, however, to complete a draft of a manuscript, and then to respond to some of the suggestions made by a staff reading committee. He was also able to look over the introduction to the study prepared by Solomon Fabricant.

Dr. Dickinson's death in September 1967 made more difficult and more time consuming than usual the task of checking and editing the manuscript. But with the help of Maude Pech and Joan Tron, the work has finally been completed.

Because Dr. Dickinson was unable to oversee the final editing, we cannot be sure that he would have approved every change that was made in the manuscript left by him. However, the editors tried hard to adhere to the viewpoint he took.

We record our heartfelt thanks to Dr. Dickinson, and to Mrs. Dickinson as well, for a task completed under great difficulties. The National Bureau is grateful, also, to the Russell Sage Foundation for grants made to finance the study. We should like to acknowledge as well the advice and assistance, throughout the study, of an advisory committee consisting of: F. Emerson Andrews, Foundation Library Center (ret.); Gary S. Becker, Columbia University; Merle Curti, University of Wisconsin; Richard Eells, Columbia University; Lyman Ford, United Community Funds and

Councils of America; Raymond W. Goldsmith, Yale University; Covington Hardee, Clark Carr and Ellis; Rembrandt C. Hiller, Jr., Sears Roebuck and Company; C. Harry Kahn, Rutgers University; Thomas Karter, Social Security Administration; Herbert E. Klarman, Downstate Medical Center, State University of New York; Benson Y. Landis (dec.), National Council of Churches; Ray M. Peterson, Equitable Life Assurance Society (ret.); John A. Pollard (dec.), Council for Financial Aid to Education; W. Homer Turner, United States Steel Foundation; Walter M. Upchurch, Jr., Shell Companies Foundation; Donald Young, Rockefeller University.

The manuscript was read and approved for publication by a committee of the Board of Directors consisting of Erwin D. Canham, Crawford H. Greenewalt, and Willard L. Thorp. In addition, Dr. Thorp wrote two formal "Director's Comments," which are appended to Chapters 4 and 9, respectively.

Geoffrey H. Moore
Vice President—Research

Philanthropy in the American Economy

An Introduction

SOLOMON FABRICANT

INTERESTING facts about the structure of our economy, as well as the generosity of our people, are revealed in Dr. Dickinson's report on the changing position of philanthropy in the United States during the period from 1929 to 1959—one of a number of publications resulting from the National Bureau's study of the economic aspects of philanthropy.[1] As we reflect upon the facts revealed in this report, important questions arise concerning the respective roles of philanthropy, collective action through government, and the pursuit of self-interest, in promoting the well-being of the community at large. To note the outstanding facts and point to some of the questions they raise is the purpose of this introduction. It will, I hope, serve also to complement Dickinson's report.[2]

[1] Some preliminary results were presented in Frank G. Dickinson's "The Growth of Private and Public Philanthropy," in Eastern States Health Education Conference, *Voluntary Action and the State,* New York Academy of Medicine, 1961, and my "An Economist's View of Philanthropy," *Proceedings of the American Philosophical Society,* April 1961. Both papers are reprinted in F. G. Dickinson (ed.), *Philanthropy and Public Policy,* New York, National Bureau of Economic Research, 1962. This volume includes also papers prepared for a Conference on Philanthropy sponsored by the National Bureau and the Merrill Center for Economics: on fiscal and other economic aspects of philanthropy, by W. S. Vickrey; on a theory of philanthropy, by K. E. Boulding; on hospitals and philanthropy, by Eli Ginzberg; and on philanthropy and the business corporation, by Covington Hardee. In addition, the book includes two papers on the conference itself: its highlights, as seen by F. G. Dickinson, and reflections on the discussion, by W. L. Thorp. Ralph L. Nelson's monograph, *Economic Factors in the Growth of Corporate Giving,* will soon be published jointly by the NBER and the Russell Sage Foundation.

[2] The present paper includes some portions of the paper read before the American Philosophical Society. I have drawn also on Chapter 7 of my *Trend of Government Activity in the United States since 1900* (NBER, 1952). My indebtedness to Dickinson, and to Nelson who prepared some of the major estimates of private giving, will be obvious. I have benefited also from discussions with the members of the NBER advisory committee on the philanthropy study and the participants in the Conference on Philanthropy; from comments on this

I

Especially noteworthy is the fact that philanthropic giving—private and governmental giving "in which generosity is the primary motive," as Dickinson puts it—rose much more rapidly than did payments for commodities and services bought. In 1929, private giving in the form of charity to individuals and of contributions to churches, schools, hospitals, and similar institutions, was about 2 per cent of the value of the gross national product. By 1959, according to Dickinson's calculations, the fraction had risen to 3 per cent. Governmental giving to meet needs classified under such budget categories as welfare, health, and education, which was 3 per cent of GNP in 1929, had jumped to 9 per cent by 1959. Total philanthropic giving, then, had risen from 5 per cent of GNP to 12 per cent over the thirty-year period. To judge from less formal estimates available for recent years, the high level of 1959 has at least been maintained since. In Dickinson's vivid language: "The economy now tithes. The scriptural one-tenth has been attained by a generous people!" [3]

Not everyone is willing to admit as "philanthropic" all, or even any, of the governmental payments included in these totals of philanthropic giving. Indeed, the doubts—which arise from strong views on national policy and not merely academic opinions concerning proper language— led to some of the most spirited moments of debate in the discussions held in the National Bureau-Merrill Center Conference on Philanthropy and Public Policy.

Yet whatever they are called, the governmental payments classified as philanthropic by Dickinson belong in a discussion of the place of philanthropy in the American economy. If not themselves philanthropic, they are, in the technical language of economists, "substitutes," and

paper, particularly by Geoffrey H. Moore and Ralph Nelson; and from a reading of the background papers prepared for the conference, of the chapter on philanthropic contributions in C. Harry Kahn's *Personal Deductions in the Federal Income Tax* (published for the National Bureau in 1960 by the Princeton University Press), and two doctoral dissertations—M. K. Taussig's *The Charitable Contribution Deduction in the Federal Income Tax* (Thesis, Massachusetts Institute of Technology, 1965), and R. A. Schwartz's *Private Philanthropic Contributions—An Economic Analysis* (Thesis, Columbia University, 1966).

[3] *Philanthropy and Public Policy,* p. 30.

probably "close substitutes," for philanthropy. The increase in the scale of these governmental payments is therefore relevant, even when the primary concern is private philanthropy.

But there are also other "substitutes" for philanthropy besides the governmental payments to which Dickinson points. Our society has developed a variety of means to cope with the needs of its less fortunate members and to enhance the well-being of all. Governmental activities classified under budget categories that do not meet Dickinson's criteria of philanthropy may also help to avoid illness, or lessen its severity, or assure a family's capacity to carry the burden when it falls upon them. And the same may be said of activities in the market sector of the economy that no one would consider philanthropic. Indeed, it is not going too far afield to recall that the moral justification of our type of economic system is its great effectiveness in harnessing self-interest for the benefit of the entire community. The economic activities covered by the market portion of GNP now serve the common good more effectively than before. This improvement is also an advance in the battle against misfortune and the wider struggle to enhance the well-being of our citizens. It also, then, is in some degree a "substitute" for philanthropic giving, and should be mentioned in discussing the changing position of philanthropy in the American economy.

People think of philanthropy in terms of the motives that spur it, of course, as well as in terms of its objectives. From this point of view, too, our perspective must be wide when we consider the position of philanthropy in our economy. For philanthropy is spread wider through economic life than most people will recognize at first sight. Philanthropic giving, we say, is motivated by generosity; and ordinary economic transactions, by self-interest. But as Dickinson is careful to note, while generosity is the primary, it is not necessarily the sole, motive of philanthropic giving. Similarly, self-interest may be primary but it is not always the only motive in ordinary economic transactions. If there is a touch of philanthropy even in the market place—just as there is a touch, or more than a touch, of self-interest among the motives in philanthropic giving—it deserves notice.

There are other questions that invite attention. Why has governmental philanthropy risen in relation to national product? Why has not private philanthropy fallen, with governmental giving rising so rapidly? Have higher income tax rates, coupled with the deductibility of philanthropic contributions on tax returns, played a large role in supporting private philanthropy?

II

If we are to understand the role of philanthropy in economic life, we must first note the diverse ways in which the philanthropic motive manifests itself in the life of a market economy such as ours.

Philanthropy, according to the dictionary, is "love towards mankind; practical benevolence towards man in general; the disposition to promote the well-being of one's fellow-men." If this is its meaning, philanthropy is present in more aspects of economic life than most of us are aware of. There is an element of philanthropy in many of our actions, which we are prone to overlook.

One reason for this is a tendency to let our definition of philanthropic purposes and philanthropic giving be influenced by the regulations of the Internal Revenue Service. We recognize, of course, that for tax purposes these regulations permit deduction of contributions to organizations but not to individuals, and we would all agree that contributions to persons, outside the family at any rate, belong in an aggregate of philanthropic giving. Few of us, however, wonder whether we should not depart in a similar way from tax regulations that permit the deduction of contributions to churches and veterans' organizations, but not of contributions to political parties or "propaganda" organizations—which also aim, or claim, to promote the well-being of man in general.

Another item omitted from the list of tax-deductible contributions— in this case because it is also omitted from the list of taxable incomes— is the income earned on the property of foundations, hospitals, universities, churches, and other nonprofit institutions, and put by them to philanthropic use. We may remember the money incomes derived from the endowments of these institutions. But the rental value of the plant and equipment they own and use for philanthropic purposes is often overlooked, perhaps because this rental is seldom recorded even in their own accounts.

Another reason why philanthropy is underestimated is that we usually define giving in a narrow way. We tend to forget that to forego income also is to give. Thus, the tax code permits the deduction, on tax returns, of contributions in cash or property, but not of contributions in the form of personal services or (in large part) of the services of property. Nobody keeps books on the time housewives or even corporate officials spend in philanthropic activities, but such contributions must make up a substantial sum, as Dickinson notes.

Every economist can point also to a less obvious sense in which philanthropy may be broader and its role larger than any ordinary figures on philanthropic giving would suggest. The clergyman or scientist who accepts an income lower than he could obtain in another respectable calling, because he prefers to occupy himself with work deemed to be of greater social value, also is making a philanthropic contribution. It is very similar to the contribution of time and money made by others in support of church or research institute. How much there is of this sort of giving is even more a matter of guesswork. I suspect there is a good deal.

Indeed, there is an element of something like philanthropy in almost every activity of economic life, when people temper their search for personal advantage with some regard for the welfare and opinions of their fellowmen. It is there in lesser degree and it is less calculated than in the choice of an occupation, but I do not believe it is negligible. No one is philosopher enough to disentangle the motives involved in restraining one's passions and one's selfishness. No one is able to decide how much of this restraint is to be credited to what is, in a literal sense, true philanthropy, how much to a calculation of one's long-run personal advantage, and how much merely to keeping within the law. However, if even a fraction of this kind of "giving" to society at large belongs in the realm of philanthropy, it is important to our assessment.

I have just said that no one is able to disentangle motives, and I cannot pretend to do so myself. But surely a philanthropic thread is woven also into many of our "purely selfish" motives. The desire to keep within the law is not entirely a wish to avoid confinement or a money fine. The fear and shame of violating the law is a reflection, in part, of one's regard for the welfare and opinions of his fellowmen. Similarly, the acceptance of a lower rate of pay than one could obtain in another occupation, because one likes to do basic research or social work, is not only a response to one's "likes." Why do people "like" to add to knowledge or to work with people needing help? It is easy to recognize the selfish

element in philanthropic giving. We should not overlook the philanthropic element in our selfish actions.

Indeed, in this broad sense philanthropy is a necessary condition of
social existence, and the extent to which it is developed influences an
economy's productiveness. For decent conduct pays large returns to
society as a whole, partly in the form of a higher level of national income
than would otherwise be possible. Underdeveloped countries are learn-
ing that, despite their hurry to reach desired levels of economic efficiency,
time must be taken to develop the kind of business ethics, respect for
the law, and treatment of strangers that keep a modern industrial society
productive. Widening of the concepts of family loyalty and tribal brotherhood to include love of man "in general" is a necessary step in the
process of economic development.

I have been pointing to the philanthropic element in our ordinary
work-a-day activities. But I must add that if philanthropic giving is
"primarily" motivated by "generosity," to repeat Dickinson's words, this
is to say also that there may be a secondary element of self-interest in
the motivation. Although we are less likely to overlook it—it is easy to
notice the mote in another man's eye—it requires more than the bare
mention I have given it.

The "economic" return a giver may expect, in addition to the "un-
selfish" satisfaction of helping others, may take the form of better relations—or the avoidance of worse relations—with customers, employees,
or the general public. Presumably, giving by business corporations is
likely to be heavily influenced by such considerations, and therefore not
easily distinguishable from advertising or employee fringe benefits. But
giving by individuals also is not always free of such motives; in contribut-
ing to a hospital building fund, for example, there may be the sensible
wish to help ensure the availability of hospital facilities in case of personal need.

A rather different kind of example is provided by contributions to
churches. Religious institutions may be viewed not only as philanthropic
organizations but also, and even primarily, as organizations producing
certain services required by their members. Seen from this standpoint,
the philanthropic giving is less than the total contribution paid to a
religious institution by the wealthier (or more faithful) parishioner. It is
only the excess over the cost of the services he received. The beneficiaries
are those who contribute less than the cost of the services they receive.

Presumably the same qualification can be put on contributions to other membership organizations, such as those of veterans, which also are included in the Internal Revenue tax-deductible list of philanthropic institutions.

Against this background, let us now take a closer look at Dickinson's estimates of private philanthropic giving, in order to identify the particular aspects of philanthropic activity covered by the estimates, and to see how well the estimates cover them.

III

Philanthropic giving, as already stated, is defined as "giving in which generosity is the primary motive." Or, to cite the fuller definition with which Dickinson begins, philanthropic giving is "giving away money (or its equivalent) to persons outside the family and to institutions without a definite or immediate *quid pro quo* for purposes traditionally considered philanthropic." After scouting out the available information, Dickinson put together estimates of the following items to make up his total of private philanthropic giving:

	Million Dollars		Percentages of GNP	
	1929	1959	1929	1959
Gifts of living donors:				
To institutions—tax deductible	1,084	8,545	1.04	1.77
To persons outside the family—not tax deductible	434	3,418	.42	.71
Charitable bequests—tax deductible	154	810	.15	.17
Gifts by business corporations—tax deductible	32	482	.03	.10
Money income and imputed income on the property of foundations and other institutions used for philanthropic purposes	517	1,675	.50	.35
Total private giving	2,221	14,930	2.13	3.09

Three questions arise: the exclusions; the adequacy of the estimates of what is included; and whether the omissions and errors in the statistics raise serious doubts about the trend in private philanthropic giving.

The estimates, it can be seen, include tax-deductible gifts by living donors, estates, and business corporations; gifts by persons to persons outside the family, which are not tax-deductible; and the cash and imputed incomes on the endowment and other property of philanthropic or partly philanthropic institutions, which are neither taxable as income nor tax-deductible when used for philanthropic purposes. Dickinson's total for 1959 is half again as large as the total of tax-deductible contributions alone.

Not included are contributions to institutions omitted from the Internal Revenue's approved list, the value of volunteer services rendered in charitable causes, and giving in which "generosity," though not the primary motive, may not be entirely negligible. In a study of the national accounts recently begun at the National Bureau, John Kendrick provides a tentative estimate for one of these items, the value of "volunteer labor." It comes to as much as 1 per cent of the official GNP in 1929 and 2 per cent in 1965.[4] Inclusion of the estimate for this item alone would raise the ratio of private philanthropic giving to GNP to 3 per cent in 1929 and 5 per cent in 1959.

Dickinson's concept of private philanthropic giving, then, is broader than the concept built into the Internal Revenue code. But it is narrower than the concept that might be associated with philanthropy viewed in all its aspects. It is close to the traditional concept partly because that *is* the traditional concept, and partly also because adequate estimates of some of the items that Dickinson would have wanted to include could not be made.

Even the items included in Dickinson's total of private giving could be estimated only approximately. The largest item, the estimate of gifts by living donors to institutions, consists of contributions in cash and kind which are tax-deductible within specified limits. The limitations are unimportant, since very few persons or families make contributions in excess of the limits. More important is the fact that the contributions are shown only when deductions are itemized on the tax return. On most returns advantage is taken of the standard deduction, for it exceeds the amount that would otherwise be deductible. The Internal Revenue's tabulations of *Statistics of Income,* the primary source of the data on contributions actually deducted, must therefore be pieced out with estimates

----

[4] He warns that the estimate is subject to considerable revision. See *47th Annual Report* of the National Bureau of Economic Research, June 1967, p. 11.

for contributions by those using the "standard deduction," and also with estimates for those whose low incomes make filing of a return unnecessary. Some error in the estimates may result also from a tendency to exaggerate deductions for tax purposes, though there is a partial offset in contributions made but forgotten by tax-time.

A check against the estimates, and some information on the uses to which the funds are put, is provided by Dickinson's table of contributions received by institutions. This covers gifts from living donors and corporations, bequests, and income on endowments. In 1958 (estimates are not available for 1959), these receipts were as follows:

	Million Dollars
Religious organizations	4,036
Parochial schools	896
Higher education	1,057
Secular health	810
Secular welfare	950
Miscellaneous	344
Total	8,093

The sum of receipts in 1958 is less than the corresponding sum of contributions reported—roundly, $8,100 as against $9,800 million. In 1930, the earliest year available, the two were roughly equal, however. Reported receipts therefore rose less rapidly than did reported contributions —about 450 per cent as compared with almost 600 per cent. The two estimates are not strictly comparable—the receipts estimate, for example, does not cover all recipient institutions, and it is in part net of collection expenses—and some discrepancy is to be expected on that account. On the whole, therefore, the check broadly confirms the order of magnitude of the level of private giving, and also—though less closely—of its rise since 1929.

Much more doubtful is the estimate of gifts to persons. Because these are not deductible under the tax regulations, there are no tax statistics with which to start. Dickinson was compelled to make the estimate by assuming gifts to persons to be a constant percentage of gifts to institutions, basing this assumption on a variety of impressions, including some derived from consumer expenditure surveys made by the Bureau of Labor Statistics for the mid-1930's, 1950, and 1960–61. It is possible that the rise of institutionally organized philanthropy, together with (and in part on account of) the increase in income tax rates, led to a shift between 1929 and 1959 from direct person-to-person giving to giving through institutions. Had such a shift taken place, the rise in the estimate of person-to-person giving would be overstated. The BLS and other information available are not sufficient to eliminate the possibility entirely.

Since a major interest of many readers will be in the trend of private giving, it is well to ask what some alternative assumptions would do to the estimate of the trend. Suppose we were to assume that no rise had occurred in the ratio of person-to-person giving to GNP, and, further, that the trend reported by receipts was closer to the truth than that reported by contributions. On these assumptions, which Dickinson discarded as rather extreme, we would reach an estimate that indicated constancy, rather than a rise, in the ratio of total private giving to GNP. It should be stressed that even this estimate would not indicate a decline in the ratio.

There is a further question. A glance at the list of institutions receiving contributions shows that religious organizations received about half the contributions reported. If religious organizations were considered to be not philanthropic but rather membership organizations producing services for their members, a viewpoint mentioned above, total private giving would be very substantially reduced. But the rate of increase in private giving would be raised slightly, not lowered, if all or a constant fraction of the contributions to religious institutions were excluded. This, of course, is because there was a decline in the share of religious contributions in the total of private giving.

To return to Dickinson's estimates: Private philanthropic giving rose from less than three billion dollars in 1929 to almost fifteen billion in 1959. This is an increase of 570 per cent in "current dollars," of almost 300 per cent in dollars of constant purchasing power,[5] and of 170 per cent in such dollars per head of the population. Real income per capita also rose, and perhaps this provides the best backdrop against which to place the rise in real private philanthropic giving per capita. It amounts to comparing the rise in private giving directly with the rise in national product or income, as Dickinson does. As already mentioned, private

[5] The decline in the purchasing power of the dollar is judged by the rise in the consumer price index.

giving as a percentage of gross national product rose—from 2.1 per cent in 1929 to 3.1 per cent in 1959, if we accept the digit after the decimal point as significant. It rose more rapidly in relation to disposable personal income—from 2.6 per cent in 1929 to 4.4 per cent in 1959. Neither standard of comparison is quite satisfactory, as national income accountants know—the estimate of giving includes bequests, for example, which are not made from current income—and this is one reason why Dickinson uses several standards. However, any reasonable alternative would show a similar trend.

As we have seen, this estimate does not cover every aspect of philanthropy in economic life, and in some respects it may cover too much. While it corresponds fairly closely to what most people would consider to be philanthropic giving, the questions raised about the effect on the estimate if marginal items not included were added, or some included were subtracted, as well as the questions about the accuracy of the items included, cast some doubt on the estimate. For these reasons it seems best to express the trend in conservative language: Private philanthropic giving probably rose as rapidly, and perhaps more rapidly, than the national product between 1929 and 1959. There is very little doubt that private giving in real terms rose more rapidly than population.

IV

Government provides many free services and "gives away money" for many purposes. There are not only payments to unfortunates but also payments to persons (poor and otherwise) blanketed into the social security system at a ripe old age, when the system was started and when its coverage was broadened; not only disaster relief to farmers but also payments under the Agricultural Adjustment programs; not only public assistance but also work-relief; not only the free services of state employment agencies but also those of the police, the courts, and the military; not only free medical care but also free parks; not only domestic aid but also foreign aid; not only cash payments to libraries and museums but also the annual value of their exemption from property and income taxes.

Dickinson guided himself by the criteria specified in his definition of philanthropic giving—that the payments or services not only be "without

a definite or immediate *quid pro quo"* but also be "for purposes traditionally considered philanthropic." What he chose to include in his estimate
of public philanthropy is indicated by the following tabulation:

	Million Dollars		*Percentages of GNP*	
	1929	*1959*	*1929*	*1959*
Veterans' programs (excl.				
aftercost of war)	261	2,503	.25	.52
Public aid	68	4,088	.06	.85
Other welfare	95	1,091	.09	.23
Health and medical	428	3,413	.41	.71
Free schools	2,260	16,454	2.16	3.41
Social insurance (excl. insur-				
ance paid for by benefici-				
aries or employers)	—	14,506	—	3.01
Public housing	—	166	—	.03
Foreign aid (excl. military)	—	1,633	—	.34
Total	3,112	43,854	2.98	9.08

This tabulation summarizes under a few categories many different programs carried on at the several levels of government, federal, state and
local. The item of public aid, for example, includes a variety of programs
under such titles as old age assistance, aid to dependent children, aid
to the blind, aid to the permanently and totally disabled, "general" assistance, work programs, and surplus food distributed to needy persons. The
full list is given in Dickinson's detailed tables, and it was of course an
even fuller and more detailed list that he consulted before deciding which
governmental program fitted his concept of philanthropy.

Even with his criteria in mind, questions arise. Included are items
some people would exclude from an estimate of public philanthropy.
The social insurance item, they would insist, is insurance, not philanthropy, even though the present beneficiaries receive far more than would
be due them on actuarial principles; veterans' programs, even excluding
the aftercosts of war, constitute a payment for services rendered; and
free schools in a democracy are no more philanthropic than free roads.
Not included by Dickinson are items some would include. One is the
value of the property-tax exemption privilege enjoyed by private philan-

thropic institutions, which (I would guess) may have had a value of something like $500 million in 1959. In the discussions of Dickinson's preliminary estimates at the philanthropy conference there was more concern about his including too much than too little. In estimating the total he considers basic, therefore, Dickinson has tried to be conservative. More important, he has accompanied his estimate with a warning that it might be too inclusive for those who prefer a narrower definition of philanthropy, and has emphasized that the details he provides make it possible to fit other, narrower, concepts of public philanthropy.

From the point of view of those who prefer a total that includes all government outlays that can be thought of as philanthropy or as alternatives to, or substitutes for, private philanthropy, Dickinson's estimate is too low. All the items included by Dickinson, since they are for "purposes traditionally considered philanthropic," help to meet needs that have spurred private philanthropic giving. But not every governmental outlay or service that is for "purposes traditionally considered philanthropic" is included in Dickinson's total if it failed to meet his other criterion—that there be no "definite or immediate *quid pro quo.*" This is one reason why Dickinson's basic total of public domestic philanthropy is less (by about 15 or 20 per cent) than the corresponding total of domestic social welfare expenditures under public programs compiled by Ida C. Merriam of the Social Security Administration—the total from which Dickinson started when he prepared his estimate.

In Dickinson's basic total of public philanthropy, then, we have an estimate of governmental outlays on a major class of rather close substitutes for private philanthropy. While there can be differences of opinion on just what items belong here, and also on just how well government philanthropy can substitute for private philanthropy, there can be no doubt that governmental outlays "for purposes traditionally considered philanthropic" have grown very rapidly since 1929, both absolutely and in relation to private philanthropy. The story is one of more governmental operation in 1959 than in 1929 of the institutions that provide services of a philanthropic character, more payments of a philanthropic character by government to persons, more contributions by government to privately run institutions to support the philanthropic services provided by these institutions, and more governmental support in the form of taxes foregone.

V

Governmental philanthropy as estimated by Dickinson does not cover all the substitutes for private philanthropy that have grown in importance since 1929. Excluded from his estimate, and also from the larger total of social welfare expenditures published by the Social Security Administration, are governmental payments for such services as water supply, sanitation, and sewage disposal, many of which are supplied at less than full cost or even without specific charge. Perhaps these are not as close substitutes as is a public dispensary for a private hospital's free clinic, in the short run at least, but the rising volume of these and other governmental services—whether supplied free or not, whether for purposes traditionally considered philanthropic or not—must be mentioned in our discussion.

A major example of this other class of substitutes for private philanthropy is the social insurance paid for by employees or paid on their account by employers. The great bulk of old age, survivors, and disability insurance (OASDI) benefits was classified by Dickinson as public philanthropy because only about 5 per cent of the benefits paid out under the system since passage of the Social Security Act was met by employer and employee premiums (social security taxes) paid on behalf of the beneficiaries. On the other hand, workmen's compensation—which also appears in Mrs. Merriam's list of social welfare expenditures—is much closer to being an actuarially sound insurance system, and was therefore excluded by Dickinson from his category of public philanthropy. Benefits under this kind of insurance, as well as the excluded 5 per cent of OASDI benefits, belong in our list of substitutes because they help to meet "philanthropic-type needs" when they arise.

Social insurance is just one member of one class of arrangements constructed to meet philanthropic-type needs. Not only governmentally sponsored but also purely private insurance policies—which are bought in the market place and which no one would classify as philanthropy—have become increasingly important. Their spread and strengthening have made a major contribution to the ability of an individual or family to cope with accidents, ill-health, and death. When Pierce Williams' pioneering study on *The Purchase of Medical Care through Fixed Periodic*

Payment was published by the National Bureau in 1932, near the beginning of Dickinson's period, this kind of insurance was of small importance. Growth since then in these and other market provisions for meeting the needs of medical care, hospitalization, and the like, has been phenomenal. By 1950 over 8 million employees were already covered by insured basic medical plans. By 1959 the number covered had doubled, and many employers were adding coverage also of major medical insurance for the protection of their employees. Blue Cross and similar types of group insurance against the costs of medical, surgical, and hospital care are "fringe benefits" into which few job applicants fail to inquire nowadays.

The growth of private pension systems is still another example of a substitute for philanthropy—in this case, old age assistance. The growth of these systems and of the funds flowing into their reserves was so rapid during the 1950's that concern began to be expressed about their impact on saving and the capital markets. Even the country's consumer loan system, which has spread and become more efficient, can be counted among the substitutes for philanthropy, for it is available to meet emergencies and educational costs, as well as other needs.

Perhaps most important has been a whole series of changes since the 1920's that have reduced the risk of ill-health, death, or unemployment, and thus have served to lessen or even eliminate the need to turn to others for help. Emerson Andrews has recalled to students of philanthropy Maimonides' words that in the duty of charity, "the most meritorious of all, is to anticipate charity, by preventing poverty. . . . This is the highest step and the summit of charity's golden ladder." [6] That we are reaching for this step is signified by numerous developments. In the governmental sector we now have a high employment policy, for example, which we have been endeavoring to improve in a variety of directions; and we continue to strengthen public health measures. In the private sector, there have been successful efforts to reduce the accident rate and to devise new methods of medical treatment. Also far reaching in its effects has been the increase, even speedier than earlier generations enjoyed, in the nation's productivity, and thus in the real income available to the average family to put aside for "a rainy day." And it is note-

[6] Quoted in F. Emerson Andrews, *Philanthropic Giving,* Russell Sage Foundation, New York, 1950, p. 35.

worthy that the poorer families have increased their incomes more rapidly than the average since 1929.

A telling example of the effect of some of these developments on philanthropic-type needs is provided by the greatly reduced incidence of orphanage, referred to by Dickinson.[7] Between 1900–11 and 1965 the decline in the death rate reduced by almost two-thirds the probability of a husband twenty-five years old dying before he had reached the age of forty-five and his first born child the age of eighteen. Even over the period of immediate concern to us, we can be sure that the reduction has been significant.

Not all the developments since the 1920's have served to lessen philanthropic-type needs. The reduction in death rates, just noted, coupled with a decline in birth rates, meant also that a larger proportion of the population now dies old and the burden of old age is correspondingly greater. On net balance, however, taking account as well as one can of the pluses and minuses, it seems fair to say that there has been a reduction in the need for private philanthropy—judged, I hasten to add, by the standards of the 1920's.

I have provided only a few illustrations, but the direction and general character of the various developments outlined are fairly clear. So, too, are their causes. Many are the natural results of free enterprise: it pays to invent better things or better ways to do things. Another set of developments may be seen as the fruit of earlier philanthropic investment in research. A major factor has been intensified governmental efforts to improve the operation of the economic system—efforts which came in response to better knowledge of the sources of poverty, higher incomes, raised standards of well-being, and the working of the democratic process.

There must have been much overlapping and interaction among the factors involved. Thus, factory inspection by governmental and compulsory workmen's compensation insurance probably had something to do with incentives to reduce industrial accident rates. The expansion of government and along with it the imposition of a heavy progressive income tax encouraged the development of private pensions and other fringe benefits. And these in turn—the rapid growth of private pension funds is a current example—have been stimulating efforts to widen government regulation.

    [7] See the paper presented by him to the N.Y. Academy of Medicine, cited above, p. 46. The figures I quote are from the Metropolitan Life Insurance Company, *Statistical Bulletin*, April 1967.

Many of these factors have also influenced philanthropic giving. The sources of the rise in the "nonphilanthropic" activities of government have in large part been the sources of the rise in governmental philanthropy. And the tax increases that supported the rise in both kinds of government activity have affected private incentives to give for philanthropic purposes.

The factors affecting philanthropic giving constitute a large subject and require more deliberation than can be given to them here, but a few things need to be said.

VI

"The disposition to promote the well-being of one's fellow-men" can lead to private giving, to governmental giving, or to efforts to improve the "social arrangements under which the free pursuit of self-interest," in George Stigler's words, "is at worst harmless and at best greatly helpful to the rest of the community." [8] The three are not entirely separable. Economic research supported by private as well as governmental grants is aimed at improving these social arrangements, and social experiments by private philanthropic organizations have often paved the way for sound improvements and extensions of governmental philanthropic activity. But the distinction will bear making.

There is little doubt that in modern times, at least, improvement of the operation of the social system has commanded most of the efforts devoted to promoting the general well-being, and in the long run has also contributed most. But these efforts can vary in intensity and effectiveness. A remarkable feature of the decades covered by Dickinson was the strengthening of these efforts, and on the whole also of their effectiveness in promoting social welfare.

Hardly less remarkable, however, was the great expansion of governmental giving: from 3 to 9 per cent of GNP. What is the explanation?

Some people might be tempted to say, complacently, that the American people have become more generous, or, complainingly, that socialistic notions have invaded the country. But neither, nor both together, make a sufficient answer.

It is a little more informative, and perhaps more objective, to list

[8] Introduction to Adam Smith, *Selections from the Wealth of Nations,* New York, 1957, p. ix.

improved knowledge of the needs of the people, higher standards of decency and well-being, more resources with which to support governmental giving, and the working of the democratic process, to which I have already referred. These factors, which underlay the rise of governmental activity generally, are also the factors that influenced governmental giving.

But much more than a list would be required if we wished to understand and appreciate the process through which governmental philanthropic giving was pushed up after 1929. As in explaining the trend of government activity generally, we would need to consider the tendencies towards increase in governmental giving already present in 1929 and ask how they were modified or strengthened by the forces that entered the scene in the years that followed.

We would have to point to change in population composition, and note how the decline in number of children per family meant a higher value put on each child, and stimulated demands by parents for longer and better schooling for their children, and more and better health, sanitation, hospital, and recreational services; and how the increase in the percentage of older people in the population, together with urbanization, made the problem of the older worker more serious and forced the establishment of old age assistance programs and old age and survivors' insurance. Increase in population and its ceaseless movement westward also brought the end of the frontier around 1890, and this—along with the decline in the rate of population growth in the 1920's and 1930's— came to be a major factor in the theories of economic maturity and stagnation that provided ammunition for proponents of government action.

Advance in science and technology also contributed, and its role would have to be included in any adequate sketch of the factors involved in the rise in governmental giving. Progress in economic science and statistics brought increased knowledge of incomes and living and working conditions, and strengthened the possibilities of dealing with social problems through governmental action. Progress in chemical and biological science made possible and stimulated government enterprise to deal with sanitation and illness. Even more important, advance and diffusion of physical and biological science and technology brought industrial change, greater economic interdependence, and urbanization, which in turn greatly expanded the number of those favoring government programs to deal with slums and unemployment. Industrialization meant also higher real income per family, and this helped raise standards of assistance by government and made it possible to meet the costs.

The recurrence of business depression played its part. We are too close to the great depression of the 1930's, and its influence then and later on social security, labor, banking, agricultural, and other legislation, to forget its role. When fluctuations in business and employment became less violent after the war, attention was shifted to economic growth and government's responsibility to foster it. More and better educational and health services per capita came to be justified as long-term investments in productive capacity.

Developments in other parts of the world could not be neglected. Innovations in social legislation and standards in their application have been imported from Europe for many years, and more recently much has been made of the growing economic, political, military, and scientific power of some of the centrally planned economies. "Socialist ideology" gained ground also in the United States, while those who opposed it favored a "positive program for democracy" to ward off radicalism by training the strong forces of government on economic and social problems. Also important, of course, were changes in the international situation, which brought war and the increased possibility of war, and better knowledge of the problems of poverty, disease, and ignorance that trouble the world. Programs for international relief, rehabilitation, and development were instituted. And the residues of war were reflected in our veterans' programs.

The major developments that unearthed old economic and social problems and created new ones, that forced the problems upon the attention of the people and expanded our knowledge of how to deal with them, that raised standards of social responsibility and increased the country's ability to meet these standards—these and other developments would belong in any adequate explanation of the rise of government philanthropy.

VII

Compared with the large expansion between 1929 and 1959 of government's efforts to promote the well-being of our people, the change in private giving from 2 to perhaps 3 per cent of GNP seems modest indeed. Nevertheless, it also is noteworthy—perhaps even surprising to some readers—and invites explanation. Why should there have been a rise, or even maintenance, of the ratio of private giving to GNP during a period when economic and social welfare improved and governmental giving jumped so sharply?

If the growth of private giving were largely a reflection of a rise of giving for religious purposes—purposes that are not directly supported by government (except in a small way through property-tax exemption) or by the market—the answer might be found in a religious revival. But philanthropic giving to religious organizations, as the statistics provided by Dickinson show, has risen no more rapidly, and probably a little less rapidly, than private contributions for other purposes. The question remains.

Part of the explanation may be something akin to a religious revival, namely, a rise in standards of well-being—or, in other words, a strengthening of the disposition to promote the well-being of our fellow-men. Another part of the explanation may be the changes in tax rates and other provisions of the tax code, already mentioned more than once, which have reduced the cost of giving, especially to those in the high tax brackets. Still another part of the answer may be the rise in the general level of income per capita, if philanthropic giving is the kind of "good" to which people tend (on the average) to devote a larger share of their income when they become richer—or, taking account of the diversity of the objectives of philanthropic giving, if private giving of this kind is a significant fraction of the total, and is growing rapidly enough to offset, or more than offset, declines that have taken place in the fraction of philanthropic giving for purposes now satisfied by government. The respective roles of these several factors are not entirely clear, but something useful can be said about each. We begin with taxes.

The rise in income tax rates between 1929 and 1959 lowered the cost to the taxpayer of "deductible" philanthropic contributions by the change in the marginal rate of tax—the tax on the top dollar of his income, approximately. Per dollar of contribution, the cost to those with taxable incomes of $100,000 or more, fell from about 86 cents in 1929 to 16 cents in 1959 or 81 per cent. For those in the lower income brackets the reduction was of course less—a decline of 58 per cent for those with incomes of $50–100 thousand, 46 per cent for incomes of $25–50 thousand, and 23 per cent for incomes of $10–25 thousand.[9] This reduction in "price" must have helped to encourage private philanthropic giving.

It is easy to exaggerate the importance of the tax incentive in the present case, however. There is no such incentive for families with incomes so low that they do not file any tax return. Nor is there any tax incentive for those who pay taxes but do not itemize their deductions. The "standard deduction," which removes the tax incentive to make philanthropic contributions, has been permitted since 1941, and by 1958 was used by two-thirds of all taxpayers. The contributions of the two groups combined equaled 30 per cent of all contributions in 1958.

Even for taxpayers who do itemize their deductions, the rise in income tax rates may have had only a modest effect, if not on their own contributions, then on the aggregate amount of all contributions, which is our concern. To judge from the rough evidence, the elasticity of response of contributions to changes in tax rates appears to be such that a given percentage reduction in the "price" of contributions would tend to be accompanied by no greater and perhaps even a smaller percentage increase in the amount contributed.[10] More important, taxpayers in the high tax brackets, for whom the reduction in price was greatest, are relatively few in number. Despite their high incomes and their relatively high contribution rates, their contributions account for only a small fraction of all contributions. In 1958, for example, the contributions reported by taxpayers with incomes of $25,000 or more equaled no more than 12 or 13 per cent of all contributions. Even a substantial percentage increase in the contributions of the upper income groups, because of large tax-rate increases, would mean a much smaller rise in the total of all contributions by "living donors."

There is evidence—to be presented by Nelson—that donations by business corporations also have been influenced favorably by tax rate changes. Some part of the increase in corporate contributions relative to corporate net profits—from 0.3 per cent in 1929 to 1.0 per cent in 1959—therefore also reflects the rise in tax rates. And we know that estate taxes and other considerations, such as the wish to retain family control of a company, have influenced giving.

While, then, we should not exaggerate the importance of taxes, neither

[9] I am indebted for these estimates to Harry Kahn.

[10] The evidence is quite mixed, as the reader will see if he consults the studies by Kahn, Vickrey, Nelson, Taussig, and Schwartz, cited in footnotes 1 and 2.

should we count them as negligible. Changes in the tax system between 1929 and 1959 very likely encouraged philanthropic giving. Taxes thus help to explain why private philanthropic giving did not decline relative to the nation's income.

VIII

The rise in income taxes between 1929 and 1959 tended, of course, to reduce disposable income, as well as the "price" of giving. In this way, the rise in taxes tended also to reduce philanthropic giving. But other factors besides taxes affected incomes. Indeed, the depressant effect of increases in income taxes on disposable income was greatly overpowered, on the average, by factors that worked to push income up, such as the increased productivity of the economy referred to earlier. Income per family, after taxes and adjusted for price changes, rose by approximately 50 per cent between 1929 and 1959. Has this rise been a significant factor in supporting private giving?

All of us know, and both tax return compilations and consumer surveys confirm, that the higher the level of family income in any year, the higher is the average amount of philanthropic contributions. It will be surprising to most people, however, that this is not true of the *ratio* of contributions to current income (before or after taxes). In the lowest segment of the income range, below about $5,000 in 1939 (when the standard deduction did not complicate the relevant statistics), the ratio was inversely correlated with income, apparently due to the fact that the lower income groups are more densely populated by old people who may be maintaining the contributions to churches and other institutions which they were accustomed to make when they were younger, sometimes paying for them out of capital. In the middle range, between about $5,000 and $25,000 in 1939, the percentage of income devoted to philanthropic purposes remained approximately constant, neither falling nor rising with income. Higher contribution rates began to appear only after an income level of about $25,000 had been reached. As already mentioned, however, not many taxpayers are in the higher income brackets. In the light of these facts, and the further fact that the income distribution was somewhat narrowed between 1929 and 1959, it does not appear that a 50 per cent increase in real income per family could have exerted more than a modest upward push on the ratio of philanthropic giving to income.

The simple comparison of taxpayers at different income levels in a given year may be misleading, however. The higher income brackets of any single year include a larger than average proportion of taxpayers who have risen to that level only temporarily, and the lower income brackets include a larger than average proportion of taxpayers who have fallen to that level only temporarily. If the contribution in any year is determined in accordance with the taxpayer's normal or average income, rather than his income of that year, the cross-sectional data would underestimate the contribution rates of the high-income brackets and overestimate the contribution rates of the low-income brackets. The effect on the contribution rate of a rise in income from one year to another would tend to be understated.

On the other hand, the use of personal foundations as a channel and reservoir between high-bracket taxpayers and philanthropic institutions may mean that for these taxpayers an unusually high income is accompanied by an above-normal contribution, and an unusually low income, by a below-normal contribution. This would reduce the bias mentioned.

Only a large allowance for the bias would significantly alter the impression that, on the whole, the rise in income has been less powerful in maintaining or raising private giving than might be presumed on the basis of cross-sectional data relating to a single year.

There are other grounds for accepting what would otherwise remain a rather uncertain conclusion. Consider, for example, what we might expect to see as we look back to times when real incomes were lower than they are now or than they were in 1929. Had income had any large effect on philanthropic giving, over the long run, the percentage of 1929 income contributed to philanthropy would have been much bigger than the corresponding percentage in 1900; bigger in 1900 than in 1870; and bigger in 1870 than in 1840. Though the information is sparse, and certainly not available in the statistical terms Dickinson has provided for 1929–59, there is little reason to believe that such a pronounced upward trend would be found in private giving.

It seems reasonable to expect the ratio to normal income of contributions (or at least of some kinds of contributions), at any given income level, to be a function of *relative* income, and the average contribution income ratio to be independent of the average absolute level of income.

If philanthropy is the "disposition to promote the well-being of one's fellow-men," it is always possible to follow its bent whatever the current condition of one's fellow-men. The entrance of government into philanthropy on a large scale, like the general rise in income, has not altered the fact that resources are always scarce, that the general well-being can always be improved, and that satisfaction of the disposition to improve it can always be rewarding.

Further, it is quite possible, even likely, that the disposition to promote the general well-being—the "taste" for philanthropic giving—was somewhat strengthened after 1929. Some of the same factors that served to expand governmental philanthropy might well have tended also to cause such a shift in tastes. This appears to have been the case not only in family giving, but also in business giving, as Nelson notes in his study of business-corporation philanthropy.

All in all, then, stability or even rise in the ratio of private giving to income since 1929 in the face of a great improvement in social welfare between 1929 and 1959, can be explained by a combination of three factors: a tax effect, a rise in real income per capita, and a shift in preferences. But we cannot be sure of the order of their importance.

If this reasoning is near the mark, it would appear that the assumption by government of a large responsibility for philanthropic giving served to keep private philanthropic giving from rising even more rapidly than it did. We can be sure, in any case, that it served to shift the direction of private philanthropic giving. As government entered a field, private philanthropy sought and found other fields in which to operate. It was mentioned at the philanthropy conference, for example, that private agencies devoted to the blind no longer concern themselves with the relief of poor blind people, but still find something to do.

Were the task of promoting the general welfare taken over entirely by government, private philanthropy—like private business enterprise—would shrink severely. Perhaps such a development can be read in the history of Soviet Russia. But while our country has expanded government philanthropy it has also continued to encourage private philanthropy, by partial subsidy through the tax system and by special arrangements, as in the case of the Red Cross.

Other questions of policy deserve to be mentioned before we conclude. But first, another word on the role of philanthropy in economic life.

IX

To say that philanthropy is a necessary condition of social existence and that the extent to which it is developed influences an economy's productiveness is not to say that philanthropy—love of man in general—is a sufficient condition of social existence, or that it is the major force in economic life.

Practical men see fewer possibilities than do others of getting the world's business done on a philanthropic basis. We are sinners more than saints. It is all too evident to the discerning eye that love of man in general, though it influences a wide range of behavior, is in limited supply, and is limited therefore in the role it can play in the economic and other aspects of life.[11]

Perhaps an analogy will clarify my point. It is one thing to follow the written and unwritten rules of the game, even when the umpire is not looking and even when the rules have been altered in a direction of which one does not approve. It is quite another thing to treat one's opponent more gently than the rules require. I have been underscoring the contribution of the first, not of the second. Indeed, I hasten to add that the strength of the philanthropic motive, and the success with which it can be called upon in the day-to-day business of life is sometimes exaggerated. This is evident when special appeals are made to businessmen not to profiteer, to consumers to avoid selfish accumulation in anticipation of price rise, or to employers and trade unions to compose their differences in the light of the public good. Study of human behavior has not made economists optimistic about men's response to such appeals. In Adam Smith's words: "It is not from the benevolence of the butcher, the brewer, or the baker, that we expect our dinner, but from their regard to their own interest. We address ourselves, not to their humanity but to their self-love, and never talk to them of our own necessities but of their own advantages." [12]

Economists might wish it to be otherwise, but their analysis stops them

[11] Cf. D. H. Robertson, "What Does the Economist Economize?", *Economic Commentaries*, London, 1956.

[12] *The Wealth of Nations*, Book I, Chapter II; p. 11 in the edition cited above, note 6.

from putting much hope in philanthropy as a large means of getting the ordinary work of the economy done.

To continue with the analogy, more progress has been made by joining together to tighten, and teaching ourselves to follow, the rules that govern us all, than by persuading the individual player to rise above the rules. It is for this reason that thoughtful men anxious to promote the well-being of their fellowmen have devoted their energies to improving "those social arrangements under which the free pursuit of self-interest is at worst harmless and at best greatly helpful to the remainder of the community."

X

The questions opened up by Dickinson's estimates of philanthropy in the American economy range widely. They include not only questions concerning the factors that have influenced philanthropic giving, and questions concerning the role of philanthropy in economic life, but also questions on policy like those put before the Conference on Philanthropy. These questions are worth repeating here:

What is the appropriate "division of labor" among government, the market, and private philanthropy, in meeting human needs most effectively? Have the appropriate lines of division changed; do they continue to change; in what direction should they change? Should government continue to subsidize (or encourage) private philanthropy through the various provisions of the tax system? Should government expand or contract its direct support; or alter the ways in which it directly supports private philanthropy? What of the respective roles of the federal, state and local governments? Should philanthropy, for purposes of governmental support, be redefined in any way? In what directions should private philanthropy concentrate its efforts, taking account of past and prospective expansion of governmental activities and of market developments (private insurance, etc.)? What media of giving should be favored by private givers? [13]

To be more specific about one or two of these questions, is there any need to support private philanthropy when government is taking over more and more of the burden of helping the needy, financing higher as

[13] *Philanthropy and Public Policy,* pp. ix–x.

well as lower education on an increasing scale, and beginning to support the sciences, arts, and humanities? Should not the trend toward public philanthropy be encouraged, and should not private philanthropy be expected to retire from the scene—except as the chief support of religious activities, which the Constitution reserves for the private purse? Or is there, on the contrary, substance to the argument that private philanthropy performs certain useful social functions that cannot be entrusted to government: that it is essential to human progress that we seek to discover and test better ways to live and work together—that this requires independence of thought, initiative, and willingness to invest in what may sometimes seem to be extreme or impractical ideas— that these requirements are not easily met by government? Should we not continue to depend on "voluntary associations," which John Jewkes once said "are the life-blood of free society; they have in the past led to much of our progress in education, social insurance and health services . . ." ? [14]

Is there substance also to the claim that there is a need to foster private philanthropy even in routine areas, such as running the hospitals— that voluntary participation in such activities, in the form of contributions of time and money, constitutes an essential exercise of the spirit of brotherhood basic to social existence—that this sense of responsibility for one another needs to be instilled in the young, if civilization is to be maintained in a world in which each quarter-century sees a new generation—that teaching our children to develop their philanthropic "instincts" is a function not only of the family, school and church, but also of the voluntary association—that, in addition, competition between private and governmental philanthropic institutions is good for both?

Even to pose such questions means to take a broad view—to look at our entire social organization, to consider its moral as well as its economic roots, and to ask how our society has responded and should respond in the future to the stresses of technological and other change. The reader will know by now that it is easier to stir up such questions than to answer them. He will not be surprised that Willard Thorp's reflections on the philanthropy conference concluded with a plea for further study.

[14] *Ordeal by Planning,* New York, 1948, p. 206.

The reader will also realize that statistics which raise such questions deserve close study. He will want to acquaint himself with their derivation and the details I have been forced to skirt. He will want to see what Dickinson himself has to say about them.

Solomon Fabricant

The Changing Position
of Philanthropy in
the American Economy
1929–59

FRANK G. DICKINSON

To Cherry

patient wife,
nurse, and critic

Preface

At the very outset, two points must be stressed. First, the period covered by this report, 1929 through 1959, witnessed unusual, it might be said almost revolutionary, changes in philanthropy, and indeed in many of our great social institutions, as the public sector of the economy grew rapidly. Second, one of the reports on philanthropy in the current series, the report on the conference held at the Merrill Center for Economics, should be examined by readers of this volume.[1] The conference report provides the reader with a broad view of the problem and sets forth some of the controversies that arose during the conference regarding the boundaries of philanthropy. Because philanthropy is not a marketplace concept, its boundaries, particularly in a period of rapid economic and social change, are very difficult to fix. Those I have chosen to employ here would not necessarily be accepted by every group of economists, for the reasons stated in the conference volume and restated herein.

Ralph L. Nelson provided much help in the preparation of the estimates of the income of private domestic philanthropy and in the

---

[1] *Philanthropy and Public Policy* (Frank G. Dickinson, ed.), New York, National Bureau of Economic Research, 1962. One of my two articles in it, "The Highlights of the Conference," summarizes various opinions regarding a definition and the scope of philanthropy.

particularly difficult task of trying to estimate the incomes of religious institutions, which are not required to report their income under our tax laws.

I am also indebted to those who took part in the Conference on Philanthropy and to three of my colleagues on the research staff of the National Bureau of Economic Research—Gary S. Becker, C. Harry Kahn, and Raymond W. Goldsmith—for helpful suggestions. In the computation of the tables in Chapters 7, 8, and 10, I was assisted by Joyce Goldy Skeels, Stephen M. Munsinger, and David P. Evans. Natalie Nayler served in many capacities in this study, and Maude Pech of the National Bureau staff has been invaluable in the later stages. James F. McRee, Jr., and Joan R. Tron edited the manuscript.

Most of all, I am indebted to Solomon Fabricant and Geoffrey H. Moore for the direction of this study from its inception.

Frank G. Dickinson

Northern Illinois University
DeKalb, Illinois

1 Basic
Concepts

The word philanthropy literally means "love of mankind." Philanthropic acts manifest the generosity of the giver. The literal meaning of the word must not be forgotten at any stage of a study of philanthropy, for our period of time or for any period of time. It does not, however, provide a ready means for circumscribing or limiting the concept itself. All acts that we perform because of love of our fellow man would be indeed difficult to encompass, so the definition should indicate some boundaries which the literal meaning of the word does not provide.

One always hesitates to try to *define* a concept as one can define a term, but one can *describe* a concept. In this study what we mean by philanthropy is *giving money or its equivalent away to persons and institutions outside the family without a definite or immediate* quid pro quo *for purposes traditionally considered philanthropic.* If one were in an ideal position to measure all payments which might be called philanthropic, he would certainly look for all types of transfer payments, excluding only the transfers between members of the family. The term family, in the sense that it is used currently by the Office of Business Economics and Bureau of the Census, i.e., persons who are living together, would probably seem too narrow in some family situations. But, as will be noted in the discussion of the data, it has not been possible to include all the amounts that are needed to describe this ideal concept of philanthropy.

This implies that an attempt is being made to measure the generosity of the American people. If the generosity is manifested toward the peoples of other countries, the data are assigned to foreign philanthropy, either private or public. The concept includes all types of transfer payments that meet the standard regardless of their size. If the funds are provided through government, the resulting expenditures are classified as public philanthropy, domestic or foreign. The decision not to restrict the concept to private sources of funds may cause some to find this concept of philanthropy too broad.

The basic emphasis, however, is on the activity itself. If it has been traditionally considered philanthropic and is transferred from a private area to a public area, it is still considered to be a philanthropic expenditure. At the beginning of the period, and before the Social Security Act began to distribute benefits, many types of local, private, secular, and religious provisions were made for the care of the aged. In addition, local and state government funds were used under some circumstances to provide for the care of the indigent aged. Now that so much of this activity has been transferred from the private to the public sphere, this concept implies only the need to distinguish between public domestic philanthropy and private domestic philanthropy. This illustration also indicates some of the flexibility inherent in both the broad design and the broad concept of philanthropy. Again, for those who prefer some other, possibly narrower, definition, the data are arranged in such a way as to facilitate rearrangements and exclusions to fit particular needs.

On the whole, it seems wiser to use a broad definition in order that more pertinent data may be brought within the compass of the study. It is much easier to remove data or classifications from a study than to insert new ones. Although our classifications may not be ideal for everyone, the intention will be to keep them in line with this purpose.

THE PERIOD 1929–59

The availability of data was only one factor in the choice of the period to be covered by this study. The year 1926, for example, would have been a better initial year for the religious aspects of philanthropy because of the thorough Census of Religious Bodies by the Bureau of the Census in that year.[1] On the other hand, the comprehensive data for social welfare expenditures, starting about 1935, suggested the choice of 1935 as the first year, but the Great Depression could not be omitted. The periods covered by two earlier National Bureau studies [2] ended in the 1920's; this fact was a minor consideration.

The basic reason was historical. The present study covers one set of activities in the social history of the American people. In preparing the general plan for the study, the 1920's seemed to loom as the end of a period in the history of philanthropy and the dawn of a new period which may well be called the "social welfare" era.

THE RESEARCH DESIGN

Philanthropy has its international as well as its domestic aspects. And in the support of philanthropic endeavors both public and private funds are intermingled. Therefore, for this study a fourfold division is clearly indicated, which I shall term the quadrants of philanthropy: private philanthropy, domestic and foreign, and public philanthropy, domestic and foreign.[3]

The reader should keep in mind also that the data will be assigned to each quadrant on the basis of who gives (public or private) and who receives (domestic or foreign), the fundamental relationship inherent in philanthropy itself.

Some of the reasons for this choice of research design will not be apparent until later in the study. Many familiar with the long history of charity, poverty, pauperism, and the various attempts over the centuries to deal with the problem and the related problems within the broader orbit of philanthropy, as well as with the contemporary situation in the late 1920's, might choose a different design. Indeed, it must be stated

[1] United States Department of Commerce, Bureau of the Census, *Religious Bodies: 1926,* Washington, 1930, 2 vols.

[2] Willford Isbell King, *Trends in Philanthropy: A Study in a Typical City,* New York, NBER, 1928, and Pierce Williams and Frederick E. Croxton, *Corporation Contributions to Organized Community Welfare Services,* New York, NBER, 1930.

[3] For a discussion of this terminology, see my chapter "The Highlights of the Conference" in *Philanthropy and Public Policy,* New York, NBER, 1962.

emphatically, that this designation of philanthropy is not necessarily the best for any other period. For example, as King noted in his study of philanthropy in New Haven, Connecticut, during the period from 1900 to 1925,[4] there were no federal government contributions to philan-

4 Willford I. King, *Trends in Philanthropy*.

thropy in New Haven as late as 1925. In a more general way, this fourfold treatment of philanthropy might have proven somewhat awkward had the period of study been the first three decades of the twentieth century instead of the second three. Indeed, for an earlier period when there were not so many persons acting as individuals or as private or public officials giving away so much money to so many persons at home and abroad, for so many purposes, the present concept would probably have been too broad.

The most essential fact in choosing a research design for this study was that philanthropy is essentially a dynamic subject because it manifests a contemporary response to a particular set of conditions. It would have been possible, of course, to exclude one or more of the quadrants and, instead, call the expenditure classified therein substitutes for philanthropy, or income transfers, or benefits guaranteed by government. As the data are developed, however, it will probably become abundantly clear that the use of such terms would have narrowly confined the treatment of a dynamic subject in a very dynamic period of social, economic, and political change, thereby blurring historical patterns.

Finally, this study emphasizes the flow of funds, that is, income and outgo. It had been hoped at the beginning to provide the asset and liability items, so that the report would, in a certain sense, become a section of the national wealth and income accounts, but limitations of time and information rendered that impracticable.

2 Sources of Private Domestic Philanthropy

We begin our estimates with the development of the materials on private domestic philanthropy. The data on and analysis of private domestic philanthropic *contributions* is presented in this chapter; the data on and analysis of *receipts* of private domestic philanthropy by the recipient institutions is presented in Chapter 3.[1]

THE SIX SOURCES

The sources of data on giving to private institutions and to individuals within the area of the domestic economy, can be divided into six classes: (1) gifts to private institutions by living donors—a rather peculiar term used in several treatises on philanthropy; (2) charitable bequests to private institutions—made before death; (3) corporate gifts; (4) foundation income from endowment; (5) nonfoundation income from endowment; (6) person-to-person giving, which excludes classes 1 and 2.

The addition of person-to-person giving (excluding transfers within

[1] In these two chapters, we have included a summary of three special topics investigated at some length by Ralph L. Nelson. These are analyses of corporate giving, family giving, and religious giving. Nelson's study of corporate giving goes into certain questions in far more detail than provided in the present book.

the family) extends the concept of philanthropy into an area which might not seem proper from some points of view. As noted, we are using a broad concept of philanthropy in this study and have not hesitated to go beyond the types and kinds of data which are developed incident to the operations of the Internal Revenue Service under the federal income tax laws. If a person makes a gift to maintain, for example, a distant relative, friend, neighbor, or even a stranger in a nursing home or in a hospital, such a gift is regarded as person-to-person giving and therefore cannot be deducted. Changes in the federal income tax laws since the end of our period ease the burden of some of these types of "gifts," and more may be made in the future. But throughout the history of federal income tax legislation, the availability of deductions for gifts has been largely restricted to gifts to organizations certified by the Internal Revenue Service.

Hence the definition of philanthropy used in this study requires that special attention be given to transfer payments from one person to another outside the family which have, within the concept employed in this study, a definite place in philanthropic activity. The decision to include person-to-person giving outside the family—gifts for which there is no ordinary *quid pro quo*—has greatly complicated our statistical problems, but we believe that extending the concept of giving beyond the scope of giving to institutions brings the subject of philanthropy into a far more realistic setting.

THE TABLES OF CHAPTER 2

An attempt has been made to eliminate as much detail as possible from the discussion and data because the basic objective is to highlight the changing role of philanthropy (using our broad concept) in the American economy, from 1929 to 1959. Accordingly, the data for the sources of private philanthropy have been condensed into basic Tables 2-1 through 2-5.

Table 2-5 presents the percentage distribution of the first five sources of philanthropic income in Table 2-1 (i.e., excluding person-to-person giving), grouped by five-year periods.

Some readers may find the grouped data in Table 2-5 useful in providing perspective before and after examining the detailed data in the

Table 2-1

Sources of Private Domestic Philanthropy, 1929-59, Background Account
(millions of dollars)

Year	Gifts of Living Donors (1)	Charitable Bequests (2)	Corporate Gifts (3)	Foundation Income from Endowment (4)	Nonfoundation Income from Endowment (5)
1929	1,084	154	32	82	435
1930	969	223	35	94	414
1931	805	220	40	89	393
1932	751	191	31	70	372
1933	700	96	27	63	352
1934	790	146	27	66	376
1935	828	106	28	68	400
1936	985	128	30	80	424
1937	1,057	127	33	105	449
1938	1,001	200	27	87	450
1939	1,177	179	31	86	452
1940	1,254	143	38	96	461
1941	1,520	175	58	103	470
1942	1,944	155	98	109	473
1943	2,449	186	159	108	477
1944	2,567	202	234	142	524
1945	2,762	192	266	148	570
1946	3,088	186	214	155	560
1947	3,559	223	241	199	550
1948	3,898	296	239	225	580
1949	3,966	206	223	242	611
1950	4,359	274	252	277	663
1951	5,051	301	343	315	716
1952	5,521	328	399	323	794
1953	6,036	355	495	333	872
1954	6,216	398	314	341	950
1955	6,735	466	415	386	1,080
1956	7,317	534	418	407	1,100
1957	7,735	602	417	449	1,200
1958	8,078	669	395	450	1,200
1959	8,545	810	482	475	1,200
1929-59[a]	102,747	8,471	6,041	6,173	19,568

(continued)

Table 2-1 (concluded)

Total (cols. 1 through 5) (6)	Person-to-Person Giving (7)	Total Private Philanthropy (col. 6 plus col. 7) (8)	Total Private Foreign Philanthropy (net) (9)	Total Private Domestic Philanthropy (col. 8 minus col. 9) (10)
1,787	434	2,221	343	1,878
1,735	388	2,123	306	1,817
1,547	322	1,869	279	1,590
1,415	300	1,715	217	1,498
1,238	280	1,518	191	1,327
1,405	316	1,721	162	1,559
1,430	331	1,761	162	1,599
1,647	394	2,041	176	1,865
1,771	423	2,194	175	2,019
1,765	400	2,165	153	2,012
1,925	471	2,396	151	2,245
1,992	502	2,494	178	2,316
2,326	608	2,934	179	2,755
2,779	778	3,557	123	3,434
3,379	980	4,359	249	4,110
3,669	1,027	4,696	357	4,339
3,938	1,105	5,043	473	4,570
4,203	1,235	5,438	650	4,788
4,772	1,424	6,196	669	5,527
5,238	1,559	6,797	683	6,114
5,248	1,586	6,834	521	6,313
5,825	1,744	7,569	444	7,125
6,726	2,020	8,746	386	8,360
7,365	2,208	9,573	417	9,156
8,091	2,414	10,505	476	10,029
8,219	2,486	10,705	486	10,219
9,082	2,694	11,776	444	11,332
9,776	2,927	12,703	503	12,200
10,403	3,094	13,497	535	12,962
10,792	3,231	14,023	525	13,498
11,512	3,418	14,930	563	14,367
143,000	41,099	184,099	11,176	172,923

aThese totals must be carefully interpreted. Since the data have not been deflated, the sum of the dollars, and to a somewhat smaller extent the percentages of GNP, are really weighted aggregates in which the weights are the various price levels prevailing in each year. This means that amounts and percentages for periods when price levels were high, get a bigger weight than they do in periods when price levels were lower.

Sources by Column
Column 1
1929-54: C. Harry Kahn, *Personal Deductions in the Federal Income Tax,* NBER, 1960, p. 66.

1956, 1958: "The Coverage of Personal Contributions in the *Statistics of Income, 1948-1958,*" Ralph L. Nelson, working memorandum.

1951, 1955, 1957: Interpolated by applying average ratio of gifts to estimated total adjusted gross income (AGI) for two adjoining years to estimated total AGI for given year. Total AGI includes that of returns on which contributions were reported, that of returns taking the standard deduction and that of nonfilers. It is arrived at by adjusting the Commerce Department's Personal Income series to a definitional basis co-extensive with that used for AGI.

1959: Estimated by applying 1958 ratio of gifts to estimated total AGI to 1959 estimated total AGI.

Column 2
1929-58: *Statistics of Income,* Treasury Department. Linear interpolation for 1951, 1952, 1955-57 (years for which data were not published).

1959: Extrapolation, assumed to be "reasonable."

Column 3
1929-35: *National Income,* 1954 ed., Department of Commerce, pp. 212-213.

1936-59: *Statistics of Income,* Treasury Department.

Column 4
Based on 1957 assets and year-of-organization data for 757 large and medium-size foundations presented in *The Foundation Directory,* p. xi, Table 1. The basic procedure involved a backward projection of foundation income from the year 1957, utilizing the above-mentioned table and stock and bond price and yield data.

1958, 1959: Extrapolations, assumed to be "reasonable."

Column 5
1929-56: Estimated using Andrews' 1949 and 1954 figures and applying ratio of Andrews to Biennial Survey of Higher Education endowment income for biennial survey years. Straight-line interpolation for intersurvey years. The total includes both cash income (estimated at 20 per cent) and imputed rents (80 per cent) of buildings and equipment received as gifts.

1957-59: Projection based on 1955 and 1956.

Column 7
40 per cent of col. 1. See text for basis.

Column 9
Table 4-1, col. 2.

Table 2-2

Background National Account Aggregates, 1929-59
(millions of dollars)

Year	Gross National Product[a] (GNP) (1)	Disposable Personal Income[a] (DPI) (2)	Gross Estates (3)	Corporate Net Income (CNI) (4)	Dividends and Interest Component of Personal Income Sector[a] (5)
1929	104,436	83,120	3,844	11,869	13,241
1930	91,105	74,374	4,109	4,649	12,439
1931	76,271	63,840	4,042	-487	11,011
1932	58,466	48,660	2,796	-3,511	9,140
1933	55,964	45,744	2,027	-639	8,268
1934	64,975	51,980	2,244	2,975	8,686
1935	72,502	58,322	2,435	5,423	8,755
1936	82,743	66,222	2,296	7,771	10,390
1937	90,780	71,000	2,768	7,830	10,597
1938	85,227	65,692	3,047	4,131	9,015
1939	91,095	70,444	2,746	7,178	9,597
1940	100,618	76,076	2,633	9,348	9,824
1941	125,822	92,982	2,778	16,675	10,291
1942	159,133	117,516	2,725	23,389	10,097
1943	192,513	133,547	2,627	28,126	10,282
1944	211,393	146,761	2,908	26,547	10,824
1945	213,558	150,355	3,437	21,345	11,559
1946	210,663	160,569	3,831	25,399	13,360
1947	234,289	170,113	4,224	31,615	14,733
1948	259,426	189,300	4,775	34,588	15,949
1949	258,054	189,654	4,993	28,387	16,916
1950	284,599	207,655	4,918	42,831	19,471
1951	328,975	227,481	5,505	43,800	20,274
1952	346,999	238,714	6,141	38,735	21,054
1953	365,385	252,474	6,776	39,751	22,592
1954	363,112	256,885	7,412	36,721	24,391
1955	397,469	274,448	7,467	47,949	26,985
1956	419,180	292,942	8,881	47,413	29,593
1957	442,769	308,791	10,294	45,073	32,219
1958	444,546	317,924	10,971	39,224	33,360
1959	482,704	337,145	11,648	47,630	37,141
1929-59[b]	6,714,771	4,840,730	147,298	721,735	502,054

Notes to Table 2-2

Sources by Column
Column 1
1929-55: *U.S. Income and Output,* Department of Commerce, 1958, pp. 118-119.
1956-59: *Survey of Current Business,* July 1964, p. 8.

Column 2
1929-55: *U.S. Income and Output,* Department of Commerce, 1958, pp. 144-145.
1956-59: *Survey of Current Business,* Department of Commerce, July 1964, p. 10.

Column 3
1929-45, 1947-51, 1954, 1957: *Historical Statistics of the United States,* Department of Commerce, 1957, series Y-333 through Y-342, p. 717.
1946, 1952, 1953, 1956, 1958: Linear interpolations.
1959: *Statistics of Income, Fiduciary Gift and Estate Tax Returns Filed during Calendar 1959,* Treasury Department, Table 1, p. 57.

Column 4
1929-59: *Statistics of Income, Corporate Income Tax Returns,* Treasury Department, respective years. Compiled net profit less net deficit of all reporting corporations. Includes income from tax exempt securities.

Column 5
1929-55: *U.S. Income and Output,* Department of Commerce, 1958, pp. 144-145.
1956-59: *Survey of Current Business,* Department of Commerce, July 1964, p. 10.

aNational account aggregates do not incorporate the latest OBE revisions (1965), which became available after these tables were completed. The revisions in percentages in this and following tables would be minor.

bSee note a, Table 2-1.

basic Tables 2-1 and 2-3. In reviewing Table 2-5, the constant relationship of two to five between excluded person-to-person giving and gifts of living donors should be kept in mind (see Table 2-1, column 7).

AGGREGATES FOR THIRTY-ONE YEARS

The estimated total amount of gifts from living donors for all the years 1929–1959 combined was $102,747 million (Table 2-1). Charitable bequests accounted for only $8,471 million during the period. Corporate gifts totaled $6,041 million, foundation income from endowment $6,173 million, and nonfoundation income from endowment $19,568 million. Thus the subtotal for the entire thirty-one years from these five sources was $143,000 million.

Table 2-3

Sources of Private Domestic Philanthropy as a Percentage of Gross National Product, 1929-59

Year	Gifts to Private Institutions					Total (col. 1 through col. 5) (6)	Person-to-Person Giving (7)	Total Private Philanthropy (col. 6 plus col. 7) (8)	Total Private Foreign Philanthropy (net) (9)	Total Private Domestic Philanthropy (col. 8 minus col. 9) (10)
	Gifts of Living Donors (1)	Charitable Bequests (2)	Corporate Gifts (3)	Foundation Income from Endowment (4)	Nonfoundation Income from Endowment (5)					
1929	1.038	.147	.031	.078	.417	1.711	.416	2.127	.328	1.798
1930	1.064	.245	.038	.103	.454	1.904	.426	2.330	.336	1.994
1931	1.056	.288	.052	.117	.515	2.028	.422	2.450	.366	2.085
1932	1.284	.327	.053	.120	.636	2.420	.513	2.933	.371	2.562
1933	1.251	.171	.048	.113	.629	2.212	.500	2.712	.341	2.371
1934	1.216	.225	.041	.102	.579	2.163	.486	2.649	.249	2.399
1935	1.142	.146	.038	.094	.552	1.972	.457	2.429	.223	2.205
1936	1.191	.155	.036	.097	.512	1.991	.476	2.467	.213	2.254
1937	1.164	.140	.036	.116	.495	1.951	.466	2.417	.193	2.224
1938	1.174	.235	.032	.102	.528	2.071	.469	2.540	.180	2.361
1939	1.292	.197	.034	.094	.496	2.113	.517	2.630	.166	2.464

Year										
1940	1.246	.142	.038	.096	.458	1.980	.499	2.479	.177	2.302
1941	1.208	.139	.046	.082	.374	1.849	.483	2.332	.142	2.190
1942	1.222	.097	.062	.068	.297	1.746	.489	2.235	.077	2.158
1943	1.272	.097	.082	.056	.248	1.755	.509	2.264	.129	2.135
1944	1.214	.095	.111	.067	.248	1.735	.486	2.221	.169	2.052
1945	1.293	.090	.125	.069	.267	1.844	.517	2.361	.221	2.140
1946	1.466	.088	.102	.073	.266	1.995	.586	2.581	.309	2.273
1947	1.519	.095	.103	.085	.235	2.037	.608	2.645	.286	2.359
1948	1.502	.114	.092	.087	.224	2.019	.601	2.620	.263	2.357
1949	1.537	.080	.086	.094	.237	2.034	.614	2.648	.202	2.446
1950	1.532	.096	.089	.097	.233	2.047	.613	2.660	.156	2.504
1951	1.535	.092	.104	.096	.218	2.045	.614	2.659	.117	2.541
1952	1.591	.095	.115	.093	.229	2.123	.636	2.759	.120	2.639
1953	1.652	.097	.135	.091	.239	2.214	.661	2.875	.130	2.745
1954	1.712	.109	.086	.094	.262	2.263	.685	2.948	.134	2.814
1955	1.695	.117	.104	.097	.272	2.285	.678	2.963	.112	2.851
1956	1.746	.127	.100	.097	.262	2.332	.698	3.030	.120	2.910
1957	1.747	.136	.094	.101	.271	2.349	.699	3.048	.121	2.927
1958	1.817	.150	.089	.101	.270	2.427	.727	3.154	.118	3.036
1959	1.770	.168	.100	.098	.249	2.385	.708	3.093	.117	2.976
1929-59[a]	1.530	.126	.090	.092	.292	2.130	.612	2.742	.166	2.575

Source: Tables 2-1 and 2-2.

[a]See note a, Table 2-1.

Table 2-4

Relation of Selected Components of Private Domestic Philanthropy to Relevant National Account Aggregates, 1929-59

Year	Gifts of Living Donors as Per Cent of Disposable Personal Income (1)	Charitable Bequests as Per Cent of Gross Estates (2)	Corporate Gifts as Per Cent of Corporate Net Income (3)	Income from Endowment as Per Cent of Dividends and Interest Component of Personal Income Sector	
				Foundation (4)	Nonfoundation (excluding imputed rents)[a] (5)
1929	1.304	4.006	.270	.619	.657
1930	1.303	5.427	.753	.756	.666
1931	1.261	5.443	-8.214	.808	.714
1932	1.543	6.831	-.883	.766	.814
1933	1.530	4.736	-4.225	.762	.851
1934	1.520	6.506	.908	.760	.866
1935	1.420	4.353	.516	.777	.914
1936	1.488	5.575	.386	.770	.816
1937	1.489	4.588	.421	.991	.847
1938	1.524	6.564	.654	.965	.998
1939	1.671	6.519	.432	.896	.942
1940	1.648	5.431	.407	.977	.939
1941	1.635	6.299	.348	1.001	.913
1942	1.654	5.688	.419	1.080	.937
1943	1.834	7.080	.565	1.050	.928
1944	1.749	6.946	.881	1.312	.968
1945	1.837	5.586	1.246	1.280	.986
1946	1.923	4.855	.843	1.160	.838
1947	2.092	5.279	.762	1.351	.747
1948	2.059	6.199	.691	1.411	.727
1949	2.091	4.126	.786	1.431	.722
1950	2.099	5.571	.588	1.423	.681
1951	2.220	5.468	.783	1.554	.706
1952	2.313	5.341	1.030	1.534	.754
1953	2.391	5.239	1.245	1.474	.772
1954	2.420	5.370	.855	1.398	.779
1955	2.454	6.241	.866	1.430	.800
1956	2.498	6.013	.882	1.375	.743
1957	2.505	5.848	.925	1.394	.745
1958	2.541	6.098	1.007	1.349	.719
1959	2.534	6.954	1.012	1.279	.646
1929-59[b]	2.123	5.751	.837	1.230	.780

[a]Imputed rents estimated as 80 per cent of nonfoundation income from endowment.

[b]See note a, Table 2-1.

Source: Tables 2-1 and 2-2.

The amount of person-to-person giving, as indicated by the scanty data available on support payments, suggests that this item was possibly 40 per cent of the gifts of living donors.[2] If this estimate is correct, the thirty-one-year total for person-to-person giving was $41,099 million. When this item is added to the subtotal of $143,000 million for the five sources, the grand total becomes $184,099 million. These enormous sums constituted 2.7 per cent of GNP for the period (Table 2-3).

OTHER NATIONAL AGGREGATES

The consolidated items from the quadrants will be compared with GNP in Chapter 10, despite the well-recognized shortcomings of GNP as a measure of the totality of economic activity. However, some items may seem more directly related to smaller national aggregates; for example, disposable personal income, which totaled $4,841 billion during the thirty-one-year period as compared with $6,715 billion for GNP (columns 2 and 1 of Table 2-2). Hence, in Table 2-4, we make such comparisons. Gifts of living donors comprise 2.1 per cent of disposable personal income and only 1.5 per cent of gross national product for the entire period. (Both trends are irregularly upward; the business cycle implications have not been examined.) Charitable bequests are shown as 5.7 per cent of gross estates (Table 2-4) and only 0.1 per cent of GNP (Table 2-3). Corporate gifts are shown as 0.8 per cent of corporate net income (Table 2-4), but as only 0.1 per cent of GNP (Table

[2] Our ratio of two-fifths of the amount given by living donors is based primarily on general observation of family giving patterns and many small samples in the field of philanthropy. We are encouraged, however, by the information gathered in the several Bureau of Labor Statistics Consumer Expenditures Surveys (1936, 1950, and 1960–61). It is true that our concept of person-to-person giving and of gifts of living donors, on which the two-fifths estimates rest, are not identical in composition to any BLS items (largely because BLS data are intentionally selective, sampling only middle-income families in cities). Even the BLS term, "support payments," had to be modified in estimating the ratio (two-fifths) between person-to-person giving and gifts of living donors; for example, alimony was eliminated from support payments. Nevertheless, the ratios of several relatively comparable Survey items indicate that our 40 per cent estimate of person-to-person giving relative to giving by living donors to institutions is not too wide of the mark, and that in all likelihood the ratio is rising over time. The estimates of gifts of living donors involved a more systematic procedure but the relative accuracy of the two estimates is, of course, not known. The 40 per cent figure should be checked at some time by a separate investigation.

Table 2-5

Percentage Distribution of Sources of Income of Private Domestic
Philanthropic Institutions by Five-Year Periods, 1929-59

Year	Gifts to Private Institutions			Foundation Income from Endowment (4)	Nonfoundation Income from Endowment (5)	Total (cols. 1 through 5) (6)
	Gifts of Living Donors (1)	Charitable Bequests (2)	Corporate Gifts (3)			
1929	60.7	8.6	1.8	4.6	24.3	100.0
1930-34	54.7	11.9	2.2	5.2	26.0	100.0
1935-39	59.1	8.7	1.7	5.0	25.5	100.0
1940-44	68.8	6.1	4.1	3.9	17.0	100.0
1945-49	73.8	4.7	5.1	4.1	12.2	100.0
1950-54	75.0	4.6	5.0	4.3	11.0	100.0
1955-59	74.5	6.0	4.1	4.2	11.2	100.0
1929-59	71.9	5.9	4.2	4.3	13.7	100.0

Note: Detail may not add to total because of rounding.
Source: Table 2-1.

2-3). Foundation income and nonfoundation income from endowment have been shown as percentages of the dividends and interest component of the personal income sector as well as percentages of GNP. Only in Table 2-4 do we make these comparisons with smaller universes than GNP. Further attention to these relationships would probably prove more confusing than helpful.

AMOUNTS GIVEN AND AMOUNTS RECEIVED

The data described in Chapter 3 indicate that recipient institutions may be grouped in six classes; religious organizations, parochial schools, higher education, secular health, secular welfare, and miscellaneous.

Other students of philanthropy have found that estimates of amounts given usually exceed the estimates of amounts received. This study considers the universe of private domestic philanthropy to be the amounts given rather than the amounts received; that is, in the consolidation of the data from the four quadrants developed in Chapter 10, the "where from" data described in this chapter rather than the "where to" data described in Chapter 3 will be used. Such a procedure seems to be necessary in a study that deals primarily with the changing role of philanthropy in the American economy. Moreover, greater accuracy is on the side of this course because most of the data are by-products of federal income taxes. How much income tax a person pays and for what purposes he can obtain reductions in the amount of income subject to tax are obviously matters of importance to the Treasury of the United States. Hence, one would expect the accounts to be much clearer on the matter of data (derived after many adjustments) from tax returns than from rather crude estimates of income derived by institutions which are for the most part not subject to tax.

GIFTS OF LIVING DONORS: DERIVATION OF ESTIMATES

The estimates of the amounts given by living donors are derived from federal income tax returns as recorded in *Statistics of Income.* The amounts consist, for the most part, of gifts which are deductible from income subject to federal income taxes.

The procedures which have been followed in developing the estimates of gifts of living donors for the entire thirty-one years are based upon a study by C. Harry Kahn.[3]

KAHN'S METHOD

Quite apart from the data compiled in *Statistics of Income,* Kahn had to make allowances for individuals who did not file federal income tax returns but contributed in the aggregate considerable amounts to private domestic philanthropic institutions. In addition, estimates had to be made for persons who did file personal income tax returns but did not itemize their deductions because they preferred to take the standard de-

---

[3] *Personal Deductions in the Federal Income Tax,* Princeton University Press for National Bureau of Economic Research, 1960.

duction. Kahn's estimates, therefore, have two important sources of error no matter how carefully the estimates are prepared.

Kahn describes his procedure in the following terms (pp. 227–229):

. . . This is the sum of reported contributions and an estimate of contributions by persons who did not file a tax return or who chose the standard deduction.

From 1924 to 1940, the estimates of unreported contributions are for those who did not file tax returns. They were computed by attributing a contribution rate to the income not covered on tax returns. We adhered throughout to the adjusted gross income concept. From total AGI we subtracted all AGI reported on tax returns as well as the amount of AGI unexplained. The difference is assumed to be the estimated AGI of nonfilers.

Since the nonfilers are those not required to file tax returns, we imputed to them a contribution rate (ratio of contributions to AGI) equal to that reported for each given year on the tax returns of the income group into which most of the nonfilers might be expected to fall. To be on the conservative side in this hypothetical estimate, all the unexplained amount was allocated to tax return filers in proportion to their income, and the "reported" rate imputed to nonfilers was calculated with this broader income base, that is, it was lowered correspondingly. The income groups in which nonfilers were assumed to fall, in each period, and the contribution rates assigned to them, are shown below:

Year	Income Groups [a] ($000's)	Contribution Rates for Nonfilers (per cent)
1924	0–3	1.5
1925–1931	0–5	1.3–1.5
1932–1939	0–3	1.8–2.1
1940–1943	0–2	2.1
1944–1954	0–2	1.7–2.0

[a] Net income groups until 1943; AGI groups thereafter. The contribution rates shown above were multiplied by the estimated AGI of nonfilers to obtain the estimates of unreported contributions for 1924–1940.

From 1941 on, estimated contributions not reported on tax returns also include estimates for persons filing returns with standard deductions. For the years 1941–1943, when the standard deduction could be taken only on returns with less than $3,000 gross income, the ratio of contributions to income on returns for 1940 in the 0 to $3,000 group was used to estimate contributions for that income group. . . . In 1944 the standard deduction became available for all tax returns, and it was therefore necessary to impute contribution rates to returns in all income groups, although the relative frequency of returns with standard deduction was greatest for low income returns. An estimate of contributions for all tax returns in 1944 was obtained by applying to 1944 reported income the estimated 1943 ratio of contributions to reported income. From this figure the reported contributions on returns with itemized deductions were subtracted, and the residual taken as the contributions that would have been reported on short-form returns if none had used the standard deduction. A contribution rate of 1.5 per cent for returns with standard deductions was thus obtained for 1944.

We used this rate for all standard deduction returns from 1944 to 1947. Since we received this ratio by assuming no change in the over-all reported contributions rate between 1943 and 1944, we may have established the level of contributions "reporting" for the years after 1944 somewhat too low. In 1948 the standard deduction was once more liberalized by a rise in its ceiling per return from $500 to $1,000 for almost all taxpayers. The resulting shift of some taxpayers from itemized deductions to the standard allowance, required an adjustment in the contributions rate on standard deduction returns, as estimated for 1944–1947. Accordingly, the amount of income shifted from the long-form to the short-form returns category was estimated, and to that amount of income we assigned the average contributions rate prevailing in 1947 on returns with itemized deductions. Thus the new estimated rate for contributions on standard deduction returns, 1948–1954, became 1.66 per cent.

To make the procedures outlined above somewhat more concrete, the figures below show for one year, 1952, how the estimate was obtained (in millions):

Estimated contributions of nonfilers:

1. Total AGI	$240,645
2. Minus: AGI reported on all returns	216,030
3. Minus: Amount unexplained	22,147
4. Equals: AGI of nonfilers	2,468
5. Line 4 × 0.019 (adjusted contributions rate of 0 to $2,000 AGI group on taxable returns)	47

Estimated contributions of those filing returns with standard deduction:

6. AGI on returns with standard deductions	141,647
7. Line 6 × 0.0166	2,358
8. Itemized contributions	3,116
Hypothetical estimate of total contributions, line 5 + line 7 + line 8	5,521

OUR USE OF KAHN'S METHODS

Since Kahn's study did not cover the years beyond 1954, we computed the estimates for 1956 and 1958 from a detailed examination of the coverage of personal contributions in *Statistics of Income* for 1948–58. The period was marked by large increases in the reporting of deductions on income tax returns, changes having a direct and important effect on the coverage of personal contributions. The number of tax returns on which contributions were itemized rose from 7.8 million in 1948 to almost 20 million in 1958, and the amount of contributions deducted rose from $1.9 billion to $5.7 billion. Whereas in 1948 about one return in seven contained an itemized deduction for contributions, by 1958 this had risen to about one in three.

Over the period, the adjusted gross income (AGI) reported on returns which itemized deductions became a larger part of the total for the country. That is, the income of nonfilers and of persons taking the standard deduction—income from which unreported contributions were made —became a smaller part of the total. The AGI against which deductions were not specifically offset declined from 76 per cent of total AGI in 1948 to 53 per cent in 1958. Also the percentage of returns that itemized deductions but omitted contributions declined. Both developments indicate that reported contributions accounted for an increasing share of total expenditures.

This trend toward increasing coverage was well established between 1948 and 1954, when Kahn's series ends. Over this six-year period reported contributions increased from less than one-half to five-eighths of estimated total contributions. Despite the large decrease in the number of persons not reporting contributions, and in their share of total AGI, the percentage of estimated unreported contributions to the corresponding estimate of AGI remained quite constant, at about 1.44.

This, of course, is not unexpected. Kahn applied a giving rate of 1.66 per cent to the AGI of returns with the standard deduction and 1.9 per cent of the AGI of nonfilers. He also deducted an "unexplained" amount of AGI, which represents, in the main, the underreporting of taxable income. This deduction, in effect, produces a lower base than the one used here to which to relate unreported contributions. Unless there was a large shift in the relative sizes of nonfiler, standard deduction, and "unexplained" AGI, the aggregate unreported rate should remain relatively constant.

To estimate unreported contributions for 1956 and 1958, the rate of 1.44 per cent was applied to the AGI not included on returns with itemized deductions. The estimate was then added to the reported contributions for these years to arrive at an over-all total. This produced a value for living donors' gifts of $7,317 million in 1956 and $8,078 million in 1958 (column 1 of Table 2-1). Also, by 1958, contributions reported on tax returns had risen to 70.5 per cent of total contributions.

The above analysis probably understates, by a small amount, the growth in the coverage of reported contributions. One aspect of this growth did not enter the calculations, namely, the increase from eighty-eight to ninety-six in the number of returns with itemized contributions as a percentage of returns having itemized deductions of any kind. This surely reflects an increased reporting of contributions; however, time and data precluded an attempt to estimate its contribution to the increased coverage.

CHARITABLE BEQUESTS

The data presented in column 2 of Table 2-1 were taken directly from the *Statistics of Income for Estate Tax Returns*. They therefore do not include the charitable bequests from estates too small to be required to file a return. The exclusion of such data is unlikely to substantially affect the total. The *Statistics of Income* did not contain tabulations of charitable bequests for 1951, 1952, 1955, 1956, and 1957. The values for these years are linear interpolations between 1950 and 1953 and between 1954 and 1958.

CORPORATE GIFTS

The data on corporate giving through 1935 were taken from Department of Commerce, *National Income,* 1954 ed., Table 36. For the period 1936 through 1958 they were taken directly from the *Statistics of In-*

come Corporation Income Tax Returns. The preliminary report for the corporate *Statistics of Income* was used for 1959.

Despite the presence of such direct and consistent data on corporate giving, one would have to say that it is understated in the published sources in two ways. First, many expenditures made by corporations that clearly add to the betterment of the community are charged in some manner or another to the costs of doing business.[4] In this category are such items as the lending or donating of company equipment. Second, considerable expenditure of company resources goes toward released time of executives and employees for charitable causes. Among the more outstanding examples of this are the executive leadership positions in community chest drives. (If this paid time equaled about 0.3 per cent of the total compensation of employees of corporations, it would exceed the amount of corporate gifts.)

FOUNDATION INCOME FROM ENDOWMENT

The first step in estimating foundation income from endowment was to develop a cumulated series of the amounts of assets of foundations. This was possible because F. Emerson Andrews had assembled a reasonably complete list of the medium and larger foundations (assets of $1 million or more in 1957) by year of organization.[5] Knowing the foundations in existence for each year, it was possible to produce an estimate of their income since 1929.

The assets of these foundations were in 1957 values and thus it was necessary to convert them into current-year values to serve as a basis for the estimate of current-year income. To do this, the assets were first divided into their equity and debt components, using fragmentary evidence on the portfolio composition of several large foundations. To the equity and debt values for 1957, stock and bond price indexes were applied to produce an equity and debt value for 1956. This linking backward was successively performed to produce the respective values for

[4] One authority on corporate giving compiled for the author a list of 100 types of corporate assistance which usually showed up in the corporate accounts as business expense. Efforts designed to sample accounting practices in the United States in this regard proved fruitless.

[5] Russell Sage Foundation, *The Foundation Directory,* New York, 1960.

each preceding year. In addition, the values of the assets of foundations organized in each succeeding year were subtracted from the total to adjust for the emergence of new foundations. In this way a current-year value figure for the foundations in existence in any given year was developed.

To compute the endowment income from these values, the current market values of the equity and debt components were multiplied respectively by the dividend and interest yield for the year. These two components of income were then added together to produce the total of estimated endowment income for the year. This is the series presented in column 4 of Table 2-1.

The above method is necessarily very crude and does not specifically deal with some important trends which would affect the series. First, it assumes a constant portfolio investment policy over this period; i.e., that foundation treasurers put the same proportions of new and reinvested funds into equity and debt at the beginning of the period as they did at the end. Casual observation suggests that there was, in fact, a trend toward investment in equities. The magnitude of this bias, however, is not at all clear. Second, it does not take into account the foundations that were liquidated over this period. This would tend to cause an understatement of foundation income in the earlier years relative to the later years. The bias toward an understatement of income in the earlier years probably also exists from the assumption of a constant debt-equity investment policy. A third bias might arise from the exclusion of small foundations from this calculation, although its direction is not apparent. There is simply no way of knowing whether the share of total foundation income received by foundations with assets below $1 million in 1957 has increased or decreased over the period.

A more precise estimate of the time pattern of foundation income is possible, and some exploration of this has been undertaken. One may obtain direct evidence on the income of the largest foundations from their annual reports. For a number of foundations it is possible to develop continuous series back through 1929. In recent years the ten or fifteen largest foundations have accounted for more than half of foundation assets and income, and complete annual financial reports are available for this large group in most cases. A more reliable series might thus be developed by combining the direct evidence of the large foundations with the kind of imputation procedure described above for the remainder. In addition, to take explicit account of the liquidation of foundations, some adjustment, based upon whatever empirical evidence is available, can be performed.

NONFOUNDATION INCOME FROM ENDOWMENT

This series represents an estimate of the income received by what might be called operating, as distinguished from financial, philanthropic institutions; that is, colleges and universities, churches, hospitals, museums, libraries, etc., which hold both endowment assets and tangible assets. The series includes both income from the securities and other assets in which endowment is invested, and also the value of the services provided by the tangible assets, that is, an imputed rent from these assets.

The procedure followed was first to find a reliable estimate for some year and then to link this estimate to a series which describes one component of this income. Estimates for total income were given by F. Emerson Andrews for the years 1949 and 1954. To develop estimates for earlier years, the ratio of Andrews' total figure for 1949 was applied to the series on higher educational endowment income for the biennial survey years preceding 1949. For intersurvey years a simple linear interpolation was made. Between 1949 and 1954 a simple linear interpolation of Andrews' beginning and ending values was made. The biennial survey endowment income for 1956 was used for that year and a cautious extrapolation was made beyond 1956.

The reasons for not developing direct estimates by major type of institution are several. First, endowment income data for hospitals and churches are largely nonexistent, and endowment income probably accounts for only a small fraction of their income from capital (less than 5 per cent of all church income in the 1936 Religious Census). Second, comprehensive estimates of the values of tangible assets for all of the major institutions do not exist after 1948, the year Rude's series ends.[6] Thereafter there is nothing on which to base imputation of rent. Third, the construction of such tangible-asset data would be a long and laborious task.

As presented, movements in the series before 1959 are the same,

[6] Robert Rude, "Assets of Private Nonprofit Institutions in the United States, 1890–1948," unpublished study, National Bureau of Economic Research, 1959.

relatively, as movements in the endowment income of higher education. There are, however, several reasons for believing that, were a directly estimated series available, its time picture would not be the same. First, the trends in the cumulation of tangible assets have probably been different for higher education, churches, and hospitals, so that the trend in imputed rents for the three categories have not been the same. Second, the ratio of financial to tangible assets among the three institutions is not the same, nor is it likely that trends in the ratio have been. How important these variations are in causing the time picture to depart from the crude estimate cannot be determined. It is felt that the estimate provides at least some notion of the order of magnitude of this component of philanthropic income.

A BRIEF SUMMARY

These comments on methods and sources of the data shown in Table 2-1 are designed to explain them, and inform the reader of the problems confronted and our attempts to solve them. Philanthropy is not a market-place type of economic activity. Hence many needed records are missing. The author expects, however, that these are a reasonably good set of data.

3 Recipient
Institutions of Private
Domestic Philanthropy

The income of private domestic philanthropy for the thirty-one years of study was estimated at $184 billion; $143 billion excluding the rough approximation of person-to-person giving. At the outset, we must frankly confess that we have not been able to find where all the money was sent; that is, we cannot account for the entire $143 billion income of philanthropic institutions. The amounts sent abroad, which are estimated in the next chapter, do not explain the discrepancy; they were relatively small, and, what is more, most were first received by institutions at home and are included in the $143 billion or the $184 billion. We are somewhat comforted, however, by the knowledge that other students of private philanthropy (Andrews, Jenkins, Kahn) were also unable to find what institutions received all the funds given.[1]

This basic inability to reconcile the "where-from" with the "where-to" data springs from the rather obvious fact that better records are kept on the amounts given. Nevertheless, Kahn questions the reliability of his own estimates of giving based on income and estate tax returns.[2] His

[1] F. Emerson Andrews, *Philanthropic Giving*, New York, 1950; Edward C. Jenkins, *Philanthropy in America*, New York, 1950; C. Harry Kahn, *Personal Deductions in the Federal Income Tax*, Princeton for NBER, 1960.
[2] *Ibid.*, pp. 46–91 and 216–229.

estimates are, in turn, difficult to reconcile with his estimates derived from consumer expenditure surveys. Two human frailties, fabricating and forgetting, may or may not be compensating errors in the national aggregates. On balance, however, the student of philanthropy is likely to regard the tax data as reasonably reliable. On the other hand, the amounts received by philanthropic institutions are not taxable. Few of the recipient institutions are required by law to make financial reports to an agency of government.

THE TABLES OF CHAPTER 3

These and related difficulties account for the organization of the data in the tables of this chapter. Table 3-1 provides for income and percentage distribution for selected years, 1930–58. The estimated income of recipient institutions is shown separately for religious organizations, parochial schools, higher educational institutions, secular health, secular welfare, and a miscellaneous category.

Table 3-2 merely provides for expressing the income of the six classes of recipient institutions as percentages of personal consumption expenditures and gross national product. In the light of previous comments on GNP and smaller national aggregates, no further reference to this table seems necessary. Table 3-3 summarizes the ratios for the same selected years between the amount given, as reported in Chapter 2, and amount received—the four-fifths reconciliation. From 1950 to 1958 the ratios varied narrowly between 0.80 and 0.83. Table 3-4 is the major table on religious groups. Last is Table 3-5, which provides for five-year groupings of the percentages of total giving to religious organizations. Some readers may prefer to glance at summary Table 3-5 before examining annual data in Table 3-4.

ONLY FOUR-FIFTHS

In general, we have succeeded in accounting for about four-fifths of the estimated amount given during the thirty-one-year period. The larger amounts are carried forward to our grand totals for philanthropy in

Table 3-1

*Estimated Income of Recipient Institutions
and Percentage Distribution,
Selected Years, 1930-58*

Year	Religious Organizations[a] (1)	Parochial Schools (2)	Higher Education (3)	Secular Health (4)	Secular Welfare (5)	Miscel- laneous (6)	Total (7)
		Income (millions of dollars)					
1930	787	153	210	97	167	60	1,474
1935	534	75	141	36	120	63	969
1940	612	115	179	56	150	100	1,212
1945	1,009	146	246	330	675	205	2,611
1950	1,962	428	447	530	650	309	4,326
1955	3,166	746	795	685	860	331	6,583
1956	3,497	801	936	808	1,015	335	7,392
1958	4,036	896	1,057	810	950	344	8,093
		Percentage Distribution					
1930	53.4	10.4	14.2	6.6	11.3	4.1	100.0
1935	55.1	7.7	14.6	3.7	12.4	6.5	100.0
1940	50.5	9.5	14.8	4.6	12.4	8.2	100.0
1945	38.6	5.6	9.4	12.6	25.9	7.9	100.0
1950	45.4	9.9	10.3	12.3	15.0	7.1	100.0
1955	48.1	11.3	12.1	10.4	13.1	5.0	100.0
1956	47.3	10.9	12.7	10.9	13.7	4.5	100.0
1958	49.9	11.1	13.1	10.0	11.7	4.3	100.0

Sources by Column
Columns 1 and 2

Table 3-4.

Column 3

Biennial Survey of Higher Education. Included are private gifts and grants for current education and plant expansion, and additions to permanent funds (endowment, annuity, student loan, and other nonexpendable funds of a philanthropic origin).

Columns 4 and 5

1930-55: Thomas Karter, "Voluntary Agency Expenditures for Health and Welfare from Philanthropic Contributions, 1930-1955," *Social Security Bulletin,* February 1958, Table 3.

1956-58: NBER itemization. The health and welfare total was divided between the two categories in the same proportions as Karter's 1955 apportionment.

Notes to Table 3-1 continued

Column 6

Mainly secular private gifts for foreign relief, charity rackets, capital grants to foundations, museums, libraries, and cultural support.

1930-40: June 1944, *Survey of Current Business.*

1945: Average of 1940 and 1950 estimates.

1950: Sum of lines 4, 6, 8, and 9 of Table 15 in Andrews, *Philanthropic Giving,* p. 73.

1955-58: NBER itemization.

Note: Detail may not add to total because of rounding.

[a]Probably includes some church-supported health and welfare, and includes parochial schools.

Chapter 10. Accordingly, no extended discussion will be presented in this study of the technical problems of preparing our "four-fifths" reconciliation. Because 1958 rather than 1959 is the latest year for which we developed a reconciliation—to the extent of 82 per cent—the data for 1958 will be featured in this discussion more than those for the selected years or for the entire three decades.

As shown in Table 3-1, religious organizations received an estimated $4,036 million in 1958; this was only 49.9 per cent of the amount received by all recipient institutions which we could trace. (Our estimates for this one large item may be far too low and could account for much of the discrepancy between funds donated and funds received.) If we add to this the 11.1 per cent received by parochial schools (religious or educational philanthropy), the portion allocated to these two groups exceeded 60 per cent in 1958. The remaining items were 13.1 per cent for higher education, 10.0 per cent for secular health, and 11.7 per cent for secular welfare; 4.3 per cent must be classified as miscellaneous. In Table 3-1 the total equals 100 per cent; this procedure should not obscure the fact that the amounts which could be traced were only 82 per cent of our estimate of the amounts given during 1958 (Table 3-3).

It should also be noted that some of the receipts of religious organizations were spent for health and welfare but are not included in the secular health and welfare columns of Table 3-1. This table also indicates that a noticeable decline in percentage of the total received was for religious institutions, from 53.4 per cent in 1930 to 49.9 per cent in 1958. The most definite and most pronounced increase was for secular health,

Table 3-2

Relation of Income of Recipient Institutions to Personal
Consumption Expenditures and Gross National Product
Selected Years 1930-58

Year	National Account Aggregate ($ million) (1)	Religious Organizations (2)	Parochial Schools (3)	Higher Education (4)	Secular Health (5)	Secular Welfare (6)	Miscel- laneous (7)	Total Recipient Income (8)
	Personal Consumption Expenditures	*Income of Recipient Institutions as Per Cent of PCE*						
1930	$ 70,968	1.11	.22	.30	.14	.24	.08	2.08
1935	56,289	.95	.13	.25	.06	.21	.11	1.72
1940	71,881	.85	.16	.25	.08	.21	.14	1.69
1945	121,699	.83	.12	.20	.27	.55	.17	2.15
1950	195,013	1.01	.22	.23	.27	.33	.16	2.22
1955	256,940	1.23	.29	.31	.27	.33	.13	2.56
1956	269,917	1.30	.30	.35	.30	.38	.12	2.74
1958	293,198	1.38	.31	.36	.28	.32	.12	2.76
	Gross National Product	*Income of Recipient Institutions as Per Cent of GNP*						
1930	91,105	.86	.17	.23	.11	.18	.07	1.62
1935	72,502	.74	.10	.19	.05	.17	.09	1.34
1940	100,618	.61	.11	.18	.06	.15	.10	1.20
1945	213,558	.47	.07	.12	.15	.32	.10	1.22
1950	284,599	.69	.15	.16	.19	.23	.11	1.52
1955	397,469	.80	.19	.20	.17	.22	.08	1.66
1956	419,180	.83	.19	.22	.19	.24	.08	1.76
1958	444,546	.91	.20	.24	.18	.21	.08	1.82

Note: Detail may not add to total because of rounding.
Source: Table 3-1 and U.S. *Income and Output,* 1958, pp. 118-119 and 144-145
(1930-55) and *Survey of Current Business,* July 1961, pp. 6, 8.

from 6.6 per cent in 1930 to 10.0 per cent in 1958. This relative shift is significant even if allowance is made for some unreliability in our percentages.

RELIGIOUS ORGANIZATIONS

Estimation of philanthropic funds received by religious institutions in the United States is a Herculean task. Government statistics in this area

Table 3-3

*Comparison of Total Estimated Giving Based on
Donors and Recipients, Selected Years, 1930-58*

| Year | Total Estimated Giving (million dollars) | | Ratio (col. 2 ÷ col. 1) (3) |
	From Donors (1)	To Recipients (2)	
1930	1,404	1,474	1.05
1935	1,110	969	.87
1940	1,623	1,212	.75
1945	3,482	2,611	.75
1950	5,295	4,326	.82
1955	8,218	6,583	.80
1956	8,896	7,392	.83
1958	9,832	8,093	.82

Source: Column 1, Table 2-1, sum of cols. 1 through 4, and
cash income position (20 per cent) of column 5. Column 2: Table
3-1, column 7.

are sparse. The legal tradition of separation of church and state pre-
cludes that religious institutions report such data to the government for
taxation or any other purposes. The lack of tax data on church assets
and liabilities, quite apart from income and outgo, was the basic obstacle
to the original plan: to develop the changing position of philanthropy
in a balance sheet and income statement of the American economy.

Only slightly more encouraging are the statistics collected by the religious institutions themselves; they are incomplete, often unavailable to
the public, frequently unreliable, and at best nonuniform. All of this is
but a reflection of the sprawling and heterogeneous nature of religious
organization in this country. There are, however, two substantial and

Table 3-4

Estimates of Giving to Religious Organizations, by
Major Religious Groups, 1929-59
(millions of dollars)

Year	Protestant (1)	Roman Catholic Churches (2)	Parochial Schools (3)	Jewish (4)	Other (5)	Total (6)	Excluding Parochial Schools (7)
1929	596	201	152	37	4	990	838
1930	554	195	153	34	4	940	787
1931	490	175	133	29	3	829	696
1932	400	151	113	24	3	692	579
1933	348	134	90	20	3	595	505
1934	358	134	66	20	3	582	516
1935	374	136	75	21	3	609	534
1936	398	141	84	25	4	653	569
1937	415	149	91	26	3	684	593
1938	423	152	98	26	4	703	605
1939	417	152	107	26	3	705	598
1940	428	155	115	26	2	727	612
1941	481	166	120	29	4	800	680
1942	529	172	124	31	5	861	736
1943	596	175	117	33	4	926	809
1944	665	183	109	38	3	998	889
1945	765	194	146	45	5	1,155	1,009
1946	911	218	183	51	6	1,369	1,186
1947	1,017	255	254	54	9	1,589	1,335
1948	1,211	305	326	62	11	1,915	1,589
1949	1,390	335	377	75	12	2,188	1,811
1950	1,503	360	428	78	20	2,390	1,962
1951	1,673	396	487	85	22	2,662	2,175
1952	1,870	401	545	91	29	2,936	2,391
1953	2,090	433	618	99	28	3,268	2,650
1954	2,296	474	690	106	29	3,596	2,905
1955	2,507	514	746	113	33	3,912	3,166
1956	2,785	538	801	133	41	4,299	3,497
1957	3,011	582	849	141	44	4,627	3,778
1958	3,236	607	896	147	46	4,931	4,036
1959	3,398	670	953	151	51	5,224	4,271
1929-59[a]	37,135	8,853	10,046	1,876	441	58,355	48,307

Notes to Table 3-4

Source: Estimates were based on membership and gifts per member for the several religious groups. Number of members were derived from religious directories; several adjustments were required. The amount of giving per member for each group was anchored on averages for churches reporting to the National Council of Churches. The fixed percentage relationship to the norm, applied uniformly every year, was based on various religious publications; in some instances they were "guesstimate."

The derivation of 1958 data may serve to describe the estimates.

Column 1   *(Protestant):*

	Members (thousands)	Gift per Member (dollars)	Total (million dollars)
National Council Reporting Group	37,529	62.68	2,352
Negro	8,337	39.49	329
		(65 per cent of reporting)	
Latter Day Saints	1,547	90.89	141
		(145 per cent of reporting)	
Other Protestant	8,800	47.11	414
		(75 per cent of reporting)	
All Protestant	56,213	57.56	3,236

Column 2   *(Roman Catholic) Parish and Diocesan:*

Number of churches	21,481
Average expense per church	$20,226
Current church expense	$434 million
Construction (1/5 religious construction)	$173 million
Total	$607 million

Column 3   *(Roman Catholic) Parochial Schools:*

Note: Direct estimates were possible only biennially (for even-numbered years); odd-numbered were interpolated.

Students	4,705,000	
Expense per student	$138.08	(estimated on basis of public school cost per pupil)
Current expense	$650 million	
Expense met by contributions	$585 million	(assumed 90 per cent of current expense)
Construction expense	$311 million	(Roman Catholic assumed 90 per cent of all private elementary and secondary school construction)
Total	$896 million	

Notes to Table 3-4 continued

Column 4		*(Jewish):*

Members   2,128,000   (assumed 38.7 per cent of Jewish population)
Gift per member $ 69.07 (assumed 120 per cent of all Protestant)
Total $147 million

Column 5 (Other, comprised mainly of Eastern Orthodox and Old Catholic Groups):

Members   1,065,000   (assumed 35 per cent of claimed membership)
Gift per member $ 43.17 (assumed 75 per cent of all Protestant)
Total $ 46 million

Note: Detail may not add to total because of rounding.

[a]See note a, Table 3-1.

Table 3-5

*Distribution of Giving to Religious Organizations, by
Major Religious Groups, Five-Year Periods, 1929-59*
(per cent)

Year[a]	Protestant (1)	Roman Catholic		Jewish (4)	Other (5)	Total (6)
		Churches (2)	Parochial Schools (3)			
1929	60.2	20.3	15.4	3.7	.4	100.0
1930-34	59.1	21.7	15.3	3.5	.4	100.0
1935-39	60.4	21.8	13.6	3.7	.5	100.0
1940-44	62.6	19.7	13.6	3.6	.4	100.0
1945-49	64.4	15.9	15.7	3.5	.5	100.0
1950-54	63.5	13.9	18.6	3.1	.9	100.0
1954-59	65.0	12.7	18.5	3.0	.9	100.0
1929-59	63.6	15.2	17.2	3.2	.8	100.0

[a]See note a, Table 3-1.
Source: Table 3-4.

dependable collections of statistics on religious groups—the annual reports of the National Council of Churches [3] and the *Census of Religious Bodies*.[4] These sources not only contain direct data but also permit estimates and extrapolations.

In formulating the estimates in Table 3-4 religious organizations were divided into Protestant, Catholic, Jewish, and all other. The membership figures in the notes to Table 3-4 give some idea of gross and relative size of religious institutions in the United States, but they must be considered rough approximations. For much the same reasons as financial figures, membership figures fall short of accuracy, because of differences in age qualifications, as well as overlapping, incomplete, and incorrect reporting. The largest of the four groups is the Protestant, with the major Protestant sects, which report to the National Council of Churches, constituting two-thirds of this larger group. Catholic membership is substantially close to the NCC component. Jewish membership is estimated in the order of 4 per cent of all Protestant, and the residual category contains only about 1 per cent of total religious organization membership.

ESTIMATING METHODS

It should be made clear that the concern here is mainly with religious funds involved in the primary functions of religious organization: worship, and propagation of the faith. Certainly no clear line can be drawn between those church activities directed toward worship and propagation of the faith and those not. Provision for hospitals, care of the unfortunate, and education are well in keeping with religious principles. It is clearly a matter of degree. From the point of view of estimates of religious organization income, however, the relative importance of these various functions takes on more distinct shadings. For example, after 1935 the hard-charity cases were handled by public agencies. Church-supported health, welfare, and education, with one exception, account for only a minor fraction of income of religious organizations.

The exception is, of course, the support of Roman Catholic schools.

[3] National Council of Churches Reports are presented annually, variously entitled *Statistics of Church Finances, Statistics of Giving,* and *Stewardship Statistics.*

[4] U.S. Bureau of the Census, 1926 and 1936. Unfortunately for our purposes, no religious census was made in either 1946 or 1956.

Indeed, the question may be raised: Are these funds philanthropic donations or are they expenditures for educational services? Catholic schooling is an integral part of Catholic life. On the other hand, there is no
denying that many children are sent to parochial schools because their
parents feel they will acquire superior educations in that way. Since the
position of parochial schools in philanthropy is at best blurred and the
income involved is sizable, a separate series on parochial schools has
been formulated.

PROTESTANT GIVING

Protestant giving for 1958, which was $3,236 million, is broken down
into four categories: NCC reporting group, Negro churches, The Church
of Latter-Day Saints, and other. Receipts of the first group were readily
obtainable from the annual National Council of Churches reports, with
only minor changes having to be made. Total 1958 income estimated
for this group was $2,352 million, or about 70 per cent of all Protestant
giving. The per-member contribution rate was $62.68. This approximate
figure is pivotal to the study, for it has been used as a base to estimate
giving by other groups for which data were not so directly available.

In the case of Negro churches, the NCC per-member figure was adjusted to take into account the year-by-year differential in Negro-white
income [5] and the different giving pattern of Negroes. The gift-per-mem-
ber item of Negro family expenditures is smaller than that of white
families on the average, but apparently a higher proportion of it goes
to religious organizations. The 1950 *Consumer Expenditure Survey*
showed that white families' gifts and expenditures averaged $174 com-
pared with the Negro families' $81. The survey did not include a break-
down of this item. However, in the South, where Negro spending patterns
strongly influenced the data, religious giving was 39.2 per cent of all
giving, as compared with 29.4 per cent for the country as a whole.

A main stumbling block to estimation of Negro church receipts was
the absence of reliable direct data on membership, for there is much
overlapping among reporting organizations. Therefore, a membership
figure was derived by applying to census data on Negro population the

[5] U.S. Bureau of the Census, *Current Population Reports,* Series P-60.

religious participation rate of all adults, year by year.[6] In this way, total income of Negro churches in 1958 was estimated to be $329 million, or $39.49 per member.

The Latter-Day Saints, the third Protestant group, were dealt with separately because of their special tithing practices and because of their zealous support of their church.[7]

Protestant groups that are not included in the above categories are mainly those known as the "Third Force in American Religion," the Adventist and Pentecostal denominations. The receipts of this growing sector of religious organizations were estimated at $413 million in 1958. This figure was derived by applying to membership data the NCC per-member rate and the ratio .75 to account for the lower income level of these groups. This is a crude estimate, but as reasonable as possible in the absence of direct data.

CATHOLIC GIVING

Roman Catholic church giving for 1958 was $607 million for churches and dioceses and $896 million for parochial schools. In the absence of any publicly available data on receipts of Catholic churches, these amounts had to be estimated. While conceivably the NCC per-member contribution rate might provide a basis for estimating Catholic giving, substantial differences in intensity of building use and other factors seemed to warrant a different tack. The method of estimation used rests on the assumption that contributions both covered expenses and facilitated growth of Catholic churches, and thus receipts were equated with expenditures. Expenditures fall under two headings: costs of current operations and new construction for parishes and dioceses, and costs of current operations and new construction for parochial schools. Current operating expenses were derived from the average per-parish expendi-

---

[6] U.S. Bureau of Census, *Censuses of Population and Current Population Reports,* Series P-25.

[7] The 1950 *Consumer Expenditure Survey,* covering two predominantly Mormon cities, bore out these characteristics. The weighted average of religious giving in Salt Lake City and Ogden, Utah, was 1.45 times the national average of all denominational giving. Consequently this ratio was applied to the NCC per-member contribution rate and, along with membership figures, produced an estimate of receipts of the Latter-Day Saints. These were $140 million in 1958.

ture figure given in the 1936 *Census of Religious Bodies*. This figure was adjusted to take into account cost-of-living differences and growth in membership per church to generate a series for 1929–59. As a base for estimates of expenditures on parish and rectory construction, the Department of Commerce's figures on new religious construction were used. Catholic construction was taken to be one-fifth of the total, a proportion indicated by the 1936 religious census.

The basic source for probable expenditures for parochial school current operations was the *Biennial Survey of Education* (Office of Education), from which per-student public school costs were derived. Adjustments were made to allow for the very significant differences between salaries and other employment costs of public schools, on the one hand, and parochial schools, on the other.[8] The public school per-student figure so adjusted was multiplied by the number of parochial school students to obtain a total expenditure for parochial school current operations. This figure was reduced by one-tenth as an estimate of the proportion covered by tuition payments. The remaining figure, then, of $584,-699,000 in 1958 is our estimate of the amount received from "collection plates" that was channeled to parochial school current operating expenditures. Expenditures on parochial school construction were derived from the Department of Commerce series on *New Private Education Construction*.

JEWISH GIVING

Jewish giving for 1958 was estimated at $147 million. Since financial data were available for only one of the three major Jewish religious bodies, figures on giving were obtained indirectly by estimating first the membership and second a contribution rate to be applied to it. Figures on active membership were formulated by reducing Jewish population figures by two factors: the proportion of adult (fourteen and over) population to total population (70.3 per cent) and an adult participation rate estimated as 55 per cent. An earlier study indicated a contribution rate of 1.2 times the all-Protestant figure.[9]

[8] See New York *Herald Tribune,* May 9, 1961, for comparative salaries of religious, lay, and public school teachers.

[9] James N. Morgan, "Voluntarism in America—Attitudes and Behavior," Survey Research Center, Economic Behavior Program, June 1961, Table 2, p. 8 (mimeographed).

OTHER RELIGIOUS DENOMINATIONS

Religious giving not accounted for by the above three groups stems largely from the Greek Archdiocese and the Russian Orthodox churches. The 1958 estimate for the series was $46 million, which was on the order of 1 per cent of the total of religious organization income.

NONPAID SERVICE

In addition to money donations and contributions, some philanthropic institutions receive income in the form of direct services. Among the more significant of these are churches, youth organizations, community welfare organizations, and hospitals. The variety of services performed, the differences in amount of time given, and the paucity of information in general make it impossible to impute a value to these contributed services.

Services donated to hospitals provide a good illustration of this type of philanthropy. While we cannot provide anything close to an annual series on the value of these services to the 7,000 hospitals in the United States, our studies do provide some idea of the magnitude of these areas of philanthropy, and point up the difficulties that stand in the way of estimation.

Hospital volunteers perform all manner of services, which, for the present purpose, fall into two categories: fund raising and daily operations of the hospital. Their services range all the way from folding mimeographed letters and addressing envelopes for fund drives to making patients more comfortable. In fact, it is difficult to imagine the American hospital system without the benefit of volunteer services.

In the absence of a wage or salary payment to these volunteer workers, only an arbitrary value can be placed upon their services. Moreover, the types and kinds of work which they perform in the American hospital system are so varied that the assignment of a cash value for these services would be most arbitrary. Some inconclusive experimental work has been done, however, to relate hours of service of volunteer workers to total hours of paid staff.

A voluntary hospital in Westchester County, New York, reported that the paid staff of approximately 350 employees worked a total of 700,000 hours during the year, whereas the volunteers gave approximately 35,000 hours of free services during the same year. The ratio of paid hours to volunteer hours was 20 to 1.

Among the unpaid services of the volunteers was the work done in the bargain box selling merchandise donated by more than 1,400 contributions, as well as helping to feed patients and assisting the nurses in the care of patients. These services will unfortunately be excluded from any compilation of total philanthropic support of this hospital which is expressed in dollars. And the hospital is only one philanthropic institution aided by unpaid helpers. We have already mentioned uncounted corporate gifts to philanthropic endeavors in the form of paid time of personnel devoted to raising funds for community chest.

The extent of understatement from this source should be given further study. For we must recognize that the recipient institutions receive valuable service above and beyond the data set forth in this chapter. The value of these nonpaid services does not, however, account for any of the missing fifth in our "four-fifths reconciliation" of the data of Chapters 2 and 3.

4 Private
Foreign Philanthropy

Private foreign philanthropy was indicated (in Chapter 2) as the smallest of the quadrants, with a total of about 0.2 per cent of GNP for the entire period.

The unique feature of this quadrant is that it shows the amounts of philanthropic funds sent abroad—personal and institutional remittances —but not their origins. In the other three quadrants, there is an attempt to present the "where-from" and "where-to" types of information. The funds which are reported as distributed around the world by individuals and private institutions in the United States come from the same sources as those for private domestic philanthropy. Thus these distributions, having been counted as part of the income of private domestic philanthropy, had to be subtracted to get a correct total.

THE SOURCES OF PRIVATE FOREIGN PHILANTHROPY

Our classifications in Chapter 2, "person-to-person giving," and to a lesser extent "living donors," are the primary sources of personal remittances for private foreign aid. Most of the estimated gifts of living donors (and of corporations) are made to institutions, but some are doubtless made to individuals. Likewise, some private foreign aid by institutions originates in foundations. To this we add information, in Table 4-1, on

Table 4-1

Private Foreign Philanthropy: Private Remittances Abroad
(millions of dollars)

Year	Total Remittances		Institutional Remittances (Net)			Personal Remittances		
	Gross (3)+(6) (1)	Net (3)+(7) (2)	Total[a] (4)+(5) (3)	Religious[b] (4)	Nonsectarian and International (5)	Gross (6)	Net (7)	Major Countries or Areas of Destination, with Percentage of Total for Foremost (8)
1929	394	343	55	42	13	339	288	China (15), Italy, Canada
1930	349	306	49	40	10	300	257	Italy (15), China, Greece
1931	307	279	45	36	9	262	234	Italy (22), Greece, China
1932	234	217	35	27	8	199	182	Italy (26), China, Poland
1933	208	191	30	21	8	178	161	Italy (24), China, Greece
1934	181	162	30	22	8	151	132	Italy (20), China, Poland
1935	182	162	27	20	7	155	135	China (23), Italy, Poland
1936	198	176	28	22	6	170	148	China (21), Italy, Greece
1937	203	175	33	24	9	170	142	Italy (18), China, Greece
1938	190	153	38	26	12	152	115	Italy (20), China, Canada
1939	187	151	43	32	11	144	108	China (21), Italy, Eire

1940	237	178	49	30	19	188	129	China (27), Italy, Canada
1941	223	179	83	33	49	140	97	China (24), Italy, Canada
1942	164	123	65	30	35	99	58	China (22), Canada, United Kingdom
1943	295	249	115	38	77	180	134	China (29), Mexico, Canada
1944	402	357	181	58	124	221	176	Mexico (42), China, Canada
1945	520	473	234	77	156	286	240	Mexico (21), Italy, United Kingdom
1946	678	650	300	150	150	378	350	Western Europe (56)
1947	704	669	290	211	79	414	379	Western Europe (64)
1948	715	683	309	248	61	406	374	Western Europe (65)
1949	553	521	221	180	41	332	300	Western Europe (58)
1950	474	444	196	163	33	278	248	Western Europe (63)
1951	416	386	157	132	25	259	229	Western Europe (61)
1952	449	417	175	144	31	274	242	Western Europe (64)
1953	516	476	215	175	40	301	261	Western Europe (65)
1954	527	486	242	206	36	285	244	Western Europe (65)
1955	473	444	187	163	24	286	257	Western Europe (67)
1956	562	503	250	218	32	312	253	Western Europe (69)
1957	577	535	238	199	39	339	297	Western Europe (66)
1958	573	525	252	207	45	321	273	Western Europe (68)
1959	609	563	265	219	46	344	298	Western Europe (67)
1929-59d	12,300	11,176	4,437	3,193	1,243	7,863	6,741	

Notes to Table 4-1

Note: Details may not add to total due to rounding.

[a]Geographically, Western Europe was the leading recipient area in 1946 and 1947 for institutional remittances. Since then, countries outside Europe and the Western Hemisphere grouped together are the largest recipients.

[b]Remittances by religious groups are available for Protestant, Roman Catholic and Jewish groups. The amount for Protestants exceeded that for the Roman Catholic and Jewish groups during the years 1929-43. After 1943 remittances by Jewish groups exceeded those of Protestants in all the years except 1951, 1952, 1955, and 1957-59.

[c]This percentage was computed from gross personal remittances.

[d]See note a, Table 2-1.

Sources: 1929-39, Unpublished data from the Department of Commerce (letter September 23, 1959); 1940-45, *International Transactions of the United States During the War 1940-45,* Economic Series #65, Department of Commerce, p. 207-208; 1946-55, *Balance of Payments, Statistical Supplement, 1958.* Department of Commerce, p. 11-13, 115-116; 1956-59, unpublished data from the Department of Commerce (letter May 31, 1961).

overseas disbursements of funds derived from private domestic philan-thropic sources, both institutions and individuals.

The relative smallness of the amounts does not make private foreign aid unimportant. For many decades before our period began, individuals and private institutions were sending funds overseas for philanthropic purposes, and Curti has presented a detailed and comprehensive history of this type of philanthropy.[1] One of the longest and proudest records has been the expenditures made in foreign countries by our churches in support of their foreign missions.

The sources permit separate presentations of the annual net amount remitted from institutions and both gross and net from individuals. Reverse remittances from institutions and persons in other countries to our private institutions are not recorded, but are presumed to have been quite small during the three decades; so net institutional remittances are called net but are assumed to equal the gross. The institutional remit-tances are made by private institutions in the United States to individuals and institutions in foreign countries—not to foreign governments, al-though some small amounts could possibly have been given without being revealed in the sources. Institutional giving in Quadrant II is classified into religious and secular remittances.[2]

[1] Merle Curti, *American Philanthropy Abroad, A History,* New Brunswick, N.J., 1963.

[2] In his double-page chart, covering both the last half of his second period and all of his third period (1919–59), Curti (*ibid.,* pp. 506–507) gives total institu-

Doubtless some of the personal remittances do not qualify under our broad concept of philanthropy. Personal remittances are payments "made by individuals to friends or relatives [abroad] for noncommercial reasons," and these "unilateral transfers" exclude payments for goods and services and transfers of capital.[3] Some funds for deposit in foreign banks have probably been unavoidably included, but these amounts, which do not conform to our concept of philanthropy, are apparently relatively small.

The percentages of national income aggregates are presented in Table 4-2. This arrangement facilitates comparisons with the basic tables on private domestic philanthropy in Chapters 2 and 3.

GROSS AND NET REMITTANCES

Data are available for both net and gross individual remittances, but only the net amount is given for institutional remittances. The Department of Commerce does not compile data on gifts to us from private institutions of other countries—on the assumption that such receipts are negligible.[4] On the other hand, the difference between the gross and the net personal remittances indicates that for some years the people of other nations have sent a considerable amount of personal remittances to the people of the United States. It is likely that some portion of these reverse personal

tional remittances (net) and divides them into four categories: nonsectarian, Jewish, Catholic, and Protestant. For our period, 1929–59, his totals are the same as the figures in column 3 of our Table 4-1. We, however, show the religious as one combined subtotal in column 4.

Curti's denominational breakdown of the total for religious institutions is made necessary by his extensive treatment of the activities of a number of institutions (and many individuals) in each of the three religious groups. We have not deemed this separation of the data for the three religious groups necessary for our purposes.

The exclusion of all personal remittances from his chart suggests that Curti excluded from his history all remittances ($7.9 billion of our $12.3 billion) which were not first placed in the hands of American institutions before remitting overseas. However, in his text Curti makes references to person-to-person giving from Americans to persons in other countries.

[3] Hal B. Lary et al., United States in World Economy, Department of Commerce, Economic Series No. 23, 1943, p. 77. Jessie L. C. Adams, "Postwar Private Gifts to Foreign Countries Total $6 Billion," Foreign Commerce Weekly, June 17, 1957, pp. 13–17, counted both personal and institutional remittances under "gifts."

[4] Lary et al., United States in World Economy, p. 78.

Table 4-2

Relation of Private Foreign Philanthropy to National
Income Aggregates
(per cent)

Year	Total Net Remittances as Per Cent of GNP (1)	Institutional as Per Cent of GNP (2)	Personal Net as Per Cent of	
			GNP (3)	Disposable Personal Income (4)
1929	.328	.053	.276	.346
1930	.336	.054	.282	.346
1931	.366	.059	.307	.367
1932	.371	.060	.311	.374
1933	.341	.054	.288	.352
1934	.249	.046	.203	.254
1935	.223	.037	.186	.231
1936	.213	.034	.179	.223
1937	.193	.036	.156	.200
1938	.180	.045	.135	.175
1939	.166	.047	.119	.153
1940	.177	.049	.128	.170
1941	.142	.066	.071	.104
1942	.077	.041	.037	.049
1943	.129	.060	.070	.100
1944	.169	.086	.083	.120
1945	.221	.110	.112	.160
1946	.309	.142	.166	.218
1947	.286	.124	.162	.223
1948	.263	.119	.144	.198
1949	.202	.086	.116	.158
1950	.156	.069	.087	.119
1951	.117	.048	.070	.101
1952	.120	.050	.070	.101
1953	.130	.059	.071	.103
1954	.134	.067	.067	.095

Table 4-2 (concluded)

Year	Total Net Remittances as Per Cent of GNP (1)	Institutional as Per Cent of GNP (2)	Personal Net as Per Cent of	
			GNP (3)	Disposable Personal Income (4)
1955	.112	.047	.065	.094
1956	.120	.060	.060	.086
1957	.121	.054	.067	.096
1958	.118	.057	.061	.086
1959	.117	.055	.062	.088
1929-59[a]	.166	.066	.100	.139

Note: Detail may not add to total due to rounding.
[a]See note b, Table 2-1.
Source: Table 4-1 and Table 2-2.

remittances actually found their way into the income of some private institutions in the United States. Although the net is more important in some respects, both the gross and net values are presented in Table 4-1.

During the early years of the twentieth century, personal remittances were commonly called "immigrant remittances," a term which reflects the composition of the remittors, who were believed to be almost entirely foreign-born persons in the United States. The history of personal remittances prior to 1929 would show a fairly close relationship with the stream of immigration.

In the years just prior to World War I, personal remittances were probably in the neighborhood of $200 million to $250 million a year according to Williams.[5] There are no similar data available for institutional remittances in the same period. There was a decline in personal remittances during World War I to an average of about $150 million annually. Personal remittances in 1919 exceeded $700 million, a figure which has not since been surpassed.

[5] John H. Williams, "The Balance of International Payments of the United States for the Year 1920," *Review of Economic Statistics,* Supplements & Advance Letters, Preliminary Volume III, 1921, p. 197.

Institutional remittances began to assume significant proportions during World War I. Of the total of $711 million reported as "net private remittances" for the period from July 1, 1914, to December 31, 1918, in the balance-of-payments data, $600 million was personal remittances and the remaining $111 million was the amount expended abroad by the American Red Cross. Bremner estimated that 130 private agencies were participating in some form of war relief by 1917.[6] The data available do not include expenditures by other agencies, such as Near East Relief, the American Friends Service Committee, Hoover's C.R.B., the Knights of Columbus, and the Jewish Joint Distribution Committee. Perhaps a total of $200 million to $250 million was remitted by private institutions during the World War I period.

GOODS AND CASH

One of the features of our private foreign aid activities not set forth in Table 4-1 was the rapid increase in the importance of goods transmitted to the people of other countries in the years immediately after World War II. In 1946, 42 per cent of the net institutional remittances was goods, mostly food and clothing, and 38 per cent of the gross personal remittances; in 1947, 46 per cent of the institutional remittances was in the form of goods and 50 per cent of the gross personal remittances. The percentages were still high in 1948 (36 and 38, respectively); then the decline began as the food and clothing shortages in the war-torn countries lessened. By 1952 the percentages of net institutional remittances in the form of goods had declined to 25 per cent, and of gross personal remittances, 23 per cent; in 1959 the percentages were 21 and 16, respectively.

THE CHANGING ROLE

During our period of study, the total gross and net private remittances were lowest in dollars ($164 and $123 million) and as a percentage of GNP (0.103 and 0.077) in 1942, under the severe wartime restrictions

[6] Robert H. Bremner, *American Philanthropy,* Chicago, 1960, p. 128.

—not during the Great Depression. The high point of $715 million was in 1948, not 1959; the peak year for total net remittances of $683 million was also 1948, and it was 1947 for gross and net personal remittances (Table 4-1). The major countries receiving personal remittances before World War II were Italy and China; column 8 of Table 4-1 indicates that the leading country received about one-fifth of the total. Since 1946, the countries of Western Europe have received about two-thirds of the total.

The religious portions exceeded two-thirds of the institutional remittances prior to World War II. Institutional remittances have adapted quickly to changes in human needs. Remittances by the nonsectarian institutions exceeded those by religious institutions only in the war years, 1941–45. Since 1947 the religious groups have again dominated institutional remittances, about 80 per cent as compared with 72 per cent for the thirty-one years; aid to the people of Israel, a new independent state, has been an important factor. The continued progress of the missionary movement by the Protestant and Catholic churches has been a remarkable feature during even the late 1950's. The maintenance of this missionary effort and the number of missionaries maintained in Africa stand as an important monument to the long history of religious institutional remittances in our period and for many decades earlier.

The grand total for the thirty-one years of all types of private foreign aid (net) was $11,200 million, 0.17 per cent of GNP. Of this over-all total, $6,741 million, or 60 per cent, was net personal remittances. Net institutional remittances were $4,437 million, or 40 per cent, and religious remittances ($3,193 million) were 72 per cent of the institutional total.

PERCENTAGES OF GNP AND DPI

In Table 4-2, net institutional and net personal remittances are expressed as percentages of gross national product. Since personal remittances may be more closely related to disposable personal income, they have been expressed as percentages of DPI in column 4—0.14 for the thirty-one-year period.

The lowest percentages of GNP and DPI were for 1942, a year of severe restrictions on foreign exchange and foreign trade. The percentages were higher in the Great Depression than in the 1950's, indicating a downward trend in private foreign aid in relation to GNP (column 3) and DPI (column 4). This decade decline reflects, we believe, the emergence of the substitute programs of public foreign philanthropy (Chapter 9). The sharp temporary rises in the percentages of the national income aggregates in 1945–49 to prewar levels also reflect the ability of private institutional foreign aid to respond quickly to the aftermath of a great war; government programs for civilian foreign aid came more slowly and continued longer. In general, private and public foreign philanthropy are broadly supplemental rather than competitive.

CHOICE BETWEEN GROSS AND NET MEASURES

A pair of tables grouping the data from Tables 4-1 and 4-2 by five-year intervals may provide some perspective and a dilemma. Table 4-3 sets the total gross from Table 4-1 equal to 100 per cent; Table 4-4 sets the total net from Tables 4-1 and 4-2 equal to 100 per cent. (As noted, the difference between net and gross reflects "reverse" personal remittances; no reverse institutional remittances are recorded.)

The total net was 87.1 per cent of the total gross in 1929, 90.3 per cent in 1930–34, 85.1 per cent in 1935–39, and only 82.2 per cent in 1940–44; it remained above 90 per cent in each of the last three five-year periods. Total net institutional remittances rose from 14.0 per cent in 1929 to 14.8 per cent in 1930–34 to 17.6 per cent in 1935–39 to 37.3 per cent in 1940–44, and to a peak of 42.7 per cent in both 1945–49 and 1955–59. This upward trend is a noteworthy feature of the changing role of institutional aid in the field of private foreign philanthropy during our period. The complementary percentages for both gross and net personal aid decreased apace. This five-year grouping also sharpens the rising trend in the religious portion of institutional giving in the total gross of private foreign aid—from 10.7 per cent in 1929 to 36.0 per cent in 1955–59. Only in the five-year period 1940–44 did nonsectarian institutional giving exceed one-fifth of the total gross.

Table 4-4 sets the total net equal to 100.0 per cent, instead of the total gross as in Table 4-3. The percentages for the total net institutional in this is, therefore, higher than in Table 4-3 because the dollars involved are expressed as a percentage of a lower total; the totals are lowered by

Table 4-3

Distribution of Gross Private Foreign
Philanthropy by Five-Year Periods, 1929-59
(per cent)

Year[a]	Total		Institutional (Net)			Personal	
	Gross (1)	Net (2)	Total (3)	Religious (4)	Nonsectarian (5)	Gross (6)	Net (7)
1929	100.0	87.1	14.0	10.7	3.3	86.1	73.1
1930-34	100.0	90.3	14.8	11.4	3.4	85.2	75.5
1935-39	100.0	85.1	17.6	12.9	4.7	82.4	67.5
1940-44	100.0	82.2	37.3	14.3	23.0	62.7	45.0
1945-49	100.0	94.5	42.7	27.3	15.4	57.3	51.8
1950-54	100.0	92.7	41.4	34.4	6.9	58.6	51.4
1955-59	100.0	92.0	42.7	36.0	6.7	57.3	49.3
1929-59	100.0	90.9	36.1	26.0	10.1	63.9	54.8

Note: Detail may not add to total because of rounding.
[a]See note a, Table 2-1.
Source: Table 4-1.

the amount of the excess of the gross personal remittances above the net, $7,863 million above $6,741 million for the three decades. The percentages in column 5 for personal net (in the second table) lie between the percentages in columns 6 and 7 for personal gross and personal net (in the first table). But the trends are not altered.

The reader is free to make his own choice—to decide whether gross or net personal remittance plus institutional remittances should measure private foreign aid here.

There is also a question about including personal remittances in philanthropy. One's purpose will probably determine one's choice. Obviously, one way out of this dilemma would have been to restrict our concept of philanthropy to giving through institutions—not $11,176, but

Table 4-4

Distribution of Net Private Foreign Philanthropy
by Five-Year Periods, 1929-59
(per cent)

Year[a]	Total Net (1)	Institutional (Net)			Personal Net (5)
		Total (2)	Religious (3)	Nonsectarian (4)	
1929	100.0	16.0	12.2	3.8	84.0
1930-34	100.0	16.4	12.7	3.7	83.6
1935-39	100.0	20.7	15.2	5.5	79.3
1940-44	100.0	45.4	17.4	28.0	54.7
1945-49	100.0	45.2	28.9	16.3	54.8
1950-54	100.0	44.6	37.1	7.5	55.4
1955-59	100.0	46.4	39.2	7.2	53.6
1929-59	100.0	39.7	28.6	11.1	60.3

Note: Detail may not add to total because of rounding.
[a]See note a, Table 2-1.
Source: Table 4-1.

only $4,437 million for the thirty-one years. The records are better, but the concept is too narrow to quantify the generosity of the American people to people in other countries.

ABROAD AND AT HOME

As noted, one of our purposes was to reveal the portion of the income of private domestic philanthropy, $184.1 billion, used for private foreign philanthropy. Consider the gross amount, $12.3 billion, as the sum sent abroad during the relevant period. It was only 6.7 per cent of the entire income of private philanthropy, and 8.6 per cent if person-to-person giving is excluded. Clearly, more than 90 per cent of the income of private philanthropy was devoted to philanthropic endeavors within the United States.

The annual percentages of gross remittances to the entire income of private domestic philanthropy sent abroad are presented in column 3 of Table 4-5. A steady downward trend rather than fluctuations above and below the 6.7 per cent level for the thirty-one-year totals dominates this series. (The percentages—not shown—were higher, of course, in relation to the total income of private philanthropy less our estimate for person-to-person giving.) The percentages declined rather steadily from 14.8 for 1930–34 to 4.2 for 1955–59, with the exception of a secondary peak of 10.5 per cent for 1945–49.

Gross personal remittances of $7.9 billion for the three decades were 19.1 per cent of our estimate of person-to-person giving, $41.1 billion. The annual percentages are set forth in Table 4-6. Again, the percentage declines rather steadily from 78.1 in 1929 to 10.1 in 1959. For five-year periods gross personal remittances as a percentage of person-to-person giving did rise slightly, to 26.3 per cent in 1945–49, an interruption in the steady downward trend. This trend is so definite that we doubt it could be attributed to the problems of estimation and the limitations of the data already described. Rather, the downward trend probably results from a number of factors, with the declining relative importance of new immigrants very significant.

Institutional remittances of $4.4 billion for the entire thirty-one years were more than one-third of private gross foreign philanthropy ($12.3 billion), and might be compared with the subtotal of $143.0 billion, the income of private philanthropy which excludes the estimate $41.1 billion for person-to-person giving—about 3 per cent for the three decades. We present no table showing this percentage relationship annually because, among other reasons, some of the charitable bequests, totaling $8.3 billion, were not made to institutions.

We submit, however, that a direct comparison of religious funds sent abroad with the income received each year by religious institutions is meaningful for the entire period. The percentages sent abroad are set forth in Table 4-7. The total income of religious organizations, excluding income to parochial schools, was $48.3 billion (Table 3-4). Of this income, $3.2 billion, or 6.6 per cent, was sent abroad. Conversely, 93.4 per cent was used in the United States. The percentage sent abroad was

Table 4-5

*Private Foreign Philanthropy: Gross Remittances
Compared with Total, 1929-59*
(millions of dollars)

Year	Total Private Philanthropy (1)	Total Gross Remittances (2)	Percentage of Total Sent Abroad (3)
1929	2,221	394	17.7
1930	2,123	349	16.4
1931	1,869	307	16.4
1932	1,715	234	13.6
1933	1,518	208	13.7
1934	1,721	181	10.5
1935	1,761	182	10.3
1936	2,041	198	9.7
1937	2,194	203	9.3
1938	2,165	190	8.8
1939	2,396	187	7.8
1940	2,494	237	9.5
1941	2,934	223	7.6
1942	3,557	164	4.6
1943	4,359	295	6.8
1944	4,696	402	8.6
1945	5,043	520	10. 3
1946	5,438	678	12.5
1947	6,196	704	11.4
1948	6,797	715	10.5
1949	6,834	553	8.1
1950	7,569	474	6.3
1951	8,746	416	4.8
1952	9,573	449	4.7
1953	10,505	516	4.9
1954	10,705	527	4.9
1955	11,776	473	4.0
1956	12,703	562	4.4
1957	13,497	577	4.3
1958	14,023	573	4.1
1959	14,930	609	4.1
1929-59[a]	184,099	12,300	6.7

[a]See note a, Table 2-1.
Source: Table 2-1, column 8; Table 4-1, column 1.

Table 4-6

Private Foreign Philanthropy: Gross Personal
Remittances Compared with Person-to-Person Giving, 1929-59
(millions of dollars)

Year	Person-to-Person Giving (1)	Gross Personal Remittances (2)	Percentage of Person-to-Person Giving Sent Abroad (3)
1929	434	339	78.1
1930	388	300	77.3
1931	322	262	81.4
1932	300	199	66.3
1933	280	178	63.6
1934	316	151	47.8
1935	331	155	46.8
1936	394	170	43.1
1937	423	170	40.2
1938	400	152	38.0
1939	471	144	30.6
1940	502	188	37.5
1941	608	140	23.0
1942	778	99	12.7
1943	980	180	18.4
1944	1,027	221	21.5
1945	1,105	286	25.9
1946	1,235	378	30.6
1947	1,424	414	29.1
1948	1,559	406	26.0
1949	1,586	332	20.9
1950	1,744	278	15.9
1951	2,020	259	12.8
1952	2,208	274	12.4
1953	2,414	301	12.5
1954	2,486	285	11.5
1955	2,694	286	10.6
1956	2,927	312	10.7
1957	3,094	339	11.0
1958	3,231	321	9.9
1959	3,418	344	10.1
1929-59[d]	41,099	7,863	19.1

[a]See note a, Table 2-1.
Source: Table 2-1, column 7; Table 4-1, column 6.

Table 4-7

Proportion of Religious Giving Sent Abroad, 1929-59
(millions of dollars)

Calendar Year	Total Religious Giving (1)	Religious Giving Abroad (2)	Percentage of Total Sent Abroad (3)
1929	838	42	5.0
1930	787	40	5.1
1931	696	36	5.2
1932	579	27	4.7
1933	505	21	4.2
1934	516	22	4.3
1935	534	20	3.7
1936	569	22	3.9
1937	593	24	4.0
1938	605	26	4.3
1939	598	32	5.4
1940	612	30	4.9
1941	680	33	4.9
1942	736	30	4.1
1943	809	38	4.7
1944	889	58	6.5
1945	1,009	77	7.6
1946	1,186	150	12.6
1947	1,335	211	15.8
1948	1,589	248	15.6
1949	1,811	180	9.9
1950	1,962	163	8.3
1951	2,175	132	6.1
1952	2,391	144	6.0
1953	2,650	175	6.6
1954	2,905	206	7.1
1955	3,166	163	5.1
1956	3,497	218	6.2
1957	3,778	199	5.3
1958	4,036	207	5.1
1959	4,271	219	5.1
1929-59[a]	48,307	3,193	6.6

[a]See note a, Table 2-1.

Source: Table 3-4, column 7, total religious giving excluding parochial schools classified as education; Table 4-1, column 4.

about 5 per cent at the beginning and at the end of our three decades, except for a noticeable peak during the period 1945–49, when the proportion sent abroad was 12.5 per cent. In the annual data the peak percentages were, for 1947 and 1948, 15.8 and 15.6, respectively. It is clear, therefore, that religious institutions in the United States did respond to the enormous demands for assistance abroad in the years immediately following World War II; the complementary percentage of the income of these institutions used within the United States declined sharply, following the cessation of hostilities, to lows of 84.2 and 84.4 per cent in 1947 and 1948. As Curti and others have pointed out, the response of religious and sectarian philanthropy in the United States during World War II was hampered by the political and transportation problems during the conflict, but the expansion after hostilities ended was very rapid.

DIRECTOR'S COMMENT—Willard L. Thorp

While Dickinson is certainly correct in suggesting that this quadrant is the smallest of the four, the data upon which he relied probably understate the generosity of Americans in the foreign field. To be sure, the estimates of person-to-person giving are much too high if one excludes transfers within the family, as is done in the estimates for domestic person-to-person giving. Probably the bulk of the personal remittances are either from immigrants or their descendants to members of their families still abroad or from Americans to American relatives abroad, including soldiers, diplomats, students and the like. One can only guess about proportions, but I suspect that remittances to nonfamily members not involving some sort of *quid pro quo* would be relatively small, say one-quarter of the total included in the estimates.

On the other hand, the estimate for giving by private institutions appears to be too small. Recent reports are that there are some 500 such nonprofit institutions providing technical assistance abroad. Remittance data are quite inadequate to measure their activity. They do not cover the actual contributions by givers, much of which are spent in the United States for overhead, recruiting and the like—costs which are included in the corresponding domestic figures. The cost of travel for their American personnel sent abroad is often a substantial part of the budgets of these institutions and is not included when paid in the United States. Furthermore, many Americans when abroad arrange to have some part of their compensation deposited in their home banks or otherwise paid in the United States. Thus part of their actual compensation never appears as a remittance. Finally, since many persons involved are volunteers themselves or may be members of some group providing only minimum subsistence payments, the real contributions made in services may far exceed the cash flow.

A survey made about 1960 by the State Department's Advisory Committee on Private Enterprise in Foreign Aid estimated that the volume of foreign assistance given annually by foundations and voluntary agencies was about $700 million and this is the figure which was used by the U.S. Government in making its annual report to the Development Assistance Committee in Paris. This suggests that recorded remittances represent no more than one-third of the amount which should properly be credited to institutions engaged in foreign philanthropy.

If one applies the two modifications which are suggested above, they tend largely to offset each other. The total for this quadrant, 1929–59, would be increased from $12,300 to $15,300 million. Using Dickinson's approach, the grand total for all four quadrants would not change, since the quadrant for private domestic philanthropy would have to be reduced correspondingly. Domestic institutional giving would be reduced by $8,900 million and domestic person-to-person giving would be increased by $5,900 million. These figures make no allowance for any undervaluation of the services actually rendered.

5 Social Welfare and Public Philanthropy

DEFINITIONS

Not all the forms of public philanthropy are as deeply ingrained in our political, economic, and social system as, for example, provision for old-age assistance. A number of questions must therefore be confronted at this point in order to lay the groundwork for the trends in public philanthropy. Are not all expenditures by government intended to promote the welfare of the people? If not, what expenditures of government should be excluded from the concept of welfare or social welfare? What is the meaning of the term public philanthropy, as used in this report? More important, what are the differences between public and private philanthropy? Are all expenditures for what are currently called social welfare (or governmental social welfare) to be considered as forms of public philanthropy?

It seems best to discuss these rather controversial questions with reference to four recent volumes, each of which has the word welfare in its title.[1] Later, reference will be made to a number of publications of the

---

[1] Vaughn Davis Bornet, *Welfare in America,* Norman, Okla., 1960; Alfred de Grazia and Ted Gurr, *American Welfare,* New York, 1961; Walter A. Friedlander, *Introduction to Social Welfare,* Englewood Cliffs, N. J., 1961; Harold L. Wilensky and Charles N. Lebeaux, *Industrial Society and Social Welfare,* New York, 1958.

Social Security Administration itself. The development of the welfare theme in these studies helps to explain the term public philanthropy as used in the present study in relation to currently used concepts of welfare and social welfare.

Bornet boldly offers a "tightly worded" definition: "Social welfare is special services supplied and material assistance given by all or part of society to a human being thought to be in need." [2] He notes that a definite boundary cannot be established because social welfare is still in a fluid state; however, a list of some of the areas he eliminates will prove helpful in understanding his concept: "(1) Education—that is, public and private schools, adult education, and public libraries. (2) Corrections—prisons, police, parole and probation officers, jurists, and courts. (3) Private hospitalization and clinical procedures, the services of physicians and nurses (except when free or part-pay) remembering that Blue Cross and similar prepayment programs are insurance paid by individuals or by companies. (4) Union-management health and/or pension plans, which are to a large extent benefits in lieu of wages. (5) Civil service pensions and retirement plans, for the government contributes in the capacity of employer. (6) United States overseas aid and technical assistance programs, given through the United Nations or extended independently; these, it has been contended, are integral parts of our foreign policy." [3]

He also apparently excludes veterans' benefits and most nonbenevolent expenditures of churches, social insurance, and the protective services of many groups.

De Grazia and Gurr present a much broader concept of welfare. They describe it as "the material and spiritual well-being of people," and distinguish between social welfare "for the good of those who need society's special attention" and general welfare "for the equal benefit of all men." They recognize that "social welfare is closely akin to other kinds of welfare and that most institutions of society provide many types of welfare." [4] Accordingly, public and private agencies are involved in social welfare activities. The test of a *quid pro quo* or its absence in the activities covered is not specifically applied. At the outset they note that a "welfare activity" may benefit either those who are economically well-

[2] Bornet, *Welfare in America*, p. 31.
[3] *Ibid.*, p. 47.
[4] De Grazia and Gurr, *American Welfare*, p. 1.

to-do or those who are impoverished, or both.[5] This major distinction marks off "welfare activity" from the long history of private and public charity as a type of activity in which the status of the individual is a determining factor; recipients of "welfare" need not be poor, only eligible.

Unlike Bornet, they do not present a list of major exclusions. But in their numerous tables the grouping of items would suggest a very wide variety of types and kinds of activities. For example, governmental expenditures for foreign aid are listed as general welfare, with technical assistance designated as governmental social welfare. Also, unlike Bornet, they list veterans' services and benefits as within the compass of the social welfare programs of the national government.[6] Moreover, social insurance, including the entire amount of Old-Age and Survivors Insurance benefits, is regarded as welfare but apparently not social welfare.

Their concept of social welfare, private and public, is indicated by their table for a typical year in the 1950's.[7] Four broad sources of funds for social welfare are presented and estimates for each of the totals are given:

Direct individual contributions, 22 per cent	$8.0 billion
Corporate and other business contributions, 2 per cent	0.7 billion
Contributions through foundations and other funds, 3 per cent	1.0 billion
Contributions through government taxation, 73 per cent	27.0 billion
Total	$36.7 billion

The first three items have already been classified under private philanthropy in our earlier chapters. The $27 billion from government includes $14 billion for education, $5 billion for veterans' programs, $3.5 billion for public health, and $4.5 billion for public assistance and social service. Social insurance is excluded.

While most government activities might be termed welfare (in the broad sense), a number of programs are considered to be "social welfare" activities. Under governmental social welfare, de Grazia and Gurr include veterans' programs (total expenditure), public assistance, health and medical programs, foreign technical assistance, public housing and community development, higher education and social services in the edu-

[5] *Ibid.*, p. 3.
[6] *Ibid.*, pp. 12, 371.
[7] *Ibid.*, p. 12.

cational system (e.g., school lunch programs, etc.), vocational rehabilitation, and a small miscellaneous category. Social insurance programs are apparently in a hybrid category, as they are sometimes included and sometimes excluded (p. 12) from social welfare (in the latter instance, designated as "general welfare"). Similarly, their treatment of education is ambiguous. The text suggests that the educational system is "general welfare," though certain social welfare activities are provided thereunder (p. 171). But the table reproduced above includes all local and state expenditures for elementary and secondary schools. De Grazia and Gurr classify only technical assistance abroad under social welfare; they consider the remainder, all military and other nonmilitary foreign aid, under "American welfare abroad"; whereas we do not consider military aid as public foreign philanthropy.

In summary, de Grazia and Gurr may have intended their table for 1950 to circumscribe their concept of public and private social welfare in a broad welfare system. If so, the four lines or categories describe activities somewhat similar to the flow of funds encompassed in our study, but with important differences. Other tables in their volume, however, raise some doubts about the similarity to our concepts.

Thus, the studies by Bornet and by de Grazia and Gurr do not entirely agree upon what should be included under welfare and general welfare, and, more particularly, under public social welfare.

Friedlander defines social welfare as follows: " 'Social welfare' is the organized system of social services and institutions, designed to aid individuals and groups to attain satisfying standards of life and health, and personal and social relationships which permit them to develop their full capacities and to promote their well-being in harmony with the needs of their families and the community." [8] He further states that no universally accepted agreement has been reached on the meaning and scope of the term. For example, although education and labor legislation contribute to well-being and physical and mental growth, they are not included under his definition of social welfare. He includes social insurance and most of the social welfare expenditures which are presented in the annual tabulations by Ida C. Merriam in the *Social Security Bulletin*. He definitely includes veterans' benefits; on the international scene he includes many of the social welfare activities of the United Nations and the technical assistance program of the State Department.

[8] Friedlander, *Introduction to Social Welfare*, p. 4.

Wilensky and Lebeaux distinguish between two concepts of social welfare, the "residual" and the "institutional." The residual concept "holds that social welfare institutions should come into play only when the normal structures of supply, the family and the market, break down." According to the authors, this concept was more popular in the United States before the Great Depression of 1929 than it is now.[9] The institutional concept, which Wilensky and Lebeaux adopt, envisions the "welfare services as normal, 'first line' functions of modern industrial society." No stigma or abnormality is implied.

The institutional concept contains five criteria for delineating social welfare. These are: formal organization, social sponsorship and accountability, absence of profit motive as a dominant program purpose, functional generalization (an integrative, rather than segmental, view of human needs), and direct focus on concern with human consumption needs.[10] Modern social welfare must really be thought of as help given to a stranger, one with whom the giver has no personal bond. The service must be socially sponsored, by government or by a "smaller collectivity." Welfare plans provided by private business, such as recreation facilities, pension plans, and nurseries for the benefit of employees, must be considered as either social welfare programs under business auspices or as nonwelfare programs even though they perform functions which are essentially similar to those performed by social welfare agencies. Much depends on the purpose; if, for example, the pension is considered a part of the wage structure, the pension is not welfare. Moreover, some programs generated by employers, such as supplemental employment benefits, doubtless create pressure for expanded public programs of unemployment compensation. However, data on industrial welfare programs are included. The fee-scaling of physicians in private practice is regarded by them as essentially a part of the professional norm or ethics of physicians; services to charity patients are therefore not welfare.

In general, welfare institutions do the job that other institutions do not. This implies a wide variety of services to meet human needs. Wilensky and Lebeaux exclude the school system from social welfare because it has a segmental approach; social welfare is characterized by an "integrative view of human needs." [11]

[9] Wilensky and Lebeaux, *Industrial Society and Social Welfare*, pp. 138, 139.
[10] *Ibid.*, p. 146.
[11] *Ibid.*, p. 144.

All governmental services are socially sponsored, but social welfare is characterized by direct concern with human consumption needs. Hence national defense and other services "inherent in the nature of the state" are excluded from social welfare, as are such intermediate activities as road building and forest conservation, where the benefits are "so remote in time or diffused among the population that they will not be privately provided." Social welfare is the direct services of government for individuals: schools and universities, subsidized housing, museums, and so on. However, when such a service "becomes highly developed, widespread in its incidence among the population, and professionally staffed by persons other than social workers," such as public education, there is some tendency to exclude it from the category of social welfare. "Tax-supported social welfare programs in the United States are termed 'public welfare,' " but incorrectly identified as relief.[12]

Apparently Wilensky and Lebeaux would not include farm aid or any of the programs of the federal government designed to aid agriculture because they are too close to our systems of production, not directly concerned with human resources. Apparently they would include most of the items (with or without the large item for public education) covered in the Merriam tabulations in the *Social Security Bulletin* (which we shall discuss later), but would also include public recreation, correctional systems, and welfare programs for Indians. They include unemployment compensation, for example, not as an antidepression measure, but as a means of alleviating individual distress.[13] They do note evidence of a tremendous increase in expenditures by local private agencies—private social welfare—for the leisure-time activity of persons in the community regardless of their income status, and for a wide variety of other purposes.

Jenkins recognizes that the government in many areas is paralleling the activity of philanthropy; he indicates a number of similarities and differences in their operation but he restricts his concept of philanthropy to the private sector.[14]

The position of Andrews is set forth in his monumental 1950 study and in briefer comments in his 1956 study.[15] In the earlier study he

[12] *Ibid.*, pp. 147, 148.
[13] *Ibid.*, p. 145.
[14] Edward C. Jenkins, *Philanthropy in America,* New York, 1950.
[15] F. Emerson Andrews, *Philanthropic Giving,* New York, 1950, Chaps. 3 and 5; and *Philanthropic Foundations,* New York, 1956.

notes: "The greatest single stride ever made in bringing into the orbit of government the services that were formerly first charges upon our philanthropies was the Social Security Act, enacted in 1935 but broadened by later amendment and still needing considerable improvement. Where it touches most closely the traditional fields of 'charity' is in its provisions, in which the states participate, for the needy aged, dependent children, and the needy blind." [16] Looking toward the future, he states: "Clearly, we are now in a period of change, and one of the most significant elements in that change is the extent to which many basic needs of man are being met by government." [17] He summarizes some of the federal grants to foreign countries in the 1940's, but states clearly: "Although our government's gifts to other nations are not private philanthropy, and many of them are not even philanthropy under its broadest definition, their amount and character need to be stated to lend perspective to private giving." [18]

Gifts by private institutions in the United States to the people of other countries are deemed private foreign philanthropy, but all aid by government, both military and nonmilitary, is excluded from his grand totals of "receipts of private philanthropy" and "estimate of current annual giving to private philanthropy." [19] In *Philanthropic Foundations* he describes and gives data for the National Science Foundation, a federal agency, and the quasi-governmental Smithsonian Institution. The assets and expenditures of these foundations, however, are not included in his summary tables; one of his criteria for a foundation is that it be a nongovernmental organization.

The purpose of Jenkins, Andrews, and other earlier students of philanthropy, it should be emphasized, was to develop data on private and to touch incidentally upon the newer items of public philanthropy.

THE MERRIAM LIST

The list of items considered social welfare expenditures under public programs, used in the annual compilations by Mrs. Ida C. Merriam of the

[16] Andrews, *Philanthropic Giving,* p. 44.
[17] *Ibid.,* pp. 46, 48.
[18] *Ibid.,* p. 77.
[19] *Ibid.,* Tables 14 and 15, p. 73.

Social Security Administration, form a much more definite starting point for our analysis of public domestic philanthropy than the literature on welfare and social welfare. It has the definite advantage of being regularly published and therefore completely available. In the description of the data in each annual publication of the Merriam totals, there is clear indication that the various concepts of governmental or public social welfare expenditures have been thoroughly considered by Mrs. Merriam and her staff, and they have settled upon this list of items after consideration of the literature, the controversies, and the differences of opinion on what constitutes social welfare.

The broad classifications in the Merriam compilation of social welfare expenditures under public programs are social insurance, public aid, health and medical programs, other welfare services, veterans' programs, education, and public housing. Moreover, the data are divided into expenditures from federal funds and expenditures from state and local funds. Some capital expenditures are included. The annual totals are compared with total government expenditures and with GNP.

Tables 5-1 and 5-2 present the data from the Merriam compilations for selected years of our period. Breakdowns for federal and for state and local social welfare expenditures under public programs are set forth in Table 5-1. Here attention should be called to the growth from a grand total of $4 billion in 1928–29 to $52 billion in 1959–60. As a percentage of GNP, the increase has been from 4.2 per cent to 10.5 per cent. Since the seven major items and subitems will be examined at a later point for the purpose of inclusion, exclusion, or modification in our tables for public domestic philanthropy, further comment on this large table will be postponed.

In Table 5-2 the expenditures for each of the seven major categories are shown as a percentage of the total expenditures and the federal percentage of the total expenditures in each of the selected years. The decline in the percentage for education from 56.8 per cent to 34.3 per cent, and the increase in the percentage for social insurance from 7.9 per cent to 37.3 per cent, provide some perspective of important changes in social welfare expenditures during our period of study; the indicated increase in the proportion of federal funds from 14.5 per cent to 46.2 per cent is a part of this historical perspective. The analysis of the data derived from these two tables will be presented later, since our concept of public domestic philanthropy is not coextensive with Mrs. Merriam's universe. Nevertheless, the Merriam concept of social welfare expenditures under public programs comes much closer to our concept of public domestic philanthropy than any of the concepts of public social welfare examined earlier in this chapter; and, as already noted, the compilations will presumably continue to be published annually.

The largest item that might reasonably be added to the Merriam list is farm relief, starting with the Agricultural Adjustment Administration expenditures born of the Great Depression in the 1930's. But the payments received by farmers for complying with changing requirements of the program are basically payments established from time to time by federal legislation for the purpose of controlling the production of livestock and crops. In times of war, the purpose has been to stimulate production. Thus the farm program really fails to qualify as a social welfare expenditure because it is part of the productive aspect of the American economy. We shall, therefore, exclude payments under the farm program and its antecedents from our data.

Public expenditures for recreation are not included in the Merriam tables. A number of comments in the annual surveys indicate, however, that this exclusion results primarily from problems of compiling the necessary data and secondarily from a decision that such expenditures should not be included. Such public expenditures are clearly public domestic philanthropy. Provision for public recreation in Yosemite National Park or Yellowstone Park, and the enjoyment of the beauty of such public places is quite as real as the utilities enjoyed by the use of the knife, the fork, and the spoon in consuming food purchased by social welfare funds.

OTHER QUESTIONS

This brief examination of concepts and data on social welfare leaves a number of questions unanswered. Our test of philanthropy is essentially found in the description of the concept itself in Chapter 1. It is giving the money away without an immediate or definite *quid pro quo*. It is difficult to conceive of the support of certain assistance programs, for example, indigency in old age as being other than a manifestation of the generosity of the people. Centuries ago it may have reflected only a

Table 5-1

Social Welfare Expenditures[a] Under Public Programs, Selected Fiscal Years 1934-35 Through 1959-60 (millions of dollars)

Program	1928-29	1934-35	1939-40	1944-45	1949-50	1954-55	1958-59	1959-60
Total	4,310	6,494.0	8,481.8	8,908.7	23,054.0	32,127.7	49,195.5	51,875.8
Social insurance	340	383.9	1,216.4	1,387.7	4,911.2	9,878.3	18,267.8	19,325.8
Old-age survivors, and disability insurance[b]			28.1	266.8	784.1	4,436.3	9,615.9	11,032.3
Railroad retirement			115.7	143.7	304.4	575.6	777.6	925.4
Public employee retirement[c]		210.0	254.5	382.8	743.4	1,379.5	2,342.5	2,569.9
Unemployment insurance and employment service[d]			551.7	185.9	2,230.1	2,114.0	3,717.9	2,824.0
Railroad unemployment insurance			18.9	4.3	119.6	158.6	200.2	215.2
Railroad temporary disability insurance					31.1	54.2	57.0	68.6
State temporary-disability insurance, total[e]				5.1	72.3	217.5	328.1	344.1
Hospital and medical benefits[f]					2.2	20.0	38.5	39.6
Workmen's compensation, total[g]		173.9	247.5	399.1	626.2	942.6	1,228.6	1,346.2
Hospitalization and medical benefits[f]		65.0	90.0	122.0	193.0	315.0	395.0	430.0
Public aid		2,997.6	3,598.7	1,030.5	2,496.2	3,003.0	3,997.9	4,100.6
Public assistance[h]		623.9	1,124.3	1,028.8	2,490.2	2,941.1	3,890.9	4,041.2
Vendor medical payments[f]						211.9	410.0	492.5
Other[i]	470	2,373.7	2,474.4	1.7	6.0	61.9	107.0	59.4
Health and medical programs[j]		543.7	697.2	1,936.9	2,344.3	2,914.0	4,052.4	4,232.1
Hospital and medical care		378.0	460.0	1,585.7	1,506.0	2,052.1	2,652.5	2,812.5

Code	Program							
	Civilian programs	339.0	415.0	485.7	1,174.0	1,449.5	1,907.4	2,173.9
	Defense Department and Medicare	39.0	45.0	1,100.0	332.0	602.6	745.1	638.6
	Maternal and child health services[k]	6.7	13.8	62.0	29.8	92.9	133.4	139.4
	Medical research[l]		3.0	15.0	51.3	99.8	287.4	375.0
	Other public health activities[m]	124.0	179.5	222.8	328.4	315.8	418.7	406.1
	Medical-facilities construction	35.0	41.0[f]	51.5[f]	428.8[f]	353.3	560.4	499.1
	Defense Department		f	f	f	8.9	34.3	30.9
	Other	35.0	41.0	51.5	428.8	344.4	526.1	468.2
500[i]	Other welfare services[i]	139.3	114.1	195.3	401.6	580.2	1,020.1	1,161.1
	Vocational rehabilitation, total	2.2	4.1	10.2	30.0	41.4	90.3	100.6
	Medical rehabilitation[f]	.2	.4	1.4	7.4	9.2	16.6	17.7
	Institutional and other care[n]	111.1	65.0	67.5	107.9	165.4	377.5	450.2
	School lunch[o]			47.4	158.7	238.3	366.3	399.3
	Child welfare[p]	26.0	45.0	70.2	104.9	135.1	186.0	211.0
550	Veterans' programs[q]	449.8	535.0	890.1	6,380.8	4,369.3	5,093.7	5,091.2
	Pensions and compensation[r]	390.2	447.8	755.9	2,092.8	2,712.3	3,325.6	3,425.8
	Health and medical services	58.9	86.2	114.5	745.8	761.1	894.6	942.1
	Hospital and medical care	56.0	72.1	96.3	585.9	722.0	836.0	867.2
	Hospital construction	2.9	14.1	16.2	156.2	33.0	45.7	57.5
	Medical research		.1	2.0	3.7	6.1	12.9	17.3
	Education		1.0	9.7	2,689.1	699.9	602.7	404.7
	Welfare and other[s]	.7		10.0	853.1	196.0	270.7	318.6
2,450	Education	1,979.7	2,316.2	3,457.2	6,507.9	11,294.3	16,607.5	17,788.3
	Elementary and secondary, total	1,850.7	2,115.4	2,679.5	5,745.7	10,046.3	14,602.9	15,587.9
	Construction[f]	115.3	50.1[t]	82.5	1,018.7	2,362.4	2,980.7	2,863.7
	Higher education and other, total	129.0	200.8	777.7	762.2	1,248.0	2,004.6	2,200.4
	Construction[f]	u	26.0	u	217.2	312.1	499.6	535.9
	Public housing[v]		4.2	11.0	12.0	88.6	156.1	176.7

(continued)

Table 5-1 (continued)

Program	1928-29	1934-35	1939-40	1944-45	1949-50	1954-55	1958-59	1959-60
Total	625	3,013.4	3,290.2	3,460.3	10,028.4	13,898.6	22,601.3	23,978.5
From Federal Funds								
Social insurance		98.9	350.2	728.9	2,059.6	6,428.8	13,028.2	14,292.4
Old-age, survivors, and disability insurance[b]			28.1	266.8	784.1	4,436.3	9,615.9	11,032.3
Railroad retirement			115.7	143.7	304.4	575.6	777.6	925.4
Public-employee retirement[c]		90.0	107.5	184.8	433.4	799.5	1,377.5	1,519.9
Unemployment insurance and employment service[d]			65.8	114.6	361.9	354.1	927.7	467.8
Railroad unemployment insurance			18.9	4.3	119.6	158.6	200.2	215.2
Railroad temporary-disability insurance					31.1	54.2	57.0	68.6
Workmen's compensation, total[g]		8.9	14.2	14.7	25.1	50.5	72.3	63.1
Hospitalization and medical benefits[f]		3.0	5.2	4.7	5.2	6.9	8.2	9.0
Public aid		2,373.7	2,244.9	420.1	1,103.2	1,504.2	2,082.1	2,116.9
Public assistance[h]			280.1	418.4	1,097.2	1,442.3	1,975.1	2,057.5
Vendor medical payments[f]						23.3	150.9	199.6
Other[j]		2,373.7	1,964.8	1.7	6.0	61.9	107.0	59.4
Health and medical programs[k]		60.0	99.2	1,241.9	661.2	964.9	1,434.8	1,414.0
Hospital and medical care		48.0	50.0	1,115.7	383.0	673.1	846.5	747.5
Civilian programs		9.0	5.0	15.7	51.0	70.5	101.4	108.9
Defense Department and Medicare		39.0	45.0	1,100.0	332.0	602.0	745.1	638.6
Maternal and child health services[l]			7.8	55.2	20.1	23.7	33.3	33.3
Medical research[m]			3.0	15.0	51.3	99.8	271.4	352.0
Other public health activities[n]			37.5	54.6	80.0	75.0	77.2	58.1
Medical-facilities construction		12.0	1.0	1.5	126.8	93.3	206.4	223.1
Defense Department			f	f	f	8.9	34.3	30.9

Other	2.1	1.0	1.5	126.8	84.4	172.1	192.2
Other welfare services	1.0	9.7	87.0	166.7	244.2	383.1	410.1
Vocational rehabilitation, total	.1	2.0	7.5	21.0	26.4	57.4	64.3
Medical rehabilitation[f]	1.1	.2	.7	3.7	5.7	10.4	11.2
Institutional and other care[o]		6.1	16.0	21.7	41.4	37.5	26.2
School lunch[p]			47.4	119.7	169.3	275.9	306.7
Child welfare[q]		1.6	16.1	4.2	7.1	12.3	12.9
Veterans' programs[r]	449.8	535.0	890.1	5,918.8	4,307.7	5,032.6	4,979.3
Pensions and compensation[s]	390.2	447.8	755.9	2,092.8	2,712.3	3,325.6	3,425.8
Health and medical services	58.9	86.2	114.5	745.8	761.1	894.6	942.1
Hospital and medical care	56.0	72.1	96.3	585.9	722.0	836.0	867.2
Hospital construction	2.9	14.1	16.2	156.2	33.0	45.7	57.5
Medical research		.1	2.0	3.7	6.1	12.9	17.3
Education			9.7	2,689.1	699.9	602.7	404.7
Welfare and other[t]	.7	1.0	10.0	391.1	134.4	209.6	206.8
Education	28.9	47.0	81.3	106.9	374.8	512.8	622.3
Elementary and secondary, total	19.9	32.5	48.0	63.9	315.4	348.9	395.5
Construction[f]	v	v	v	5.2	139.3	80.7	74.8
Higher education and other, total	9.0	14.5	33.3	43.0	59.4	163.9	226.8
Construction[f]	v	v	v	5.9	5.4	1.0	1.2
Public housing[w]		4.2	11.0	12.0	74.0	127.7	143.5
From State and Local Funds							
Total	3,480.6	5,190.6	5,448.4	13,025.6	18,229.1	26,594.2	27,897.3
Social insurance	285.0	866.2	658.8	2,851.6	3,449.5	5,239.6	5,033.4
Public employee retirement[c]	120.0	147.0	198.0	310.0	580.0	965.0	1,050.0
Unemployment insurance and employment service[d]		485.9	71.3	1,868.2	1,759.9	2,790.2	2,356.1

(continued)

Table 5-1 (concluded)

Program	1928-29	1934-35	1939-40	1944-45	1949-50	1954-55	1958-59	1959-60
State temporary disability insurance, total[e]				5.1	72.3	217.5	328.1	344.1
Hospital and medical benefits[f]					2.2	20.0	38.5	39.6
Workmen's compensation, total[g]		165.0	233.3	384.4	601.1	892.1	1,156.3	1,283.2
Hospitalization and medical benefits[f]		62.0	84.0	117.3	187.8	308.1	386.8	421.0
Public aid		623.9	1,352.8	610.4	1,393.0	1,498.8	1,915.8	1,983.7
Public assistance[h]			843.2	610.4	1,393.0	1,498.8	1,915.8	1,983.7
Vendor medical payments[f]						188.6	259.1	292.9
Other[j]			509.6					
Health and medical programs[k]		483.7	598.0	695.0	1,683.1	1,949.1	2,617.6	2,818.1
Hospital and medical care		330.0	410.0	470.0	1,123.0	1,379.0	1,806.0	2,065.0
Maternal and child health services[l]		6.7	6.0	6.8	9.7	69.2	100.1	106.1
Medical research[m]							16.0	23.0
Other public health activities[n]		112.0	142.0	168.2	248.4	240.8	341.5	348.0
Medical facilities construction		35.0	40.0	50.0	302.0	260.0	354.0	276.0
Other welfare services		137.2	104.4	108.3	234.9	336.0	637.0	751.0
Vocational rehabilitation, total		1.2	2.1	2.7	9.0	15.0	32.9	36.3
Medical rehabilitation[f]		.1	.2	.7	3.7	3.5	6.2	6.5
Institutional and other care[o]		110.0	58.9	51.5	86.2	124.0	340.0	424.0
School lunch[p]					39.0	69.0	90.4	92.6
Child welfare[q]		26.0	43.4	54.1	100.7	128.0	173.7	198.1
Veterans' programs[r]					462.0	61.6	61.1	111.9
Education		1,950.8	2,269.2	3,375.9	6,401.0	10,919.5	16,094.7	17,166.0
Elementary and secondary, total		1,830.8	2,082.9	2,631.5	5,681.8	9,730.9	14,254.0	15,192.4
Construction[f]		115.3	50.1	82.5	1,013.5	2,223.1	2,900.0	2,788.9
Higher education and other, total		120.0	186.3	744.4	719.2	1,188.6	1,840.7	1,973.6
Construction[f]		v	26.0	v	211.3	306.7	498.5	534.7
Public housing[v]						14.6	28.4	33.2

Notes to Table 5-1

[a]Expenditures from Federal, state, and local revenues (general and special) and trust funds and other expenditures under public law; includes capital outlay and administrative expenditures, unless otherwise noted. Includes some expenditures and payments outside the United States. Fiscal years ended June 30 for Federal Government, most states, and some localities; for other states and localities, fiscal years cover various twelve-month periods ended in the specified year.

[b]Excludes net payments in lieu of benefits (transfers) under the financial interchange with the railroad retirement system.

[c]Excludes refunds of employee contributions to those leaving the service; Federal expenditures include payments to retired military personnel and survivors. Data for administrative expenses not available for Federal noncontributory programs.

[d]Includes unemployment compensation for Federal employees, for ex-servicemen, and for veterans under the Servicemen's Readjustment Act of 1944 and the Veterans' Readjustment Assistance Act of 1952 and payments under the temporary extended unemployment insurance programs.

[e]Cash and medical benefits, including payments under private plans where applicable in the four states with programs. Includes state costs of administering state plans and supervising private plans; data for administrative expenditures of private plans underwritten by private insurance carriers or self-insured not available.

[f]Included in total shown directly above; excludes administrative expenditures, not available separately but included for entire program in preceding line.

[g]Cash and medical benefits paid under Federal workmen's compensation laws and under state laws by private insurance carriers, by state funds, and by self-insurers. Excludes administrative costs of state agencies before 1949-50 and all administrative costs of private insurance carriers and self-insurers. Beginning 1959-60 includes data for Alaska and Hawaii.

[h]Old-age assistance, aid to dependent children, aid to the blind, aid to the permanently and totally disabled, and, from state and local funds, general assistance; includes vendor medical payments. For 1939-40, total includes $1 million in administrative costs and Federal Emergency Relief Administration funds for which distribution by source of funds is not available.

[i]Work program earnings, other emergency aid programs, and value of surplus food distributed to needy families.

[j]Excludes expenditures (1) for domiciliary care in institutions other than mental or tuberculosis (included under institutional care); (2) for health and medical services provided in connection with state temporary disability insurance, workmen's compensation, public assistance, vocational rehabilitation, and veterans' programs (included in total expenditures for these programs; and (3) made directly for international health activities and for certain subordinate medical programs, such as those of the Federal Aviation Agency, the Bureau of Narcotics, the Bureau of Mines, the National Park Service, and the U.S. Civil Service Commission.

[k]Services for crippled children and maternal and child health services.

[l]Medical research expenditures of the U.S. Public Health Service, the Food and Drug Administration, the Atomic Energy Commission, the National Aeronautics and Space Administration, and the Department of Defense.

Notes to Table 5-1 (concluded)

[m]Excludes expenditures for water supply, sanitation services, and sewage disposal but includes regulatory and administrative costs of these services; also includes expenditures for medical equipment and supplies for civil defense.

[n]Expenditures for homes for dependent or neglected children and for adults other than veterans and the value of surplus food for nonprofit institutions.

[o]Federal expenditures represent cash apportionment and the value of commodities purchased and distributed under the National School Lunch Act and the value of surplus commodities distributed under other agricultural programs. Beginning 1954-55, includes the special school milk program; nongovernmental funds are also available from private organizations and from payments by parents (in 1959-60 parents' payments totaled $556 million).

[p]Includes foster-care payments and payments for professional and facilitating services; excludes expenditures of public institutions and public day-care centers, capital expenditures by courts and by youth authorities, payments from parents and relatives, and direct appropriations by state legislatures to voluntary agencies and institutions.

[q]Federal expenditures exclude bonus payments and expenditures from veterans' life insurance trust funds; state and local expenditures refer to state bonus and other payments and services; local data not available.

[r]Includes burial awards and subsistence payments to disabled veterans undergoing training.

[s]Includes vocational rehabilitation, specially adapted homes and automobiles for disabled veterans, counseling, beneficiaries' travel, loan guarantees, and domiciliary care.

[t]State data available only.

[u]Data not available.

[v]Federal and state subsidies (and administrative costs) for low-cost housing.

Source: 1928-29, *Historical Statistics of the United States, 1960,* pp. 193-94; 1934-35 to 1959-60, Ida C. Merriam, "Social Welfare Expenditures, 1959-60," *Social Security Bulletin,* November 1961, pp. 4-5. (1934-35 incorporates some later revisions by Merriam.)

religious ethic in a scheme of family solidarity. Now it rests on a very broad basis. One could argue that there is a *quid pro quo;* that we give privately and through the provision of public revenues for the support of the aged because we might some day grow old ourselves, or, if already old, become indigent. Such an attempt to construe private or public provision for old-age indigency as being outside the realm of philanthropy because there is the possibility of some *quid pro quo* in the distant future seems to be quite unrealistic in the present.

It is perhaps a little more difficult to show that Old-Age and Survivors Insurance benefits under the social security law fall in the same category. As will be noted later, however, an average of something like

Table 5-2

Percentage Distribution of Social Welfare Expenditures Under Public Programs, Selected Fiscal Years 1928-29 Through 1959-60

Program	1928-29	1934-35	1939-40	1944-45	1949-50	1954-55	1958-59	1959-60
Social insurance	7.9	5.9	14.3	15.6	21.3	30.7	37.1	37.3
Public aid	a	46.2	42.5	11.6	10.8	9.3	8.1	7.9
Health and medical	10.9	8.4	8.2	21.7	10.2	9.1	8.2	8.2
Other welfare services	11.6[a]	2.1	1.4	2.2	1.7	1.8	2.1	2.2
Veterans' programs	12.8	6.9	6.3	10.0	27.7	13.6	10.4	9.8
Education	56.8	30.5	27.3	38.8	28.2	35.2	33.8	34.3
Public housing			b	0.1	0.1	0.3	0.3	0.3
Total	100.0	100.0	100.0	100.0	100.0	100.0	100.0	100.0
Federal funds as per cent of total	14.5	46.4	38.8	38.8	43.5	43.3	45.9	46.2

Source: Table 5-1.

[a]Some public aid expenditures included in "other welfare services."

[b]Less than 0.05 per cent.

Table 5-3

Totals for Public Domestic Philanthropy, 1929-59

Year	Veterans Program		Public Aid, Other Welfare, Health, and Free Schools		Social Insurance and Public Housing		Total	
	Million Dollars (1)	Per Cent of GNP (2)	Million Dollars (3)	Per Cent of GNP (4)	Million Dollars (5)	Per Cent of GNP (6)	Million Dollars (7)	Per Cent of GNP (8)
1929	261	.250	2,851	2.730			3,112	2.980
1930	285	.313	2,882	3.161			3,167	3.476
1931	342	.448	2,991	3.922			3,333	4.370
1932	373	.638	3,207	5.485			3,580	6.123
1933	280	.500	3,585	6.406			3,865	6.906
1934	195	.300	4,241	6.527			4,436	6.827
1935	222	.306	4,675	6.448			4,897	6.754
1936	240	.290	3,657	4.420			3,897	4.710
1937	246	.271	4,002	4.408	90	0.099	4,338	4.779
1938	252	.296	4,317	5.065	388	0.455	4,957	5.816
1939	258	.283	4,455	4.890	676	0.742	5,389	5.916
1940	261	.259	4,547	4.519	727	0.723	5,535	5.501
1941	260	.207	4,669	3.711	738	0.587	5,667	4.504
1942	267	.168	4,788	3.009	665	0.418	5,720	3.594
1943	244	.127	4,966	2.580	565	0.293	5,775	3.000
1944	285	.135	5,212	2.466	579	0.274	6,076	2.874
1945	1,130	0.529	5,506	2.578	1,710	0.801	8,346	3.908
1946	3,348	1.589	6,443	3.058	2,982	1.415	12,773	6.063
1947	4,812	2.054	7,746	3.306	2,803	1.196	15,361	6.556
1948	4,868	1.876	9,043	3.486	2,689	1.037	16,600	6.399
1949	4,664	1.807	10,595	4.106	3,190	1.236	18,449	7.149
1950	3,964	1.393	11,768	4.135	3,273	1.150	19,005	6.678
1951	3,104	.944	12,386	3.765	3,438	1.045	18,928	5.754
1952	2,386	.688	13,204	3.805	4,152	1.197	19,742	5.689
1953	2,016	.552	14,158	3.875	5,235	1.433	21,409	5.859
1954	2,032	.560	15,303	4.214	6,658	1.834	23,993	6.608
1955	2,211	.556	16,609	4.179	7,612	1.915	26,432	6.650
1956	2,356	.562	18,392	4.388	8,605	2.053	29,352	7.002
1957	2,454	.554	20,605	4.654	10,908	2.464	33,967	7.671
1958	2,518	.566	22,894	5.150	13,409	3.016	38,821	8.733
1959	2,503	.519	25,046	5.189	14,672	3.040	42,221	8.747
Total[a]	48,637	.724	274,743	4.092	95,764	1.568	419,143	6.242

Note: Detail may not add to total because of rounding.

[a]See note a, Table 2-1.

Sources: Columns 1 and 2: Table 6-3 (columns 7 & 8),
  Columns 3 and 4: Table 7-12 (columns 9 & 10),
  Columns 5 and 6: Table 8-2 (columns 15 & 16).

95 per cent of the benefits can be classified as windfall benefits in the sense of not having been theoretically prepaid by the employee and the employer, and should be considered public philanthropy. So viewed, OASI is, on the average, 95 per cent old-age assistance despite some claim of a *quid pro quo* in that a person, by belonging to a system and paying token taxes into it, is "assured" of his own benefits.

A detailed enumeration of all expenditures of government during each of the thirty-one years in our survey and a classification of them under public philanthropy or for some other purpose, such as military, would probably provide little, if any, additional clarification of the concepts employed in our study. The federal budget for defense has been large absolutely and relatively during most of our period. Although such expenditures provide income for literally millions of Americans, such payments can hardly be construed as welfare payments, devoid of a *quid pro quo*. Providing for the common defense is a basic attribute of sovereignty, indispensable to government itself. It is apparent that the drafters of the United States Constitution thought of welfare as an additional objective of the new federal government, as stated in the Preamble: ". . . provide for the common defence, promote the general Welfare . . ." and in Article 1, Section 8, "provide for the common defence *and* general Welfare" (italics added). In our review of the literature we have not encountered an instance of military expenditures being classified as philanthropy or social welfare.

Finally, it is not the intention of this study to provide a philosophy of philanthropy beyond that necessary for the task at hand, namely, to describe the changing position of philanthropy in the American economy during the last three decades. The basic trait of the American people being manifested is generosity, increasingly through public institutions but without obliterating the traditional private institutions. There are, undoubtedly, alternative views to which our tables of figures can be adapted. Our procedure will be to examine the Merriam list line by line and set forth the reasons why we feel that certain of the items must be eliminated and the amounts in other lines modified to obtain the data for the totals for public domestic philanthropy.

Table 5-3 presents the totals from each of the three chapters on public domestic philanthropy that follow (Chapters 6, 7, and 8), and the grand total, by way of introduction to the detailed discussion.

The increase from 1929 to 1959 was from $3,112 million and 3.0 per cent of GNP to $42,221 million and 8.7 per cent of GNP. The aggregate for the entire period was $419,143 million and 6.2 per cent of GNP. The annual series for Quadrant III reveals an early peak of 6.9 per cent of GNP in 1933, a sharp rise from 3.0 per cent in 1929. After 1933, the percentage declines slowly and then sharply during the World War II years and keeps below 6.9 per cent until 1949, when the percentage was 7.1. The 7 per cent level was not attained again until 1956, with increases to 8.7 per cent in 1958 and 1959.

In the three chapters that follow, we go on to explain the sources and derivations of these figures. Because veterans' benefits are the oldest and one of the largest of the items of social welfare expenditures, they will be examined first.

6 Veterans' Benefits
as Public Philanthropy

The Veterans Administration provides a medical care program for veterans, and operates and administers a wide variety of benefits, such as compensation and pensions for disabled veterans and dependents of deceased veterans, vocational rehabilitation and education, and guaranteed or insured loans.[1] Over 22.5 million men and women were veterans as of mid-1960. Another fifty-eight million of the 180 million Americans were members of the families of veterans or dependent survivors of deceased veterans, so that 81 million of the 180 million Americans in 1960 were directly or indirectly, actually or potentially protected by one or another part of the VA's program.

In its broad program the agency utilized a field network of 170 hospitals, 80 outpatient clinics, 18 domiciliaries, 67 regional offices, and 3 insurance offices. (The operation of the large life insurance program is, for the most part, a buying and paying operation and outside the scope of our discussion.) In the fiscal year ending 1960, more than $5 billion was expended from the appropriated funds, and 172,000 persons were employed. In that year, 120,000, or 8 per cent, of the nation's patients were admitted to VA hospitals or to non-VA hospitals under VA auspices. Moreover, domiciliary care was provided to almost 17,000 disabled veterans without resources for self-support.

[1] *Annual Report, Administrator of Veterans Affairs,* 1960, Washington, 1961.

Something of the broad scope of the operations of the Veterans Administration is indicated by a 20 per cent sample of all VA patients in hospitals at the end of October 1959. Of these, 33.2 per cent were veterans receiving care for service-connected disabilities; these veterans are unconditionally eligible for VA care. Second, 9.1 per cent were veterans with service-connected compensable disabilities who were receiving care for nonservice-connected disabilities; these veterans are eligible for VA care if a bed is available. Third, the remaining 57.4 per cent were veterans receiving care for nonservice-connected disabilities; these veterans are eligible for VA care if a bed is available, and they sign an affidavit certifying their inability to defray the cost of hospitalization.[2] Of the 64,900 comprising the 57.4 per cent who did not have a compensable service-connected disability, approximately 39,000 were receiving care for disabilities which are unquestionably classified as "chronic," i.e., tuberculosis, psychosis, or some other condition that had already required ninety days or more of continuous hospitalization as of the day of sample census.[3] Of the remaining nonservice-connected group, one-half of the patients were receiving or had applied for VA pensions for a nonservice-connected disabling condition. Eligibility for a VA pension implies medical indigency in the following respects: the veteran must have a disabling condition that interferes with earning a livelihood, must not have an annual income in excess of $1,400 if single, or in excess of $2,700 if with dependents.

The task of the present study is to examine the array of data presented in the annual reports of the Veterans Administration to determine which expenditures should be called public philanthropy and which should be assigned to the aftercosts of war. The basic division of these categories will be made on the basis of whether the disability involved is service-connected or nonservice-connected. This rule will be followed in the examination of ten classes of veterans' benefits (see Table 6-1). For one class, medical and hospital care, compensation for service-connected disabilities (33.2 per cent in the October 1959 sample) is not a form of public philanthropy but deferred compensation, an aftercost of war; compensation for the nonservice-connected, however, is clearly a form of public philanthropy, without a *quid pro quo*. In this broad program additional compensation is allowed for a wife, children, and

2 *Ibid.*, p. 19.
3 *Ibid.*, p. 20.

dependent parents if the veteran has been 50 per cent or more disabled by conditions incurred in or aggravated by his military service. Two excerpts from the 1960 *Annual Report* indicate the scope of these non-service-connected benefits:

> Pensions for nonservice-connected disabilities are payable to veterans eligible for pension under Chapter 15, title 38, U.S.C. . . .
> The compensation and pension program provides compensation to veterans for loss of earning power arising from injury or disease resulting from military service; provides compensation to widows and other dependents for the death of a veteran in or as a result of disability not related to service or the needs of their widows and children as a result of death of the veterans.[4]

Hence, in presenting details of the twofold classification, it will be necessary to note, among other things, the amounts spent for living veterans, deceased veterans, and disabled veterans. For example, when the last surviving veteran of the Civil War died on December 19, 1959, at the age of 117, there were still expenditures to be made, because on the compensation and pension rolls at that time there were fifty-one widows of Civil War veterans and two widows of Mexican War veterans. Certain war orphans have also been granted training benefits under the legislation.

FOR ALL WARS

Some benefits were provided for the veterans of the Revolutionary War. The *Annual Report, Administrator of Veterans Affairs,* 1960 reports that the aggregate to date of federal benefits from compensation and pension appropriations to the veterans of the Revolutionary War was $70 million. (Except for the final series, all data in this chapter are for fiscal years.) The total for the War of 1812 was $46 million, with some expenditures as late as 1946. The grand totals before June 30, 1960, for the Indian War was $115 million and for the Mexican War $62 million; there were expenditures in the fiscal year of 1960 for the living and deceased veterans of the former and for the deceased veterans of the latter. The grand total for the veterans of the Civil War was $8,202 million; Spanish American War, $4,260 million; World War I, $17,111

[4] *Ibid.,* pp. 57, 53.

million; World War II, $19,595 million; the Korean conflict, $1,424 million; the Regular Establishment, $1,216 million; and not classified by wars, $16 million. These compensation and pension items totaled $52,117 million. The grand total for the entire period of expenditures from all general and special fund appropriations for veterans of all wars was $104,759 million.

These expenditures were made pursuant to federal legislation by the Veterans Administration, and by earlier agencies, e.g., the Veterans Bureau. They are summarized in 123 columns of Table 95 of the *Annual Report, Administrator of Veterans Affairs*. In particular, annual expenditures from general and special fund appropriations have increased from some $631 million in 1929 to $5,389 million in fiscal 1960. These totals, of course, exclude the expenditures by state governments for bonus payments and other veterans' benefits. Moreover, there are also excluded from these totals the $19 billion of expenditures from supply, trust, and working funds which are over and above the $105 billion cumulative total through fiscal year 1960. Some reference, however, will be made to both of these excluded items in the discussion which follows.

This separation into the two categories (service-connected and non-service-connected) was made possible by the cooperation of the staff of the Veterans Administration in Washington, particularly Controller J. M. Hansman, and Mr. M. C. Forester and Mr. W. J. Fallwell of his staff. It should be clearly understood that the basic plan for this separation is ours. Many of the categories could be readily classified, but for others the separation or classification required special consideration or special tables.

TEN BENEFIT GROUPS FOR FOUR SELECTED YEARS

The expenditures from general and special fund appropriations were assembled into ten groups (lines 2 through 10 and 12 of Table 6-1) for the fiscal years 1929, 1939, 1949, and 1959, and divided into aftercosts of war and welfare (public philanthropy). Line 11, the sum of lines 2 through 10, contains roughly 95 per cent of the adjusted total expenditures in line 1 for each of these four selected years; about 5 per cent (line 12) remained unallocated. The separation in line 12 into the two

Table 6-1

Estimated Distribution of Veterans Administration (Adjusted) Expenditures From Appropriated Funds According to Aftercosts of War (Service-Connected) and Welfare (Nonservice-Connected), Selected Fiscal Years 1929-59
(millions of dollars)

Line No.		1929			1939			1949			1959		
		Total	War	Wel-fare	Total	War	Wel-fare	Total	War	Wel-fare	Total	War	Wel-fare
1	Adjusted total expenditures	631	365	266	555	300	255	6,648	2,266	4,382	5,019	2,564	2,455
2	Compensation	194	194		233	233		1,467	1,467		2,071	2,071	
3	Pensions	226		226	184		184	424		424	1,154		1,154
4	Insurance	121	121		38	38		95	95		53	53	
5	Education and training							2,704		2,704	574		574
6	Vocational rehabilitation							335	335		22	22	
7	Unemployment allowances							510		510			
8	4 per cent loan gratuity							28		28			
9	Construction	4	2	2	11	3	8	124	42	82	45	15	30
10	Medical and hospital care	55	30	25	70	16	54	574	195	379	881	291	590
11	Subtotal	600	347	253	536	290	246	6,261	2,134	4,127	4,800	2,452	2,348
12	All other	31	18	13	19	10	9	387	132	255	219	112	107

Notes to Table 6-1

Source: Fiscal 1959 totals, from Administrator of Veterans Affairs, *Annual Report,* 1960, Source Note 95; as follows for each line:

Page	Col.	Column Caption	*1959 Total* (millions of dollars)
Line 1. Total Expenditures			5,019
286	2	General and special fund appropriations. (The balance of the grand total of $6,282 is captioned "supply fund, trust and working funds"–$938.) From this $5,344, two items were first excluded; p. 302-7 Loan Guaranty (Public Law 346) Other, $121 million, a loan fund; p. 304-8 Direct loans to veterans, $204 million, a loan fund.	
Line 2. Compensation		Service-connected–entire amount charged to aftercost of war.	2,071
292	1	Compensation and pension appropriations (hereafter, c. & p.a.) for the regular establishment, total	109
292	6	c. & p.a., World War I, living veterans, service-connected disability compensation	217
292	2	c. & p.a., World War I, living veterans, emergency officers' retirement pay	4
294	2	c. & p.a., World War I, deceased veterans, service-connected	65
294	6	c. & p.a., World War II, living veterans, service-connected	1,126
294	8	c. & p.a., World War II, living veterans, retired reserve officers	0.012
294	9	c. & p.a., World War II, living veterans, Army of the Philippines (Public Law 301)	7
296	2	c. & p.a., World War II, deceased veterans, service-connected	293
296	4	c. & p.a., World War II, deceased veterans, Army of the Philippines (Public Law 301)	24
296	7	c. & p.a., Korean conflict (Public Law 28), living veterans, service-connected	179

Notes to Table 6-1 (continued)

Page	Col.	Column Caption	*1959 Total* (millions of dollars)
296	10	c. & p.a., Korean conflict (Public Law 28), deceased veterans, service-connected	48

Line 3. Pensions

		Nonservice-connected—entire amount charged to welfare	1,154
288	4	c. & p.a., War of 1812, total	0.0
289	1	c. & p.a., Indian wars, total	0.7
289	4	c. & p.a., Mexican War, total	0.003
290	1	c. & p.a., Civil War, total	4
290	4	c. & p.a., Spanish-American War, total	116
292	7	c. & p.a., World War I, living veterans, nonservice-connected disability pension	686
294	3	c. & p.a., World War I, deceased veterans, nonservice-connected	238
294	7	c. & p.a., World War II, living veterans, nonservice-connected	71
296	3	c. & p.a., World War II, deceased veterans, nonservice-connected	32
296	8	c. & p.a., Korean conflict (Public Law 28), living veterans, nonservice-connected	5
296	11	c. & p.a., Korean conflict (Public Law 28), deceased veterans, nonservice-connected	1

Line 4. Insurance

		Service-connected—entire amount charged to aftercost of war	(53)
306	1	Military and naval insurance, benefits	3
306	2	Military and naval insurance, transferred to U.S. government life insurance fund	0.2
306	5	National service life insurance, appropriation, benefits	0.8

Notes to Table 6-1 (continued)

Page	Col.	Column Caption	1959 Total (millions of dollars)
306	6	National service life insurance, appropriation, transferred to National Service Life Insurance fund	12
306	9	Servicemen's indemnities	36
308	1	Veterans special term insurance, appropriation	0.0
308	3	Service disabled veterans insurance, appropriation	0.0
308	4	Service disabled veterans insurance, transferred from veterans insurance and indemnities appropriation	0.0

Line 5. Education and Training

		Nonservice-connected—entire amount charged to welfare	(574)
298	2	c. & p.a., readjustment benefits (Public Law 346) (hereafter, r.b.), education and training, subsistence allowance	0.0
298	3	c. & p.a., r.b., education and training, tuition	0.0
298	4	c. & p.a., r.b., education and training, supplies, equipment and fees	0.0
302	2	r.b., education and training (Public Law 346), subsistence allowance	0.050
302	3	r.b., education and training (Public Law 346), tuition	0.3
302	4	r.b., education and training, supplies, equipments, and fees	0.026
302	5	r.b., education and training allowance (Public Law 550)	566
304	2	r.b., war orphans educational assistance and special training allowance (Public Law 364)	8

Line 6. Vocational Rehabilitation

		Service-connected—entire amount charged to aftercost of war	(22)
298	8	c. & p.a., subsistence allowance (Public Laws 16 and 894)	15
300	3	Veterans' miscellaneous benefits, vocational rehabilitation (Public Laws 16 and 894), tuition	0.0
300	4	Veterans' miscellaneous benefits, vocational rehabilitation (Public Laws 16 and 894), supplies and equipment	0.0

Notes to Table 6-1 (continued)

Page	Col.	Column Caption	*1959 Total* (millions of dollars)
304	5	r.b., vocational rehabilitation (Public Laws 16 and 894), tuition	6
304	6	r.b., vocational rehabilitation (Public Laws 16 and 894), supplies and equipment	0.9
310	5	Vocational rehabilitation (World War I)	0.0

Line 7. Unemployment Allowances

		Nonservice-connected—entire amount charged to welfare	(0.0)
298	5	c. & p.a., r.b., readjustment allowances, unemployment	0.0
298	6	c. & p.a., r.b., readjustment allowances, self-employment	0.0
304	3	r.b., readjustment allowances (Public Law 346), unemployment	0.001
304	4	r.b., readjustment allowances (Public Law 346), self-employment—$0.000,038 (credit)	-0.0

Line 8. Loan Guaranty

		Nonservice-connected—charged to welfare	(-0.003)
302	6	r.b., loan guaranty (Public Law 346), 4 per cent gratuity—$0.003 (credit)	-0.003

Line 9. Construction

		These benefits fall into two categories, aftercost of war ($15) and welfare ($30). Divided into aftercost of war and welfare on basis of percentage of veterans receiving hospital care during that year who were treated for service-connected and nonservice disabilities (Table VA2). Of all patients receiving hospital care 54 per cent were treated for service-connected disabilities in 1929, 23 per cent in 1939, 34 per cent in 1949 and 33 per cent in 1959.	45
287	3	Hospital and domiciliary facilities (construction and related costs)	45
287	4	National Industrial Recovery Act of 1933 (allotment to Veterans Administration, 1933-39)	0.0
287	5	Public Works Administration Act of 1938 (allotment to Veterans Administration, 1938-43)	0.0

Notes to Table 6-1 (continued)

			1959 Total (millions of
Page	*Col.*	*Column Caption*	dollars)

Line 10. Medical and Hospital Care

Service-connected and nonservice-connected – these benefits fall into two categories, aftercost of war ($291) and welfare ($590). Division of expenditures for medical and hospital care into aftercost of war and welfare based on the same percentages in Table VA2 referred to in line 9 above – the percentages of veterans treated for service- and nonservice-connected disabilities   881

286	4	Administration and other benefits (part)	881
286	5	Medical and hospital services	0.0
286	7	National Home for Disabled Volunteer Soldiers	0.0
287	1	State and Territorial homes	0.0

Line 11. Subtotal

This line needs no explanation but it serves two purposes.   4,800
First, for the four fiscal years shown on the table the subtotal is about 95 per cent of the total expenditures, for aftercost of war, and for welfare. This leaves amounts in line 12, "All Other" of about 5 per cent of the totals of line 1. The problem of line 12 is different because it was not found possible to distribute these items directly between the aftercost of war and welfare. Hence, the items in "all other" are distributed according to the subtotal as revealed in line 11.

Line 12. All Other

$219, divided into aftercost of war ($112) and welfare ($107)   219
by procedure described in line 11 above.

286	4	Administration and other benefits (part)	178
286	6	Maintenance for expenses for pensions	0.0
287	2	Canteen Service, revolving fund	0.0
287	7	c. & p.a., participants in yellow fever experiments	0.005
298	7	c. & p.a., adjusted service and dependent pay	0.001
298	9	c. & p.a., statutory burial awards	33

Notes to Table 6-1(concluded)

Page	Col.	Column Caption	1959 Total (millions of dollars)
298	10	c. & p.a., unclassified as to purpose	1
298	11	c. & p.a., special allowance (sec. 405, Public Law 881)	0.06
300	2	Veterans miscellaneous benefits, statutory burial awards	0.0
300	5	Veterans miscellaneous benefits, homes for paraplegics	0.0
300	6	Automobiles and other conveyances for disabled veterans	0.0
300	7	Vocational rehabilitation revolving fund (World War II and Korean conflict)	0.004
304	1	r.b., automobiles and other conveyances for disabled veterans	1
304	7	r.b., homes for paraplegics	3
308	6	Soldiers' and sailors' civil relief	1
310	6	Allotments and allowances (part)	0.0
310	7	Marine and seamen's insurance	0.0
310	10	Miscellaneous (part)	1

There are forty-seven columns in Table 95 which are not referred to above. Of this total, twelve are subtotals where the corresponding total columns have been used: page 288-5,6; page 289-2,3,5,6; page 290-2,3,5,6; page 292-2,3. Seventeen of the columns are total columns where it was necessary to use the subtotal columns: page 286-1; page 287-6,8; page 288-1,2; page 292-4,5; page 294-1,4,5; page 296-1,5,6,9; page 298-1; page 300-1; page 302-1. One column, page 288-3, has no data for our years. Expenditures for the supply fund, trust fund, and working funds (page 286-3) are not included in this compilation and hence the sixteen subtotals for this column are not referred to: page 306-3,4,7,8; page 308-2,5,7,8,9,10; page 310-1,2,3,4,8,9.

Part of column 6, page 310 (allowances) is included in the table above in line 13; the remainder, the portion expended as allotments, is part of column (3), page 286 which is not included in this compilation. Similarly, part of column 10, page 310 is included in line 13; the remainder, expenditures from trust funds, and working funds (items 34 and 41 on pages 280-81 and all items on pages 282-83 of the 1960 Annual Report) is included in column 3, page 286 and not included in this compilation.

All of column 4, page 286 is included in lines 11 and 13 of the table. Line 10, Medical and Hospital Care, is available annually in *Historical Statistics of the United States, Colonial Times to 1957,* Series Y 821, and for more recent years in the *Statistical Abstract.* (This provides the division of column 4, page 286 in lines 11 and 13; the Y 821 series, as does line 11, includes also page 286-5,7, and page 287-1,2.)

categories (described in the table footnotes) was in the same proportions as the 95 per cent totaled in line 11. The note to Table 6-1 lists the captions of the columns of source Table 95 grouped together into the ten categories in our table.

Fiscal year 1959 can be used as an illustration. Of the $5,019-million total ($5,344 million less $325 million for loans), $2,564 million was classified as expenditures for aftercosts of war and $2,455 million for public social welfare or public philanthropy; that is, 51 per cent of the adjusted total expenditures from appropriated funds was disbursed for purposes which fall in our category of aftercosts of war (service-connected) and 49 per cent in our category of public philanthropy (non-service-connected). The corresponding separation for the other three years shown in Table 6-1 are 58 and 42 per cent for fiscal year 1929, 54 per cent and 46 per cent for fiscal year 1939, and 34 per cent and 66 per cent for fiscal year 1949. The fact that as much as 66 per cent is classified as welfare or public philanthropy for 1949 is obviously traceable to the large number of men engaged in World War II and the provision for various veterans' benefits in legislation during the 1940's. The presentation of the breakdowns for the four selected years will, we trust, provide sufficient detail to explain the procedures that have been followed for each of the thirty-one years covered in our period.

An examination of this table line by line shows that all expenditures classified as "compensation" and "insurance" have been considered aftercosts of war (service-connected) and therefore not classified as public social welfare or public philanthropy. On the other hand, the other large item, "pensions," is nonservice-connected and hence exclusively classified as welfare or public philanthropy. The same is true of "education and training" and "unemployment allowances."

The members of the staff of the Veterans Administration prepared for us a percentage distribution of the number (not costs) of veterans treated in hospitals and other medical facilities of the Veterans Administration in each year, 1929–60, for service-connected and for nonservice-connected disabilities. Table 6-2 below was utilized in preparing Tables 6-1 and 6-3. The percentage of veterans treated for service-connected disabilities ranged from a high of 54 per cent in 1929 and 1930 to a low of 22 per cent in 1940 and 1941. These percentages were influenced by changes in statutory definitions. The amounts of the annual expendi-

Table 6-2

Patients Receiving Hospital Care Authorized
by the Veterans Administration, 1929-60

Year[a]	Total Patients	Veterans Treated for Service-Connected Disabilities[b]	
		Number	Per Cent of Total
1929	29,897	16,024	54
1930	30,556	16,418	54
1931	35,145	15,773	45
1932	43,469	15,199	35
1933	33,844	13,925	41
1934	38,733	11,451	30
1935	41,728	12,168	29
1936	41,251	11,906	29
1937	46,235	12,182	26
1938	50,640	12,394	24
1939	53,745	12,534	23
1940	56,450	12,670	22
1941	58,241	12,825	22
1942	56,103	13,324	24
1943	56,850	14,580	26
1944	63,890	18,476	29
1945	70,246	23,375	33
1946	87,257	28,806	33
1947	104,443	35,525	34
1948	103,576	34,872	34
1949	107,073	35,919	34
1950	102,303	34,596	34
1951	100,517	35,597	35
1952	103,774	36,182	35
1953	102,323	39,092	38
1954	108,357	40,711	38
1955	110,257	41,078	37
1956	112,660	40,195	36
1957	110,715	39,063	35
1958	112,920	38,515	34
1959	113,115	37,575	33

[a]As of June 30, 1929-54; as of May 31, 1955-57; as of November 30, 1958, and as of October 31, 1959.

[b]Does not include service-disabled veterans being treated for nonservice-connected conditions, which amounted to 9.1 per cent of the patient load in 1959.

Source: See text.

Table 6-3

Public Expenditures for Veterans Programs Classified as Aftercosts of War and Welfare, 1929-59 (millions of dollars)

Fiscal Year	Veterans Administration Expenditures (appropriated funds)				State Government Expenditures (5)	Total Veterans Welfare		
	Total (adjusted) (1)	Per Cent Aftercost of War (2)	Aftercost of War (1) x (2) (3)	Welfare (1) - (3) (4)		Fiscal Year (4) + (5) (6)	Calendar Year (7)	Per Cent of GNP (8)
1929	631	58	365	266		266	261	.250
1930	639	60	383	256		256	285	.313
1931	714	56	400	314		314	342	.448
1932	789	53	418	371		371	373	.638
1933	781	52	406	375		375	280	.500
1934	496	63	312	184		184	195	.300
1935	557	63	351	206		206	222	.306
1936	580	59	342	238		238	240	.290
1937	579	58	336	243		243	246	.271
1938	582	57	332	250		250	252	.296
1939	555	54	300	255		255	258	.283

Year								
1940	.259	261	262		262	296	53	558
1941	.207	260	260		260	293	53	553
1942	.168	267	261		261	295	53	556
1943	.127	244	273		273	333	55	606
1944	.135	285	216		216	528	71	744
1945	.529	1,130	354		354	1,731	83	2,085
1946	1.589	3,348	1,906	47	1,859	2,566	58	4,425
1947	2.054	4,812	4,790	159	4,631	2,838	38	7,469
1948	1.876	4,868	4,835	616	4,219	2,272	35	6,491
1949	1.807	4,664	4,902	520	4,382	2,266	34	6,648
1950	1.393	3,964	4,427	462	3,965	2,643	40	6,608
1951	.944	3,104	3,500	335	3,165	2,110	40	5,275
1952	.688	2,386	2,707	143	2,564	2,274	47	4,838
1953	.552	2,016	2,065	114	1,951	2,291	54	4,242
1954	.560	2,032	1,968	103	1,865	2,280	55	4,145
1955	.556	2,211	2,097	62	2,035	2,295	53	4,330
1956	.562	2,356	2,325	89	2,236	2,423	52	4,659
1957	.554	2,454	2,386	39	2,347	2,347	50	4,694
1958	.566	2,518	2,521	121	2,400	2,497	51	4,897
1959	.519	2,503	2,516	61	2,455	2,564	51	5,019
1960			2,490	112	2,378	2,577	52	4,955
Total[a]	.724	48,637	50,019	2,983	47,036	43,664	48	90,700

Notes to Table 6-3

Note: Detail may not add to total because of rounding.
[a]See note a, Table 2-1.

Sources by Column

Column 1
Annual Report of the Administrator of Veterans Affairs, 1960, Table 95, column 2
(p. 286) minus columns 7 (p.302) and 8 (p. 304).

Column 2
See Table 6-1. Annual percentages: correspondence with Veterans Administration,
February 2, 1961, April 4, 1962, and April 18, 1962.

Column 5
See Table 5-1 for source and selected years. Data for 1950 and 1955-60 are revised
estimates.

Column 7
Fiscal-year data converted to calendar-year basis by two-year moving average.

Column 8
See Table 2-2 for Gross National Product.

tures for construction and for medical and hospital care in Table 6-1
assigned to aftercosts of war were determined by the percentage of veterans treated for service-connected disabilities during the year. This
division is more satisfactory for the larger item, medical and hospital
care, than for the capital item, construction. Data were not available
on the actual costs of treating service-connected disabilities and annual
depreciation capital costs.

PUBLIC PHILANTHROPY ONLY HALF OF TOTAL

The final results are presented in Table 6-3. It presents for each of the
thirty-two fiscal years and the adjusted federal expenditures from general and special fund appropriations, the percentages, and amounts (in
millions) for aftercosts of war and for welfare or domestic public philanthropy. In column 5 the remaining part of the expenditures for veterans,

all of which we classify as public philanthropy, are those found in the Merriam compilation under veterans' welfare expenditures (including bonuses) by state governments. They are, of course, relatively small and only for post-World War II years, but they are a part of the total for veterans' benefits classified as public domestic philanthropy.

The totals in column 6 do not, of course, agree with the corresponding entries in the Merriam compilations for veterans' programs; ours are lower. The basic classifications in the Merriam compilations for veterans' programs are pensions *and compensation,* health and medical services, education, and welfare and other. In contrast, we classified "compensation" as an aftercost of war. The amount was $2,071 million in fiscal 1959; this item accounts for more than two-thirds of the excess in 1959—and in most of the years—of the Merriam totals for veterans' programs above our totals. As already noted in Chapter 6, our concept of public domestic philanthropy—no *quid pro quo*—is somewhat narrower than the Merriam concept of social welfare expenditures under public programs. In general, our entire concept of philanthropy (social welfare) for veterans is far below the Merriam totals. The major differences between our two sets of classification of all veterans expenditures are set forth in Table 6-1.[5]

For the thirty-two fiscal years 1929–60 the federal total of $91 billion has been separated into $44 billion for aftercosts of war and $47 billion for welfare (columns 3 and 4 of Table 6-3). On the other hand, for fiscal year 1949, the percentage of expenditures classified as aftercosts of war was the lowest, 34 per cent, and for welfare the highest, 66 per cent. At the other extreme, the expenditures for fiscal 1945 were divided 17 per cent for welfare and 83 per cent for aftercosts of war. For the entire thirty-two-year period, the percentage of aftercosts of war was 48 and for welfare 52. The expenditures by state governments totaled $2,983 million, which, added to the adjusted federal total of $90,700 million, gives a combined total of $93,683 million. As already noted, all state expenditures are classified as nonservice-connected, or public philanthropy.

[5] Worksheets for the complete reconciliation for fiscal 1959 with the Merriam compilations—her $5,032 million and our adjusted total of $5,019 million ($5,344 million less $325 million for loans)—are not specifically shown in the footnotes to our tables.

CALENDAR YEARS 1929–59

Since the data on private philanthropy have been set forth on a calendar-year basis, public domestic philanthropy data for fiscal years were re-computed by a two-year moving average to convert fiscal-year data into estimates for calendar years. For veterans programs these estimates for the thirty-one calendar years totaled $48,637 million (Table 6-3). This procedure does, of course, introduce the possibility of a small margin of error. (Obviously, the data for the first and last of the thirty-two fiscal years enter the moving average computations only once, whereas those of the thirty intervening years enter twice; the difference between the totals for fiscal and calendar years is $1,382 million, one-half of the entry for fiscal 1929 and fiscal 1960.)

Although the dollar series for calendar years will be related to GNP, the abrupt rise from $285 million in 1944 to $1,130 million in 1945 and to the peak of $4,868 million in 1948 indicates the immediate impact of World War II on this form of public domestic philanthropy. The annual expenditures diminished immediately after the Korean conflict and were at the $2,500-million level for the last two years of our period of study.

7 Public Aid,
Other Welfare, Health,
and Free Schools

Each of the four types of public philanthropy presented in this chapter will be discussed as a separate item: public aid, other welfare services, health and medical programs, and free schools. They are grouped together in one chapter for convenience—primarily to allow for treatment in a separate chapter of social insurance, the largest (in 1958 and 1959) and most complex of the remaining items in public domestic philanthropy.

An important element in the changing pattern of public philanthropy that relates to this chapter is the demise of the poorhouse as a major vehicle. Several factors, however, make it infeasible to depict the trend with any rigor. One is the lack of consistent data on the population of poorhouses over the years of study. Another is the fact that the trend was well under way before our period of study begins. The ratio of persons dwelling in poorhouses to 100,000 population fell from 132.0 in 1880 to 100.0 in 1900, and then to 71.5 in 1923 (*Statistical Abstract*). Yet the fact that poorhouse population statistics no longer serve as a measure of public philanthropy is a salient feature of our study. This is partly because it reflects the change in the level of government from which public philanthropy is dispensed. Major responsibility for the care of the needy and infirm has shifted over the years from local and county governments to the state and finally the federal levels, and institutional care is a device employed proportionately more by the lower than the higher levels of government. A second and closely related aspect of the decline in the role of the poorhouse in public philanthropy is that it points up the change in the nature of public welfare from a socialized type of charity to more sophisticated and impersonal forms, such as social security and categorical assistance. (This is not to say, however, that poorhouses are no longer with us. In 1950, for instance, nearly 300,000 persons lived in poorhouses.)

PUBLIC AID

Table 7-1 presents the findings of a source that is very important in our estimates: the Baird study of public and private aid in selected urban areas during 1929–40. Table 7-2 presents the findings of a study of public and private relief by Whiting and Woofter that covers both the rural and urban United States in 1932–36. While these compilations are significant in themselves, they are presented also because they complement the Baird study and permit extrapolation of its findings to earlier years and to the entire, not merely urban, United States. The United States totals for public assistance derived from the combined Baird and Whiting and Woofter studies are given in Table 7-3. Addition of administrative costs produces the final totals for the 1929–40 period for the public assistance component of public aid of this study. Table 7-3 also presents the estimating compilations for these figures. Table 7-4 gives the relevant series from one of the several most important sources of data on public assistance, the *Social Security Bulletin, Annual Statistical Supplement*, 1960, Tables 125 and 126. Summary Table 7-5 represents the last step in the building up of a total public aid series for the period. For the 1929–40 period it combines the public assistance series from Table 7-3 with other public aid, which is limited under our concept of public philanthropy to surplus food distributions to needy families. It also gives the 1941–59 totals for both public assistance and public aid. The final table in the public aid category presents a bird's-eye view of the changing proportions of federal, state, and local assumption of public assistance expenditures over selected years, 1936–59.

SCOPE AND PROCEDURE

In general we follow the divisions of public aid employed in the Merriam compilations, although some of her items are not included in our estimates on public aid because they do not come under our definition of public philanthropy. Thus our public aid figures consist of two subdivisions: public assistance and other. Public assistance covers relief (direct and work) and categorical assistance (aid to the blind, aid to dependent children, and so on). In the "other" subdivision only "surplus commodities distributed to needy families" is included in our figures from among the several items for this subdivision in the Merriam series.

Drawing up final estimates for public aid would have been a relatively simple procedure for eliminating from the Merriam figures the items that do not fall under our concept of public philanthropy, except that the first four years of our study are not covered in the Merriam estimates. Consequently a major task in the public aid section has been the compiling of figures for this gap that are comparable with the relevant components in the Merriam data for later years. It should be noted that there are Merriam estimates for fiscal 1929. However, public aid and other welfare services for that year are merged together and roughly estimated at $500 million, which seems excessive.[1] Since the enactment of the Social Security Act in 1935, some of these terms have come to have precise meaning, particularly public assistance, a very important part of public aid; the terms used during 1929–36, however, seem strange now because they came out of the distant past of the "poor law" era, with very little change for a century preceding 1929. Comprehension of this change in terms is made easier if the Social Security Act of 1935 is considered, in part, an outgrowth of and a substitute for the earlier "poor laws."

During the decade starting in 1929, there were momentous changes in the volume of relief payments, the sources of the funds, and the various kinds and types of new laws, particularly federal laws to counter the distress of the Great Depression.[2] The changeover from private local

---

[1] Ida C. Merriam, "Trends in Public Welfare and Their Implications," *Papers and Proceedings, American Economic Review,* Vol. 47, 1957, p. 477; Bureau of the Census, *Historical Statistics of the United States, Colonial Times to 1957,* Washington, 1960, Series H-13 and H-17, p. 193.

[2] The 1930's presented a unique set of problems, and some rather unique methods of dealing with them were established on an emergency basis. It would seem likely that if the nation were confronted again with such widespread un-

and public local and state funds to finance relief in 1929 (the first year of our period) to federal and federal-state programs after 1932 produces a complexity of problems of estimation for the period 1929–35. The estimates which follow are not uniformly satisfactory from any point of view, but an attempt must be made to fill the gap of these very important years in the development of public domestic philanthropy.

THE BAIRD STUDY

The Baird study produced estimates for both public and private aid for 116 urban areas, covering the ten years starting in 1929.[3] These are presented in Table 7-1. The areas, eighty-one of which were counties, contained about 37 per cent of the total population and about two-thirds of the urban population of the United States in 1930 and 1940. The fairly constant proportions of the total population in the two census years would seem at the outset to provide an easy method of obtaining estimates for the entire nation. The author warns, however, that geographic shifts in the population did occur. Moreover, the 116 urban areas included 57 per cent of the population of the Middle Atlantic states and only 19 per cent of the population of the South Atlantic and South Central states.

"Public general relief" seemed to Baird to be the best general term to encompass what historically has been called poor relief, outdoor relief, general emergency relief, or general assistance. Two subgroups are used: direct relief and work relief. Special ("categorical") types of public assistance—old-age assistance, aid to dependent children, and aid to the blind—are an additional relief category. Changing concepts and definitions in an almost revolutionary decade in the history of public philanthropy create hazards when an attempt is made to splice the old and the new data into a time series. We hope that funds and staff will

employment for such a long period of time, the maturing system of unemployment compensation might be used far more extensively than any counterpart of the emergency programs of the 1930's. One should not, however, attempt to circumscribe the inventiveness of the future.

[3] Enid Baird with the collaboration of John M. Lynch, *Public and Private Aid in 116 Urban Areas 1929–38* (with supplement for 1939 and 1940), Public Assistance Report No. 3, Bureau of Public Assistance, Social Security Board, Washington, 1942, p. 12. The collection of data in seventy-six cities was started by the Russell Sage Foundation in 1929, extended by the United States Children's Bureau and projects of the Works Progress Administration, and transferred to the Social Security Board in 1936. *Ibid.*, p. 3.

be made available so that the Merriam series will someday bridge the 1929–35 period, utilizing the Baird study among others, so that the annual (calendar and fiscal year) series will be continuous from 1929 forward.[4]

Despite its limitations, the Baird analysis is by far the most comprehensive source for the period in question and, within limits, does provide a "splice." Moreover, it provides perspective on one of the basic changes being described in this study, namely, the changeover from an earlier era in which there was still considerable dependence upon private funds to a new era of increasing dependence upon public funds. It was in the decade starting in 1929 (not the period starting in 1935) that the position of public philanthropy came largely to overshadow the role of private philanthropy (see Chapter 10). Even though the Baird study did not cover the entire United States, its use would be justified for the above reasons.

From 1929 through much of 1932 the public relief programs operated in the 116 areas were under the provisions of local and state laws; federal funds were meager before 1933–34. Public programs of old-age assistance, aid to dependent children, and aid to the blind, which were to play a prominent role in later years, were of limited importance, except in 1929, until some years after the passage of the Social Security Act in 1935. (Note columns 3 and 8 of Table 7-1, and Table 7-4.) The private charity agencies, even before 1929, had placed the relief function in a position secondary to the service function; but when widespread suffering began during the Great Depression, the private organizations tried to organize themselves quickly so that they could provide direct relief.

Direct relief and work relief may be compared in columns 4 and 5 of Table 7-1. Direct relief in the 116 urban areas exceeded work relief by a substantial amount each year. The highest amounts for each were for 1935—$537 million and $237 million.

Direct relief clearly falls within the compass of the term domestic public philanthropy because no work was required of the recipient; there was no *quid pro quo*. On the other hand, work relief might possibly be a borderline case, although most work relief provided in this particular

---

[4] Many supporting tables would also be required to present the missing subtotals for the entries in Merriam's master table, perhaps 150 or 200. Such a study would have enabled us to improve our use of her summary data.

Table 7-1

Amount and Distribution of Public and Private Assistance and
Earnings Under Specified Federal Work Programs,
116 Urban Areas, 1929-40

			PUBLIC FUNDS			
Year	Total Public and Private[a] (1)	Total Public (2)	General Relief[b] Total (3)	Direct Relief (4)	Work Relief (5)	Earnings under Federal Work Programs Civil Works Program[c] (6)
			Millions of Dollars			
1929	47.2	35.8	16.4	16.4	g	
1930	75.7	57.6	35.5	33.6	1.9	
1931	177.8	126.3	90.8	68.8	22.1	
1932	319.4	260.5	217.3	165.4	51.9	
1933	535.5	505.8	401.9	291.4	110.5	61.7
1934	914.6	898.5	614.3	400.5	213.8	239.5
1935	990.9	978.2	773.8	537.0	236.7	
1936	1,260.0	1,248.4	300.1	297.4	2.7	
1937	1,099.6	1,088.1	284.5	283.3	1.2	
1938	1,432.3	1,421.4	324.7	h	h	
1929-38[i]	6,853.0	6,620.5	3,059.2	2,418.5[j]	640.7[j]	301.2
1939	1,273.3	1,262.6	329.9	h	h	
1940	1,071.1	1,060.8	283.6	h	h	
1929-40[i]	9,197.4	8,943.8	3,672.7	3,032.1[j]	640.7[j]	301.2
			Percentage Distribution			
1929	100.0	75.8	34.8	34.7	.1	
1930	100.0	76.1	46.9	44.4	2.5	
1931	100.0	71.0	51.1	38.7	12.4	
1932	100.0	81.6	68.0	51.8	16.2	
1933	100.0	94.5	75.1	54.4	20.7	11.5
1934	100.0	98.2	67.1	43.8	23.3	26.2
1935	100.0	98.7	78.1	54.2	23.9	
1936	100.0	99.1	23.8	23.6	.2	
1937	100.0	99.0	25.9	25.8	.1	
1938	100.0	99.2	22.7	h	h	
1929-38[i]	100.0	96.6	44.6	35.3[j]	9.3[j]	4.4
1939	100.0	99.1	25.9	h	h	
1940	100.0	99.0	26.5	h	h	
1929-40[i]	100.0	97.3	40.0	33.0	7.0	3.3

PUBLIC FUNDS

Earnings under Federal Work Programs Projects Operated by the WPA[d] (7)	Special Types of Public Assistance[e]				Private Funds[f] (12)
	Total (8)	Old-age Assistance (9)	Aid to Dependent Children (10)	Aid to the Blind (11)	
	Millions of Dollars				
	19.4	g	17.8	1.6	11.4
	22.1	1.0	19.1	1.9	18.1
	35.5	10.3	23.0	2.2	51.5
	43.2	15.5	25.2	2.5	58.9
	42.3	15.2	24.3	2.7	29.6
	44.7	17.0	24.4	3.2	16.1
143.6	60.8	31.6	25.4	3.9	12.8
856.5	91.8	57.1	29.6	5.1	11.7
647.9	155.8	112.2	37.3	6.3	11.5
898.9	197.8	141.8	48.0	8.0	10.9
2,546.7	713.4	401.7	274.2	37.4	232.5
710.8	221.8	155.4	57.7	8.7	10.7
526.6	250.6	178.0	63.3	9.2	10.4
3,784.1	1,185.7	735.1	395.2	55.4	253.6
	Percentage Distribution				
	41.0	k	37.7	3.3	24.2
	29.2	1.4	25.2	2.6	23.9
	19.9	5.8	12.9	1.2	29.0
	13.6	4.9	7.9	.8	18.4
	7.9	2.8	4.6	.5	5.5
	4.9	1.9	2.7	.3	1.8
14.5	6.1	3.2	2.5	.4	1.3
68.0	7.3	4.5	2.4	.4	.9
58.9	14.2	10.2	3.4	.6	1.0
62.7	13.8	9.9	3.3	.6	.8
37.2	10.4	5.9	4.0	.5	3.4
55.8	17.4	12.2	4.5	.7	.9
49.1	23.4	16.6	5.9	.9	1.0
41.1	12.9	8.0	4.3	.6	2.7

Notes to Table 7-1

Note: For footnotes for 1939 and 1940 not given below, see *Public and Private Aid,* p. 42.

a Excludes cost of administration; of materials, equipment, and other items incident to operation of work programs; and of transient care.

b Includes statutory aid to veterans administered on basis of need.

c Figures from the WPA, Division of Statistics; represent earnings of all persons employed under the program, including the administrative staff.

d Figures from the WPA, Division of Statistics; represent earnings of persons employed on projects operated by the WPA within these areas; figures are not available for earnings of persons employed on projects other than those operated by the WPA.

e Includes figures for areas in states with plans approved by the Social Security Board and for areas in states not participating under the Social Security Act.

f Includes direct and work relief and aid to veterans.

g Less than .05 million; in 1929 work-relief totaled $24,784 and old-age assistance $8,909.

h Figures not available.

i See note a, Table 2-1.

j Work relief for 1938-40 included with direct relief since separate figures are not available; information indicates that work relief represents a negligible proportion of general relief in those years.

k Less than 0.1 per cent.

Source: Reproduced from *Public and Private Aid in 116 Urban Areas 1929-38* (with Supplement for 1939 and 1940), by Enid Baird with the collaboration of John M. Lynch, Public Assistance Report No. 3, Bureau of Public Assistance, Social Security Board, 1942, Tables 2 and 8, pages 12 and 42.

decade does appear to have been within the scope of domestic public philanthropy. Essentially it was relief granted to a recipient who performed some work in exchange for aid, but the line of demarcation between direct relief and work relief in this field of general relief was rather nebulous. Many nonfederal agencies applied a work test and accepted minor services from many recipients, but did not require any systematic work program. It would seem, therefore, that the bulk of the work relief really involved no *quid pro quo* for the public agency. At least, it would not be possible to separate out and place a value on the relatively small benefits received by the public agency making the payment for work relief. Hence in this study all work relief as well as direct relief is classified as domestic public philanthropy, as is also public assistance (column 8 of Table 7-1).

AN IMPORTANT EXCLUSION

The term "work relief" was not applied in the Baird analysis to the earnings of persons employed on various projects of the Civil Works Administration or the Works Projects Administration, since such earnings were determined on the basis of wage rates and hours of employment rather than budgeted needs for relief purposes. It is likely that much of the earnings of persons on these works programs did not involve the usual *quid pro quo* for the public agency because the intention of the program was to provide a form of work relief. Stated in another way, had the public agencies contracted for the types or kinds of construction work undertaken by some of these programs, the value received by the public agency would have been greater. Possibly the assumption that some portion, say, half, of these earnings was truly earnings and not philanthropy, and the other half truly of relief character and therefore philanthropy, might be more reasonable than considering either all of the earnings or none of them as a form of work relief. Since it is our general intention to exclude expenditures by government which might probably be questioned if they were classified under public philanthropy, it seems wiser to exclude from philanthropy all, not merely some portion, of the earnings on the organized public works programs of various types.[5] The decision to exclude such earnings from public philanthropy therefore probably results in an understatement for the years starting in 1933. Some of these earnings are shown in columns 6 and 7 of Table 7-1, but they are excluded from our totals for domestic public philanthropy.

[5] Both the earnings on federal works programs and direct relief payments provided by federal, state, and local governments are treated as income originating in the federal government by Simon Kuznets in *National Income and Its Composition, 1919–1938,* New York, National Bureau of Economic Research, 1941, p. 815; he treats the facilities constructed under the federal works programs as part of federal government gross capital formation in *Capital in the American Economy: Its Formation and Financing,* Princeton University Press for NBER, 1961, p. 187. Because Kuznets makes no distinction between federal, state, and local programs of work relief and direct relief, this treatment is not definitive for our purposes. The excluded total earnings of persons employed under federal work programs (Civilian Conservation Corps, National Youth Administration, Works Projects Administration, Civil Work Program, and other federal agency projects financed from emergency funds) for 1933–43 in millions of dollars were: 1933, $386; 1934, $1,039; 1935, $867; 1936, $2,438; 1937, $1,814; 1938, $2,229; 1939, $2,118; 1940, $1,670; 1941, $1,225; 1942, $581; 1943, $51. *Social Security Bulletin, Annual Statistical Supplement,* 1960, Table 125, p. 90.

Baird's urban relief series excluded data on the amounts of relief provided by "unorganized private charity and direct assistance extended by labor unions, fraternal organizations, private industrial and business welfare groups and local church and school organizations." [6] This is perhaps a serious gap in coverage of the data on private relief funds (column 12 of Table 7-1) for the early years of the 1929–38 decade; the omission was, however, of decreasing importance toward the end of the decade. Nevertheless, the contrast between the increasing role of public philanthropy and the diminishing role of private philanthropy in public assistance is sharply drawn.

Some public programs with relief attributes were omitted from the expenditure data in the Baird study largely because they were not available for the 116 urban areas.[7] First, the emergency education, student aid, and transient programs of the Federal Emergency Relief Administration (FERA), mainly concentrated in 1934 and 1935, were omitted; the magnitude ($186 millions, 1933–37) of this omission, however, is not very great. Second, since the operations of the Civilian Conservation Corps were primarily in rural areas of the United States, the expenditures for the program (dating from April 1933) were omitted. Third, certain local data on student aid and work programs of the National Youth Administration, established in 1935, were omitted; this omission is also not of great magnitude because the total expenditure by the end of 1938 was only $180 million for the entire United States. Fourth, surplus agricultural commodities distributed by the Federal Surplus Commodities Corporation and its predecessor, the Federal Surplus Relief Corporation, were omitted. These foodstuffs and other commodities were distributed in urban areas by welfare organizations throughout the country; some dollar data were gathered as a result of the food-stamp plan, but not enough to estimate monthly distribution for the 116 urban areas. This fourth omission is perhaps of more consequence quantitatively than any of the preceding. Fifth, the integrated series on public assistance compiled and published by the Social Security Board, including data for "other federal emergency projects financed by relief funds," [8] was omitted.

[6] *Public and Private Aid,* p. 7.

[7] *Ibid.,* p. 7.

[8] For the latter, see *Social Security Bulletin,* February 1941, p. 66–70; also *Social Security Bulletin, Annual Statistical Supplement,* 1960, Table 125.

PUBLIC AND PRIVATE ASSISTANCE IN URBAN AREAS

The relationship between these forms of public and private philanthropy in the 116 urban areas throws considerable light upon the increasing importance of the former and decreasing importance of the latter. This relationship is set forth in Table 7-1, columns 3 and 8, for public philanthropy, and the private funds are taken from column 12. In 1929, public philanthropy accounted for $35.8 million of the $47.2 million of total public and private philanthropy, or 75.8 per cent; the balance, 24.2 per cent, was private philanthropy. Approximately three-fourths of the expenditures for public and private assistance was from public funds in 1929, the first year covered in this study. The public percentage of the combined total rose slightly to 76.1 in 1930, then dropped to 71.0 in 1931, rose again to 81.6 in 1932, and jumped to 94.5 per cent in 1933. After 1933 the percentages shown in Table 7-1 indicate that at least 98 per cent of the funds were from public sources for this type of philanthropy, which historically was called poor relief, direct relief, public relief, outdoor relief, and so on. The Baird analysis provides a reasonably satisfactory indication of the growing proportion of public expenditures and the declining proportion of private expenditures for the 116 urban areas in the field of public and private relief and assistance. This conclusion supports one of the general conclusions of our study.

URBAN AND RURAL RELIEF EXPENDITURES

The Division of Social Research of the Works Project Administration developed a relief expenditures series for rural-town areas which covers the years 1932–36. The expenditures in the 85 rural-town sample areas provide the rural counterpart to the urban series of 116 areas compiled by Baird. The urban and rural-town data were combined and generalized, and then weighted on the basis of population covered for each series to provide estimates of total public assistance, 1932; private assistance, 1932–36; and rural assistance, 1932–36 (as well as monthly estimates for the fourfold classifications, public-private, rural-urban).[9] Public assistance payments included general relief; aid to the aged, blind,

[9] For methodology of developing the combined series, see Theodore E. Whiting and T. J. Woofter, Jr., *Summary of Relief and Federal Work Program, Statistics, 1933–1940*, Works Projects Administration, Washington, 1941, Appendix C, pp. 55–57.

and dependent children; and Farm Security Administration grants. (Expenditures for the Works Projects Administration, the Civil Works Program, and the special programs of the Federal Emergency Relief Administration were not included.)

Table 7-2 presents these estimates for the period 1932–36. Public assistance was estimated at $418 million in 1932, with 84 per cent of public assistance expenditures in urban areas. The urban proportion of total public relief declined in the following years, with relief being ex-

Table 7-2

Public and Private Assistance Relief Payments
in Rural and Urban United States, 1932-36
(millions of dollars)

	1932	1933	1934	1935	1936
Total relief	506	876	1,246	1,517	691
Urban	437	690	917	1,129	498
Rural	69	186	329	388	193
Percentage urban	86.4	78.8	73.6	74.4	72.1
Public relief	418	831	1,223	1,498	675
Urban	351	648	896	1,112	483
Rural	67	183	327	386	192
Percentage urban	84.0	78.0	73.3	74.2	71.6
Public Relief as per cent of total	82.5	94.9	98.2	98.8	97.7
Private relief	88	45	23	19	16
Urban	86	42	21	17	15
Rural	2	3	2	2	1
Percentage urban	97.7	93.3	91.3	89.5	93.8

Notes: Public relief includes general relief, poor relief, special types of public assistance (aid to the aged, aid to the blind, and aid to dependent children); and Farm Security Administration grants.

Rural-town areas include counties without a city of 25,000 or more, and in the New England states, townships of less than 5,000. These areas included 46 per cent of the 1930 population of the continental United States.

Source: Theodore E. Whiting and T.J. Woofter, Jr., *Summary of Relief and Federal Work Program Statistics, 1933-1940,* Works Projects Administration, 1941, Table 6, pp. 31-32.

tended to some rural areas for the first time because of the 1934 drought and the Farm Security Administration grants. Urban areas received 78 per cent of total public assistance in 1933, 73 per cent in 1934, 74 per cent in 1935, and 72 per cent in 1936. Information is not available on the urban proportion of total public assistance in 1929–31; probably it was even higher than in 1932 (84 per cent). In estimating total public relief expenditures (Table 7-3) for 1929–32, we shall assume that during this period the urban proportion was about six-sevenths of the national total.

Public assistance data for 1933–36 (Table 7-2) are based mainly on official reports and hence generally agree with the comparable data reported in current Social Security Administration publications. (See Table 7-4, column 6, 1933–36: for 1933, the total is almost identical; for 1934–36, it differs by less than 5 per cent.)

Private relief was comparatively insignificant in the rural areas. In 1932 it is estimated that only $2.2 million was expended; in 1933 the peak amount of $2.6 million was expended. Of the total private relief expenditures, 98 per cent was in urban areas in 1932, 93 per cent in 1933, 91 per cent in 1934, 90 per cent in 1935, and 94 per cent in 1936. Thus private relief was even more concentrated in urban areas than was public relief.

Calendar-year expenditures for public aid, with and without earnings on federal work projects, are presented in the *Social Security Bulletin, Annual Statistical Supplement,* 1960, in Table 125 (see Table 7-4). The data start with 1933 but contain no indications for the years 1929–32 needed in our series. Table 7-3 gives the data by which estimates were computed for these missing years.

EXTRAPOLATION OF SOCIAL SECURITY
ADMINISTRATION SERIES TO 1929

Some of the data developed by Whiting and Woofter have been used with the Baird data to derive additional national estimates for public assistance, particularly before 1933; in turn, these are tied in with data for 1933–40 in Table 7-3. Additions were then made to these national estimates for administrative costs and the value of surplus food distributed to needy families (Table 7-5).

In Table 7-3 the public assistance series for the 116 urban areas is given in column 1; this is the sum of public expenditures for general

Table 7-3

Estimated Totals for Public Assistance, 1929-40
(millions of dollars)

| Year | 116 Urban Areas (1) | Estimated U.S. Totals | | Social Security Adminis- tration Totals (4) | Esti- mated Adminis- trative Costs (5) | Total Including Adminis- trative Costs (6) |
		Population Adjustment (2)	Population and Urban Adjustments (3)			
1929	36	97	63		6	68
1930	58	156	101		9	110
1931	126	341	221		20	241
1932	261	704	456		41	497
1933	444	1,200	888	837	75	912
1934	659	1,781	1,318	1,342	122	1,464
1935	835	2,256	1,669	1,665	145	1,810
1936	392	1,059	783	681	59	740
1937	440	1,190	880	840	72	913
1938	523	1,412	1,045	1,008	87	1,094
1939	552	1,491	1,103	1,068	91	1,159
1940	534	1,444	1,068	1,053	85	1,138

Note: Detail may not add to total because of rounding.

Sources by Column

Column 1
Public assistance excluding earnings, Table 7-1 column 3 plus column 8.

Column 2
Column 1 divided by 0.37, as population in the 116 urban areas was approximately 37 per cent of the U.S. total in 1930 and 1940 (Enid Baird, *Public and Private Aid in 116 Urban Areas,* p. 4).

Column 3
According to Baird (p. 4) about two-thirds of the urban U.S. population in 1930 and 1940 was in her 116 urban areas. According to Whiting & Woofter (Table 7-3), 84.0 per cent in 1932, 78.0 per cent in 1933, 73.2 per cent in 1934, 74.2 per cent in 1935, and 71.6 per cent in 1936 of the public expenditures for relief were made in urban areas; accordingly we have assumed that 6/7 of the expenditures for public relief were in urban areas in 1929-32 and that 3/4 were for 1933-40. For 1929-32, then, column 3 = column 1 ÷ 2/3 x 6/7; and for 1933-40, column 3 = column 1 ÷ 2/3 x 3/4.

Notes to Table 7-3 continued

Column 4

Social Security Bulletin, Annual Statistical Supplement, 1960, Table 125, page 90, total assistance.

Column 5

According to *Security, Work and Relief Policies,* National Resources Planning Board, 1942, p. 598, administrative costs for categorical assistance were 9.1 per cent of payments in fiscal 1932 and 1934 and 9.0 per cent in 1933 (by extrapolation we have assumed 9.1 per cent for 1929-31); 8.7 per cent for 1935; 8.6 per cent in 1936-38; and 8.5 per cent in 1939. These percentages have been applied to column 3 for 1929-39, to estimate administrative costs. The 1940 figure is the amount reported to the author by the Social Security Administration.

Column 6

1929-32 equals columns 3 plus 5; 1933-40 equals columns 4 plus 5. This is our final series for these years for public assistance.

relief and special types of public assistance (columns 3 and 8 of Table 7-1). The crude adjustment for population, which implies no urban concentration of relief expenditures, is presented in column 2. The totals are clearly too high for all years. The estimation procedure for column 3 (see notes to Table 7-3) allows for the urban concentration.

Administrative costs for public assistance are available from 1940 to date. For the earlier years, 1929–39, they were estimated, using incomplete data for the fiscal years. These costs are available for the special types of public assistance programs for the fiscal years 1932–39.[10] Administrative expenses expressed as a percentage of payments for these programs declined from 9.1 per cent in 1932 and 1934 to 8.5 per cent in 1939. The assumption was made that administrative costs for general relief programs were in the same proportion as for the categorical programs. For the years not covered, 1929–31, it was assumed that the general relationship in the immediately following years (9.1 per cent) prevailed. These percentages for the fiscal years were applied to the estimated assistance payments for the corresponding calendar years to estimate administrative costs.

Estimated administrative expenses are presented in column 5 of Table 7-3; the total, including administrative expenses, is given in column 6. Until the data become available on the amount of the distribution of free

[10] *Work, Security and Relief Policies,* National Resources Planning Board, 1942, p. 598.

food (and administrative expenses) from the Department of Agriculture, the data in column 6 stand as our best (but incomplete) set of estimates of the amount of public expenditures for public aid, 1929–40. The single addition to public assistance (column 4 of Table 7-5) of the value of distributed free food in preparing the estimates for public aid results from our decision to attempt to exclude earnings from public works programs with definite scales of pay and hours of work from the concept of public philanthropy in the area of general relief. Table 7-3 was extended to 1940 for the purpose of utilizing all of the years in the Baird study. The most important figures in this table are the 1929–32 figures in column 3, which were used to develop the data in column 6.

SUMMARY TABLES ON PUBLIC ASSISTANCE

The payments for 1933 to 1959, excluding administrative expense, are presented in Table 7-4. The payments for old-age assistance before the Social Security Act was enacted in 1935 were $26 million in 1933; they rose to $1,883 million in 1959. Aid to dependent children rose from $41 million to $1,003 million; aid to the blind from $5 million to $91 million; aid to the permanently and totally disabled, the fourth categorical program, began in 1950 with $8 million and increased to $260 million; and last, general assistance (a nonfederal program except for FERA program in the 1930's) decreased from $759 in 1933 to $344 million dollars in 1959. (Column 8 of Table 7-4 is repeated in column 1 of Table 7-5 after 1932.)

Expenditures for surplus food comprise the expenditures for public aid as that term is used in this treatment of public philanthropy; that is, other forms of public aid in the Merriam compilations are excluded.[11]

[11] "Other" in the Merriam compilation includes surplus food distributed to needy families, work relief program earnings (WPA, NYA, and CCC), Farm Security Administration grants and administration of loans, RFC relief grants to states and municipalities, Civil Works Administration programs, and the FERA relief programs. Of these we include as public philanthropy the FERA programs, subsistence payments under the FSA (under "other assistance," Table 7-4), and surplus foods distributed to needy families (Table 7-5).

In the Merriam compilation for fiscal 1935 (our Table 5-1), the expenditures for "other" (the second subhead under public aid) dwarfs the amount for public assistance—$2,374 million and $624 million. FERA expenditures, which totaled $1,738 million in fiscal 1935, are included in the Merriam series under "other" public aid. In our series on public assistance (Table 7-4), however, FERA expenditures are included in general assistance (column 5), with relief under special programs separately shown in column 7.

The totals for the entire period, 1929–59, are presented in column 5 of Table 7-5. Public aid increased from $68 million to $4,088, from 0.07 per cent of GNP to 0.80 per cent.

FEDERAL SHARE INCREASING

The proportion of expenditures for public assistance from federal, state, and local funds is not available for 1929–35. The percentage distribution for selected years 1936–59 is presented in Table 7-6. The federal percentage rose sharply from 13.4 in 1936 to 23.2 in 1939, and to 52.2 in 1959. The percentage from the state governments declined slowly from 51.4 in 1936 to 50.6 in 1939, and then rapidly to 35.7 in 1959. The percentage from local governments, which probably reached its peak early in the Great Depression, declined from 35.2 in 1936 to 26.2 in 1939; it flattened out to the 12 to 10 per cent level after 1944. This table is further evidence of the shift in the financing of public philanthropy away from local and, to a lesser degree, state sources,[12] toward federal sources after the social security program matured.

OTHER WELFARE SERVICES

"Other welfare services" is a residual and, accordingly, difficult to utilize in our attempt to compile comprehensive data on domestic public philanthropy. It is the smallest of Merriam's six major divisions. (It should not be confused with "other public assistance," a subitem along the sec-

---

[12] Other sources were examined but not used. The *National Income Supplement* to the *Survey of Current Business,* 1954, Table 36, page 212, presents a series on direct relief, under government transfer payments, for welfare purposes for state and local governments. The annual amounts for direct relief (slightly lower than ours) were: $71 million in 1929, $105 million for 1930, $176 million for 1931, $317 million for 1932, $558 million for 1933, $745 million for 1934, $954 million (plus $2 million federal) for 1935, $635 (plus $36 million federal) million for 1937, and $965 million (plus $23 million federal) for 1938. The government transfer payments reported in this source do not provide sufficient detail for our present purposes. The major difference is the exclusion of FERA, especially in fiscal 1934–36; it is rather consistent with the Merriam treatment of FERA. The notes to the table indicate that most of the transfer payments from the federal government were for social insurance funds and military or veterans' benefits. We could have used FERA on a calendar-year basis as a simple addition to the OBE series—our public assistance series.

Table 7-4

Public Assistance Payments, 1933-59
(millions of dollars)

Year	Old-Age Assistance (1)	Aid to Dependent Children (2)	Aid to the Blind (3)	Aid to the Permanently and Totally Disabled (4)	General Assistance (5)	Subtotal (6)	Other Assistance[a] (7)	Total Public Assistance Payments (8)
1933	26	41	5		759	831	6	837
1934	32	41	7		1,201	1,281	61	1,342
1935	65	42	8		1,433	1,548	118	1,665
1936	155	50	13		439	657	24	681
1937	310	70	16		407	804	36	840
1938	392	97	19		476	985	23	1,008
1939	430	115	21		483	1,049	19	1,068
1940	475	133	22		405	1,035	18	1,053
1941	542	153	23		273	990	12	1,003
1942	595	158	25		181	959	6	965
1943	653	141	25		111	930		930
1944	693	135	25		89	942		942

Year								
1945	727	150	26		87	990		990
1946	822	209	31		121	1,183		1,183
1947	990	295	36		165	1,486		1,486
1948	1,133	364	41		199	1,737		1,737
1949	1,380	475	48		282	2,186		2,186
1950	1,470	554	53	8	295	2,380	15	2,395
1951	1,474	562	56	58	195	2,345	50	2,395
1952	1,533	554	61	91	172	2,411	53	2,464
1953	1,597	562	66	115	151	2,492	56	2,547
1954	1,593	594	68	137	198	2,589	64	2,653
1955	1,608	639	71	156	214	2,689	68	2,757
1956	1,677	663	77	177	198	2,791	70	2,861
1957	1,773	755	84	201	213	3,026	74	3,099
1958	1,830	895	87	228	307	3,347	86	3,434
1959	1,883	1,003	91	260	344	3,581	99	3,680
Total 1933-59[b]	25,858	9,450	1,106	1,431	9,398	47,244	958	48,201

[a]Other Assistance: 1933-37, relief under special programs of the Federal Emergency Relief Administration ($115 million in 1935, $4 million in 1936, and less than $0.5 million in 1937); 1935-42, subsistence payments certified by the Farm Security Administration ($3 million in 1935, $20 million in 1936, and $36 million in 1937); and 1950-59, vendor payments for medical care from general assistance funds, from special funds, and, for one state for October 1950-June 1954, from funds for the special types of public assistance; data for such expenditures partly estimated for some states.

[b]See note a, Table 2-1.

Source: *Social Security Bulletin, Annual Statistical Supplement*, 1960, Table 125, p. 90 (1933-43) and Table 126, p. 91 (1944-59).

Table 7-5

Public Assistance and Public Aid, 1929-59
(millions of dollars)

| Year | Public Assistance | | | Surplus Food Distributed to Needy Families | Total Public Aid (3) + (4) |
	Payments (1)	Administrative Costs (2)	Total (3)	(4)	(5)
1929	63	6	68		68
1930	101	9	110		110
1931	221	20	241		241
1932	456	41	497	17	514
1933	837	75	912	71	983
1934	1,342	122	1,464	149	1,612
1935	1,665	145	1,810	110	1,921
1936	681	59	740	27	766
1937	840	72	913	28	941
1938	1,008	87	1,094	51	1,145
1939	1,068	91	1,159	70	1,229
1940	1,053	85	1,138	111	1,249
1941	1,002	94	1,096	142	1,238
1942	965	87	1,052	99	1,151
1943	930	79	1,009	40	1,049
1944	942	76	1,019	10	1,029
1945	990	78	1,068	1	1,069
1946	1,183	90	1,272	a	1,273
1947	1,486	107	1,593	a	1,593
1948	1,737	124	1,861	a	1,862
1949	2,186	148	2,335	3	2,338
1950	2,395	168	2,563	6	2,569
1951	2,395	181	2,576	4	2,580
1952	2,464	197	2,661	a	2,662
1953	2,547	206	2,754	6	2,760
1954	2,653	218	2,871	37	2,908
1955	2,757	233	2,990	76	3,066
1956	2,861	249	3,110	84	3,194
1957	3,099	275	3,370	77	3,447
1958	3,434	302	3,736	91	3,827
1959	3,680	325	4,005	83	4,088
Total[b]	49,041	4,045	53,087	1,396	54,482

Notes to Table 7-5

Note: Detail may not add to total because of rounding.

^aLess than $0.6 million.

^bSee note a, Table 2-1.

Sources by Column

Column 1

1929-32, Table 7-3, column 3; 1933-59, Table 7-4, column 8.

Column 2

1929-39, Table 7-3, column 5; 1940-59, calendar year amounts reported to the author (July 6, 1962) by Thomas Karter, Division of Program Research, Social Security Administration.

Column 4

Obtained by averaging successive fiscal year data. Fiscal 1933-34, *Security, Work and Relief Policies,* National Resources Planning Board, 1942, p. 598; fiscal 1935-60, reported (June 13, 1962) to the author by Social Security Administration.

Table 7-6

Percentage Distribution of Expenditures for Assistance Payments by Source of Funds, Selected Years, 1936-59
(per cent)

Year	Federal	State	Local	Total
1936	13.4	51.4	35.2	100.0
1937	21.5	49.4	29.1	100.0
1938	22.2	50.3	27.5	100.0
1939	23.2	50.6	26.2	100.0
1944	41.4	45.8	12.8	100.0
1949	45.1	44.3	10.6	100.0
1954	50.6	37.4	12.0	100.0
1959	52.2	35.7	12.1	100.0

Source: *Social Security Bulletin, Annual Statistical Supplement,* 1960 Table 132, p. 102.

ond major division, "public aid"; that division is the subject of the first section of this chapter.)

Moreover, this residual welfare category is primarily a compilation of state and local expenditures, especially for the early part of our three decades; for fiscal 1935 only $2.1 of the $139.3 million total was federal, and for the two large subitems—institutional and other care, and child welfare—state and local expenditures were $110 million and $26 million. At this juncture the absence of supporting data to explain the sources, terms, and combinations of local, state, and federal expenditures in the Merriam compilations becomes a major statistical handicap in our use of these compilations as a master check list of items. These are among the considerations which account for the relatively brief treatment of "other welfare services."

The notes to Merriam's tabulation (our Table 5-1) state that the following public expenditures are included: vocational rehabilitation (including medical rehabilitation), institutional and other care ("expenditures for homes for dependent or neglected children and for adults other than veterans and the value of surplus food for nonprofit institutions"), school lunch program, and child welfare (including foster-care payments and direct appropriations by state legislatures to voluntary agencies and institutions). This list is our guide.

Revised estimates for "other welfare services" are available for the fifth years, beginning with fiscal 1935, and annually since fiscal 1955; unrevised data were used for the other fiscal years, 1936–54. For the first year of our period, 1929, the estimate has not been revised; moreover, other welfare services are included with public aid in the 1929 figures, with a total for the two items of $500 million.[13] In the preceding section a calendar-year series was developed for public assistance and public aid, with estimates for the early years based on sample studies, since national data were not available. Total public aid in calendar 1929 was estimated to be $70 million—Table 7-5 indicated $68 million. The unrevised Merriam estimate of $500 million for both public aid and other welfare is apparently very high. Subtracting the estimated $70 million for public aid from the $500 total would leave $430 million for

[13] Bureau of the Census, *Historical Statistics of the United States,* Washington, Series H-13 and H-17, p. 193, and Ida C. Merriam, "Trends in Public Welfare and Their Implications," *Papers and Proceedings, American Economic Review,* Vol. 47, 1957, p. 477.

other welfare services, whereas by fiscal 1935 the estimated total for this category was only $139 million (Table 7-13, column 1). Hence, for other welfare services also, it was necessary to prepare independent estimates of expenditures for 1929.

Table 7-13 in the appendix to this chapter compares the several sources that were considered for estimating other welfare service expenditures for the years 1929–34. Derivation of the estimates for this early period are given in Table 7-14. These estimates of the early years are carried over to Table 7-15, which is the summary table for the "other welfare services" category. Calendar-year estimates for selected succeeding years are also given in this table along with the Merriam data from which they were derived.

HEALTH AND MEDICAL PROGRAMS

Our series estimates for health and medical programs from 1929 to 1959 are presented in their entirety in Table 7-12. They are based essentially on the revised Merriam figures, although the military medical care and Defense Department items were omitted from our totals. Derivation of calendar-year estimates from the Merriam revised series and, in part, unrevised series, and extraction of the two items mentioned above, are given in Table 7-7 for selected years from 1929 to 1960.

It will be noted, however, that the Merriam data do not cover a period of major significance to public philanthropy—1929–35. Unlike some other periods, it is highly implausible to assume that expenditures in this period experienced a continuous rate of growth from the earlier to the later years. It is much more likely that health and medical expenditures decreased for several years after 1929 and then moved upward to the 1935 level.

Our estimates for 1929 to 1934 are based on this assumption. We were able to derive estimates of health and medical expenditures for 1929 and 1932 from data presented by Musgrave and Culbertson, and to link them to the Merriam estimates for 1929 and 1935.[14] Since the 1929 estimate obtained from this study for health and sanitation expend-

---

[14] R. A. Musgrave and J. M. Culbertson, "The Growth of Public Expenditures in the U.S., 1890–1948," *National Tax Journal*, June 1953.

Table 7-7

Health and Medical Programs
Derivation of 1929-34 Estimates
(millions of dollars)

Fiscal Year	Musgrave (1)	Unrevised Merriam (2)	Revised Merriam (3)	Merriam Estimate (4)	Calendar Year (5)
1929	458	470	445	445	428
1930				410	393
1931				375	358
1932	350			340	368
1933				395	423
1934				450	477
1935		642	505	505	
1940	434	799	652		

Sources by Column

Column 1

R.A. Musgrave and J.M. Culbertson, "The Growth of Public Expenditures in the United States, 1890-1948," *National Tax Journal*, June 1953.

Columns 2 and 3

Table 7-8, columns 1, 3, and 5.

Column 4

1929 and 1935, column 3; 1932, same percentage of column 1 as in 1929; other years interpolation from 1932.

Column 5

Average of current and succeeding fiscal years. Fiscal-year data converted to calendar-years basis by two-year moving average.

itures of federal, state, and local governments was very close to the Merriam revised estimates for that year ($458 and $445 million), it was assumed that the 1932 figures would bear the same relationship as if a Merriam estimate were available for that year. It was also assumed that fiscal 1932 was the turning point in the trend of health and medical expenditures. Since the Merriam figure for 1929 was 97.2 per cent of the Musgrave and Culbertson figure, our figure for 1932 was determined as 97.2 per cent of the 1932 Musgrave and Culbertson figures, or $340 million. From this estimate interpolations were made backward to 1929 and forward to 1934 to produce a fiscal-year series. Calendar-year esti-mates were then derived, as shown in Table 7-8. It is clear that the dis-parity in the 1940 figures in the first three columns rules out an interpola-tion for 1929 to 1935 based on Musgrave's data alone.

Musgrave and Culbertson do not give a 1929 health and sanitation figure for combined federal, state, and local governments because no apportionment of social welfare expenditures for local governments was possible for that year. Therefore, an estimate for the missing item was extrapolated by assuming that local government health and sanitation expenditures bore approximately the same relationship to those of federal and state governments in 1929 as they did in 1923 and 1932—years for which expenditures for all three governmental levels were given. The extrapolation procedure is shown in the accompanying tabulation.

| | Health and Sanitation Expenditures (million dollars) | | |
	Local Government (1)	Federal and State Governments (2)	(1) ÷ (2) (3)
1923	303.4	33.9	8.95
1932	314.8	35.3	9.20
Average of 1923 and 1932	—	—	9.08
1929	—	45.4	

Local government expenditures in 1929 = 9.08 × $45.4 million = $412.2 million; and combined government expenditures = $45.4 mil-lion + $412.2 million = $457.6 million.

FREE SCHOOLS

There are two major compilations available on which to base estimates for public philanthropy channeled to free education during the period 1929–59: the Office of Education (OE) series (given in the *Biennial Survey of Education*) and the Merriam series. Both series measure the same thing: support, through public bodies, of education. However, the OE figures were preferred for several reasons.

Table 7-8

Health and Medical Programs
Derivation of Calendar Year Estimates
(millions of dollars)

Fiscal Year	Unrevised Merriam Estimates		Revised Merriam Estimates			Calendar Year Estimates (6)
	Total (1)	Percentage Increase over Preceding Year (2)	Total (3)	Medicare and Defense Department (4)	Civilian Programs (5)	
1929	470		445		445	
1935	642		544	39.0	505	514
1936	665	3.6			523	
1940	799		697	45.0[a]	652[a]	634
1941	755	-5.5			616[a]	
1945	996		1,937	1,100.0[a]	837[a]	882[a]
1946	1,103	10.7			926[a]	
1950	2,388		2,344	332.0[a]	2,012[a]	2,134[a]
1951	2,674	12.0			2,254[a]	
1955			2,914	611.5	2,302	2,381
1956			3,035	573.8	2,461	2,613
1957			3,402	637.4	2,765	2,877
1958			3,726	737.5	2,988	3,131
1959			4,052	779.4	3,273	3,418
1960			4,232	669.5	3,563	

[a]Includes some Defense Department medical facilities construction not separately available.

Sources by Column
Column 1
Historical Statistics, U.S. Department of Commerce, Series H-16, p. 193.

Column 3
Health and Medical Programs: 1929: *Social Security Bulletin,* November 1961, Table 5, p. 10; 1935-60: Table 5-1 and its source.

Notes to Table 7-8 continued

Column 4

Sum of hospital and medical care by Defense Department, medical facilities construction by Defense Department and Medicare.

Column 5

1935, 1940, 1945, 1950, 1955-60: column 3 minus column 4. 1936, 1941, 1946, 1951: estimated by applying annual percentage increase from unrevised series.

Column 6

Estimated by averaging successive fiscal year totals in column 5.

The Office of Education figures have the advantage of being continuous throughout the period of the study. The Merriam estimates (unrevised) contain a gap between 1929 and 1935, although they have the advantage of being consistent with many other series in the public domestic quadrant of the study. It would seem feasible, then, to interpolate missing years on the basis of the OE data. But coinciding years (see Table 7-11 figures for 1929, 1935, and 1940) showed an erratic relationship between the two series, and a straight-line interpolation of the Merriam estimates was not indicated by the OE series. Thus it was decided to use the Office of Education figures, since they provide a reasonably consistent measure of public support of education over a period of time, and one of the major concerns of this study is the *change* in philanthropy during the years studied.

It was necessary, however, to extract from the OE figures some amounts already accounted for in other series of the quadrant. Tables 7-9 and 7-10, in addition to presenting the several OE series from which our estimates were derived, also show the extraction of previously counted funds. Thus Table 7-9, column 1, gives revenue receipts of public elementary and secondary schools, while columns 2 and 3 present expenditures on school lunch and school health programs, respectively. Since school lunch funds are included in our "other welfare services" series and school health expenditures appear in our "health and medical" estimates, the sum of columns 2 and 3 is subtracted from column 1 to form our elementary and secondary school series, which is carried to the summary table for public support of education (column 1 of Table 7-11). With regard to higher education, Table 7-10 presents receipts from government sources for general and educational operations and for

Table 7-9

Free Schools
Derivation of Elementary and Secondary Education Estimates
School Years 1928-60
(millions of dollars)

School Year Ending	Public Receipts (1)	School Lunch (2)	School Health (3)	Total of (2) + (3) (4)	Public Receipts, Net Total (5)
1928	2,025		8.9	9	2,016
1930	2,088		9.2	9	2,079
1932	2,067		9.5	10	2,057
1934	1,810		9.8	10	1,800
1936	1,971		11.5	12	1,959
1938	2,223		14.7	15	2,208
1940	2,260		17.9	18	2,242
1942	2,416	23	20.1	43	2,373
1944	2,604	34	22.2	56	2,548
1946	3,060	57	24.8	82	2,978
1948	4,311	116	27.7	144	4,167
1950	5,437	159	30.6	190	5,247
1952	6,423	153	44.8	198	6,225
1954	7,847	239	59.0	298	7,549
1956	9,664	293	74.2	367	9,297
1958	12,145	323	85.6	409	11,736
1960	14,673	399	98.5	497	14,176

Sources by Column
Column 1

Revenue receipts of public elementary and secondary schools from federal, state, and local governments. *Biennial Survey of Education.*

Column 2

Historical Statistics of the U.S. and our Table 5-1. Figures for certain years include value of surplus food sent to some other nonprofit institutions.

Column 3

Social Security Bulletin, November 1961, Table 5, p. 10. Partly interpolated.

Column 4

Column 2 plus column 3.

Column 5

Column 1 minus column 4.

Table 7-10

Free Schools,
Derivation of Higher Education Estimates,
School Years, 1928-60
(millions of dollars)

School Year Ending	Public Receipts		Total (3)	Veterans Tuition and Fees (4)	Net Total Col. 3 Minus Col. 4 (5)
	Educational and General (1)	Plant Fund Operations (2)			
1928	175		175		175
1930	173	31	204		204
1932	200	28	228		228
1934	143	32	175		175
1936	184		184		184
1938	192	38	230		230
1940	218	43	261		261
1942	252	15	267		267
1944	510	11	521		521
1946	453	77	530	61	469
1948	933	91	1,025	365	660
1950	1,089	362	1,451	307	1,144
1952	1,146	194	1,340	148	1,192
1954	1,259	180	1,440	44	1,395
1956	1,492	267	1,759	16	1,744
1958	1,998	503	2,501	5	2,496
1960	2,582	440	3,022	3	3,019

Note: Detail may not add to total because of rounding.
Source: *Biennial Survey of Education.*

plant fund operations. From the sum of these two columns is subtracted funds covering veterans' tuition and fees which already appear in our series on public expenditures on veterans (see Chapter 6). The difference becomes our series for higher education, and these funds are carried to column 2 of Table 7-11.

In addition to the two series on public expenditures on education and their total for both school and calendar years, Table 7-11 presents the Merriam series on education for selected years, so it may be compared with our school-year estimates derived from OE data.

Table 7-11

Public Support of Education 1929-59
(millions of dollars)

School Year Ending	Elementary and Secondary Schools (1)	Higher Education Institutions (2)	School Year Totals (3)	Calendar Year Totals (4)	Merriam Revised Series (fiscal year) (5)
1928	2,016	175	2,191		
1929			2,237	2,260	2,450
1930	2,079	204	2,283	2,283	
1931			2,284	2,285	
1932	2,057	228	2,285	2,209	
1933			2,131	2,054	
1934	1,800	175	1,975	2,017	
1935			2,059	2,100	1,980
1936	1,959	184	2,143	2,216	
1937			2,290	2,364	
1938	2,208	230	2,438	2,454	
1939			2,470	2,486	
1940	2,242	261	2,503	2,537	2,316
1941			2,571	2,606	
1942	2,373	267	2,640	2,748	
1943			2,855	2,963	
1944	2,548	521	3,069	3,164	
1945			3,259	3,353	3,457
1946	2,978	469	3,447	3,793	
1947			4,138	4,483	
1948	4,167	660	4,827	5,219	
1949			5,610	6,001	
1950	5,247	1,144	6,391	6,649	6,508
1951			6,905	7,162	
1952	6,225	1,192	7,417	7,804	
1953			8,181	8,567	
1954	7,549	1,395	8,944	9,470	
1955			9,992	10,523	11,294
1956	9,297	1,744	11,041	11,845	12,385
1957			12,636	13,436	13,972
1958	11,736	2,496	14,232	14,972	15,449
1959			15,713	16,454	16,608
1960	14,176	3,019	17,195		17,788

Notes to Table 7-11

Note: Detail may not add to total because of rounding.

Sources by Column
Column 1

Column 5 of Table 7-9.

Column 2

Column 5 of Table 7-10.

Column 3
Even years column 1 plus column 2; odd years, interpolations.

Column 4
Two-year moving average of column 3.

Column 5

Table 5-1.

These were the dominant factors and methodological consequences of the choice of OE figures. Additional differences between them and the Merriam estimates should be mentioned. The OE estimates for elementary and secondary education are based upon expenditures of state and local school systems in the then forty-eight states and the District of Columbia. The Merriam estimates include the education of dependent children overseas, education of persons in federal schools, and expenditures of Canal Zone schools. In the higher-education figures, the Merriam series includes and the Office of Education excludes depreciation allowances for plant and equipment. (The same applies to veterans' subsistence allowances.) Capital outlays for land and equipment are excluded in the Merriam series but included in the OE series.

Finally, a check of Table 5-1 will indicate that we have covered in this chapter all the Merriam items on social welfare expenditures under public programs except what she considers social insurance and public housing. Hence data for these two categories will be presented in Chapter 8, the second chapter on domestic public philanthropy.

The final summary figures for the four categories of social welfare are presented in Table 7-12; the total for each year is also presented as a percentage of GNP for that year.

Table 7-12

Public Aid, Other Welfare, Health and Medical, Free Schools, and Gross National Product, 1929-59

Year	Public Aid		Other Welfare		Health and Medical		Free Schools		Total	
	$ mil. (1)	Per Cent of GNP (2)	$ mil. (3)	Per Cent of GNP (4)	$ mil. (5)	Per Cent of GNP (6)	$ mil. (7)	Per Cent of GNP (8)	$ mil. (9)	Per Cent of GNP (10)
1929	68	0.065	95	.091	428	.410	2,260	2.164	2,851	2.730
1930	110	0.121	96	.105	393	.431	2,283	2.506	2,882	3.163
1931	241	0.316	107	.140	358	.470	2,285	2.996	2,991	3.922
1932	514	0.879	116	.198	368	.630	2,209	3.778	3,207	5.485
1933	983	1.757	125	.223	423	.756	2,054	3.670	3,585	6.406
1934	1,612	2.481	135	.208	477	.734	2,017	3.104	4,241	6.527
1935	1,921	2.650	140	.193	514	.709	2,100	2.896	4,675	6.448
1936	766	0.926	137	.166	538	.650	2,216	2.678	3,657	4.420
1937	941	1.036	135	.149	562	.619	2,364	2.604	4,002	4.408
1938	1,145	1.343	132	.155	586	.688	2,454	2.879	4,317	5.065
1939	1,229	1.349	130	.143	610	.669	2,486	2.729	4,455	4.890
1940	1,249	1.241	127	.126	634	.630	2,537	2.522	4,547	4.519
1941	1,238	0.984	142	.113	683	.543	2,606	2.071	4,669	3.711
1942	1,151	0.723	157	.099	732	.460	2,748	1.727	4,788	3.009
1943	1,049	0.545	172	.090	782	.406	2,963	1.539	4,966	2.580
1944	1,029	0.487	187	.088	832	.394	3,164	1.497	5,212	2.466

Year										
1945	1,069	.500	202	.095	882	.413	3,353	1.570	5,506	2.578
1946	1,273	.604	245	.116	1,132	.537	3,793	1.801	6,443	3.058
1947	1,593	.680	288	.123	1,382	.590	4,483	1.913	7,746	3.306
1948	1,862	.718	330	.127	1,632	.629	5,219	2.012	9,043	3.486
1949	2,338	.906	373	.145	1,883	.730	6,001	2.325	10,595	4.106
1950	2,569	.903	416	.146	2,134	.750	6,649	2.336	11,768	4.135
1951	2,580	.784	461	.140	2,183	.664	7,162	2.177	12,386	3.765
1952	2,662	.767	506	.146	2,232	.643	7,804	2.249	13,204	3.805
1953	2,760	.755	550	.151	2,281	.624	8,567	2.345	14,158	3.875
1954	2,908	.801	594	.163	2,331	.642	9,470	2.608	15,303	4.214
1955	3,066	.771	639	.161	2,381	.599	10,523	2.648	16,609	4.179
1956	3,194	.762	740	.177	2,613	.623	11,845	2.826	18,392	4.388
1957	3,447	.778	845	.191	2,877	.650	13,436	3.035	20,605	4.654
1958	3,827	.861	964	.217	3,131	.704	14,972	3.368	22,894	5.150
1959	4,088	.847	1,091	.226	3,413	.707	16,454	3.409	25,046	5.189
Total 1929-59[a]	54,482	.811	10,377	.155	41,407	.617	168,477	2.509	274,743	4.092

Sources by Column

Column 1

Column 5 of Table 7-5.

Column 3

Column 4 of Table 7-15, with interpolations for missing years.

Column 5

Column 6 of Table 7-8, with interpolations for missing years, and column 5 of Table 7-7. The figure for 1959 should be 3,418, as in

Column 5 continued

Table 7-8. The very slight error was discovered while checking the proofs, too late to be worth correcting.

Column 7

Column 4 of Table 7-11.

Note: Gross National Product: column 1 of Table 2-2.

[a]See note a, Table 2-1.

APPENDIX TO CHAPTER 7

The problem of comparability of data is substantial. With the exception of national income, all data examined were for fiscal years. Because it is a miscellaneous, residual category, it is difficult to determine if the same programs are included in the *Census of Governments'* "other public welfare" as in Merriam's "other welfare services," or to select from the detailed functional categories in financial reports of cities or state those which are properly "other welfare." For example, expenditures reported as "aid to mothers" apparently should be considered as aid to dependent children under public assistance, while "care of children" is "child welfare" under "other welfare services." [15] Veterans' aid is another difficult category. Local and state "aid to soldiers and sailors" in these early years of our period are probably included in relief or public assistance (Geddes, p. 6), but possibly may also be found in other welfare services. Our series of veterans' benefits includes no local expenditures, and no state expenditures before 1946. Thus, in the 1930's, when veterans' aid was not always clearly segregated at the local level, there is no double counting, but relief and burial for needy veterans are included in public assistance.

NATIONAL INCOME: TRANSFER PAYMENTS

The Office of Business Economics reports state and local transfer payments for "veterans' aid and bonuses, payments for the care of foster children in private family homes, and payments to nonprofit institution" (*National Income,* 1954, Table 36, p. 212). This series is shown in Table 7-13, column 3. The inclusion of veterans' aid and bonuses is the major apparent difference of this series from the Merriam compilation; however, it is not certain that all institutional care is included, nor all child welfare. The *National Income* series is about two-thirds of the Merriam figure for 1935 and about three-fourths in 1940. The reported $75 million in 1929 may thus be reasonably assumed to be a minimum

---

[15] Anne E. Geddes includes in relief expenditures the "aid to mothers" item from the *Financial Statistics of Cities,* but not "care of children." The implication is that the latter is to be considered as "other welfare." *Trends in Relief Expenditures, 1910–1935,* Research Monograph X, Works Progress Administration, Washington, 1937, pp. 6–7.

figure. If it were to be assumed that the 65 per cent ratio in 1935 was also valid in 1929, the total for calendar 1929 comparable to the Merriam series would be $115 million.

CENSUS OF GOVERNMENTS

The *Census of Governments* [16] has a category "other public welfare" in addition to public assistance, health and hospitals, education, and others.[17] Apparently this does not include veterans' benefits and it seems to be roughly comparable to Merriam's other welfare services item, but detailed explanation of the category is not available. (Fiscal-year totals reported by the *Census of Governments* for "other public welfare" are shown in Table 7-13, columns 4 and 5. Column 4 is the total, which is considerably higher than the Merriam series (column 1), in the years where they overlap. The difference, however, is mainly in the figure for the federal government; hence the state and local expenditures are shown separately in column 5. These can be compared with the Merriam figures in column 2.

In 1935, the Merriam figures for state and local expenditures are considerably higher than that of the *Census of Governments* for 1934 or 1936 ($137 million versus $93 and $96 million), but in 1940 it is slightly lower ($104 million versus $107 million).

The pattern of the *Census of Governments* series as compared with the Merriam figures for 1935 and 1940 makes it difficult to estimate a value for 1929 from these data. Interpolating between the reported totals for 1927 and 1932 would suggest a range for 1929 of $80–$85 million. The wide difference between this series and the Merriam totals in 1935 and 1940 suggests caution, although the major factor accounting for the difference—federal expenditures—was of minor importance in 1929. Examining the *Census of Governments* state and local totals—$72 million in 1927 and $78 million in 1932—would suggest $73 million in 1929 if the 1940 relationship between the two series held, or $108 mil-

---

[16] This series is an estimate derived by the Governments Division of the Census Bureau from the *Financial Statistics of Cities* and the *Financial Statistics of States.*

[17] *Historical Statistics of the United States;* Series Y-425, Y-557, pp. 723 and 727. State and local expenditures are separately available in Bureau of the Census, *Historical Statistics on State and Local Government Finances 1902–1953,* State and Local Government Special Studies Number 38, Washington, 1955, Table 1, p. 17.

Table 7-13

Various Estimates of Other Welfare Services,
Fiscal Years 1927-40
(millions of dollars)

Fiscal Year	Merriam Total (1)	Merriam State and Local (2)	OBE Transfer Payments (calendar year) (3)	Census of Governments Total (4)	Census of Governments State and Local (5)	Index: Cities 100,000+ (1929=100) (6)
1927				82	72	88.9
1928						99.4
1929			75			100.0
1930			81			96.9
1931			87			108.7
1932			90	79	78	105.7
1933			91			97.9
1934			89	183	93	104.4
1935	139.3	137.2	91			109.2
1936			90	266	96	
1937			92			
1938			93	265	101	
1939			91			
1940	114.1	104.4	86	265	107	

Sources by Column
Columns 1 and 2

Table 5-1.

Column 3
National Income, 1954, Supplement to Survey of Current Business, Table 36, p. 212.

Columns 4 and 5
Historical Statistics of the United States Colonial Times to 1957, Series Y-425, and
Y-557, pp. 723 and 727.

Column 6
Financial Statistics of Cities, 1927-35.

lion if the 1935 relationship held. Federal expenditures would probably
add another million dollars. (Merriam repc.ts a total of $2 million fed-
eral expenditures in 1935.) No..e of the series thus far examined has
been fully consistent with the available Merriam estimates for 1935 and

1940, but they do suggest for 1929 the magnitudes involved, with a range of $74–$115 million.

FINANCIAL STATISTICS OF CITIES AND STATES

Whereas in the *National Income* and *Census of Governments* series no detailed breakdown is available of the "other welfare" item, in utilizing the *Financial Statistics of Cities* and *Financial Statistics of States* the problem is that of selecting the appropriate functional categories from which to build up an "other welfare services" total.

Three items are included in other welfare services expenditures by cities: care of poor in institutions, care of children, and other charities.[18] The last category accounted for about 15 per cent of the total of $29 million reported in 1929 (Table 7-14, column 1), with the balance about equally divided between the two major categories. Population figures are available for the cities reporting expenditures. In 1927–31 the report covered cities with a population of 30,000 and over, representing about 36 per cent of the total United States population in 1927–29 and 39 per cent in 1930–31. Beginning in 1932, the report was restricted to cities with a population of 100,000 and over; the population covered in 1932–35 represented about 30 per cent of the total United States population.

The detail permitted an expenditure series for other welfare services to be compiled for cities with populations over 100,000. The total reported in 1929 was $26.6 million, and in 1935 $29.0 million. This series is expressed as an index in column 6 of Table 7-13, with 1929 equal to 100. Expenditures during the period 1929–35 did not evidence a consistent pattern. If this index is used to extrapolate backward the Merriam total for 1935 of $139.3 million, the resulting estimate is $128 million for 1929. State expenditures increased relatively more than city expenditures for other welfare services during the years 1929–31 (state data are

[18] Under governmental-cost payments for "charities," the *Financial Statistics of Cities* includes outdoor poor relief, care of poor in institutions, care of children, and other charities; and under "miscellaneous special aid to classes," aid to soldiers and sailors, and aid to mothers. Outdoor poor relief clearly belongs under public assistance and public aid rather than other welfare services. Aid to mothers is care for dependent children in the home, other than in institutions. Aid to soldiers and sailors is relief and burial aid. Following Anne Geddes procedure (*Statistics of Cities*, p. 7), these last two categories are assumed to be included under relief or public aid; thus care of poor in institutions, care of children, and other charities are the functional expenditures assumed to be included in cities' "other welfare services."

Table 7-14

Other Welfare Services
Estimated Local, State, and Federal Expenditures, 1927-36
(thousands of dollars)

Fiscal Year	Large Cities Expenditures (1)	Per Cent of Total U.S. Population (2)	Estimated Total Local Expenditures (1) ÷ (2) (3)	State Expenditures (4)	State and Local Expenditures (3) + (4) (5)	Federal Grants (6)	Total Expenditures (5) + (6) (7)	Calendar Year Estimates (8)
1927	25,376	36.0	70,489	16,181	86,670			
1928	28,366	36.0	78,794	17,300	96,094			
1929	28,558	36.5	78,241	17,683	95,924	1,200	97,124	94,684
1930	27,970	38.6	72,461	18,487	90,948	1,296	92,244	96,432
1931	31,233	38.9	80,290	18,924	99,214	1,406	100,620	107,189
1932	28,074	30.2	92,960	19,126	112,086	1,672	113,758	115,686
1933	25,990	29.8	87,215	28,689	115,904	1,710	117,614	125,302
1934	27,727	29.7	93,357	38,252	131,609	1,382	132,991	135,224
1935	28,989	29.9	96,953	38,988	135,941	1,516	137,457	139,626
1936	30,026	29.9	100,421	39,724	140,145	1,650	141,795	

Notes to Table 7-14

Sources by Column
Columns 1 and 2
Financial Statistics of Cities, 1927-36.

Column 4
Financial Statistics of States, 1927-31. Expenditures for 1932, 1934, and 1936 were estimated by applying percentage increase in state expenditures for these years over 1927 expenditures as reported in *Census of Governments;* 18.2 per cent, 136.4 per cent and 145.5 per cent. This percentage increase was added to the $16,181,000 reported in 1927. 1933 and 1936 are interpolations.

Column 6
"Federal Grants to State and Local Governments," 1960-61, *Social Security Bulletin,* June 1962, Table 1, p. 24. The series is not available for 1929 and not entirely comparable for 1935. For these years, it was extended on the basis of the adjacent year's increase.

Column 8
Calendar year expenditures were estimated by averaging successive fiscal years. Fiscal-year data converted to calendar-year basis by two-year moving average.

not available for the years 1932–36); hence, this is probably a high estimate for total expenditures.

On the basis of the population percentages, the total expenditures by cities were expanded to arrive at an estimated total of local government expenditures. These estimates are presented in column 3 of Table 7-14. A similar expansion of urban expenditures for relief was presented earlier but rejected; since relief was concentrated in urban areas, this procedure produced an overestimate. Other welfare services are probably also somewhat concentrated in cities, though not to the same extent as public assistance. The poorhouse, for example, is perhaps most often associated with county government. In 1910, when the last Census of Benevolent Institutions was conducted, there were only 1,667 persons in municipal government homes or institutions (exclusive of hospitals and sanitoriums). In county institutions there were 7,605 persons, mostly in institutions for the care of children. (State institutions, even in 1910, had 34,587 persons.) [19] *Financial Statistics of Cities* does, however, include expenditures of overlying county governments for cities having 300,000 or more

[19] U.S. Bureau of the Census, *Benevolent Institutions, 1910,* Washington, 1913, pp. 82–84.

population.[20] While these qualifications should be kept in mind, it was impossible to quantify the adjustment that should be made in estimating total local expenditures for other welfare services from costs reported in large cities, nor is it even certain what the net effect of the various factors would be.

The problem of isolating other welfare services from the functional categories reported by states is more difficult. We have included care of children; institutional care of the blind, deaf, and mute; and two small items, care of the poor (other than outdoor relief) and other charities.[21] The totals for these items, 1927–31, are shown in column 4 of Table 7-14. State data are not available for the period 1932–36. A change in the functional categories for both state and city expenditures beginning in 1937 makes it difficult to compare "other welfare expenditures" in the earlier years with the comparable items after 1936.

State expenditures for 1935 were estimated at $39 million, using the reported 1927–31 series and the *Census of Governments* series of state expenditures for "other public welfare." [22]

---

[20] U.S. Bureau of the Census, *Financial Statistics of Cities Having a Population of Over 30,000, 1929,* Washington, 1932, pp. 14–15.

[21] *Financial Statistics of States* includes, under charities, care of poor (outdoor and "all other"); care of children (in state institutions and all other); care of blind, deaf, and mute (subdivided, state institutions and all other); and other charities. Outdoor poor relief is a public assistance category; other care of the poor is predominantly institutional care, and included in other welfare services; the dollar amounts for this item are quite small, totaling $171,000 in 1929. Care of children and of blind, deaf, and mute in state institutions is obviously "institutional care" under "other welfare services." Noninstitutional care of children apparently should be considered child welfare under other welfare services rather than aid to dependent children under public assistance. (The states also report "aid to mothers"; this is the item analogous to aid to dependent children and it is considered to be public assistance.) Noninstitutional care of the blind, deaf, and mute is classified under public assistance, as it does not fit in any of the subitems under other welfare services but can be regarded as a special type of public assistance.

[22] State expenditures for other public welfare reported by the *Census of Governments* increased 18.2 per cent by 1932 as compared with 1927. The series from *Financial Statistics of States* (Table 7-14, column 4), experienced a similar rise— a 17.0 per cent increase by 1931 as compared with 1927, or (assuming a dollar increase in 1932 equal to that in the previous year) an estimated 19.7 per cent for the same period, 1927–32. The similarity of growth of the series for these years gives some support for using the *Census of Governments* as an index to extend column 4 of Table 7-14.

Expenditures reported by the *Census of Governments* for states increased 136.4

Column 5 of Table 7-14 presents the estimated total state and local expenditures for other welfare services. To complete the series, estimates of federal expenditures in this area are necessary, although, especially in the early 1930's, such expenditures were minor. In the Merriam series for 1935, they were only $2.1 million of the $139.3 million total. An entirely comparable series for federal government "other welfare services" expenditures was not immediately available, but, as indicated, this is not crucial. An approximation of federal expenditures was made by using a series on federal grants to state and local governments for "other welfare services." [23]

OUR ESTIMATES

Columns 7 and 8 of Table 7-14 presents our series for "other welfare services" for the early years (fiscal and calendar) of our period, 1929–35. The total for fiscal 1929 is $97 million. This is in substantial agreement with the ranges suggested by the alternative estimates explored in Table 7-13 and discussed above. The procedure yields a total of $137.5 million for 1935, which is very close to the Merriam total of $139.3 million and provides a rough check on our estimation procedure. Calendar-year estimates were derived by averaging successive fiscal years. (Calendar-year 1935 is $140 million by this procedure, which is the same amount we obtained from the Merriam series for calendar 1935.)

The calendar-year 1929 estimate of $95 million represents an overestimate of the extent to which other welfare services were concentrated in cities, and hence a simple population magnification of city data results in overestimation. But offsetting this is the fact that the data from which this estimate was built up do not include administrative expenses.

per cent by 1934 and 145.5 per cent by 1936, with 1927 as the base year. Applying these percentages to the $16.2 million reported in 1927, Table 7-14, column 4, yields $38.3 million for 1934 and $39.7 million for 1936 and, by interpolation, $39 million for 1935. (A similar procedure was used for 1932 and 1933 to complete the series.)

[23] "Federal Grants to State and Local Governments, 1960–61," *Social Security Bulletin,* June 1962, Table 1, p. 24. Notes to this table indicate that for 1930–35 this category includes vocational rehabilitation and state and territorial homes for disabled soldiers and sailors. The latter might be considered to belong more properly to veterans' programs, but during the 1930's, as stated above, it seems to be included in public assistance or, especially the institutional care, under other welfare services. This series begins in 1930. The 1929 and 1936 figures are estimated by assuming an increase similar to that in the adjacent year.

Table 7-15
Other Welfare Services, Calendar-Year Estimates,
Selected Years 1929-59
(millions of dollars)

Fiscal Year	Merriam Unrevised Estimates		Revised Merriam Estimate (3)	Other Welfare Calendar Year Estimates (4)
	Total (1)	Percentage Increase over Preceding Year (2)		
1929				95
1930				96
1931				107
1932				116
1933				125
1934				135
1935	113		139.3	140
1936	114	0.9	140.5	
1940	171		114.1	127
1941	209	22.2	139.3	
1945	285		195.3	202
1946	305	7.0	208.6	
1950	616		401.6	416
1951	661	7.3	431.3	
1955			580.2	639
1956			698.4	740
1957			782.6	845
1958			907.1	964
1959			1,020.1	1,091
1960			1,161.1	

Sources by Column
Column 1
Historical Statistics of the United States Colonial Times to 1957, Series H-17, p. 193.

Column 3
1935, 1940, 1945, 1950, and 1955-60, Table 5-1 and its source; 1936, 1941, 1946, and 1951 increase over preceding year estimated by applying percentage increase from column 2.

Column 4
1929-1934, Table 7-14, column 8; 1935, 1940, 1945, 1950 and 1955-59 fiscal-year data converted to calendar-year basis by two-year moving average.

(Administrative expenses were available only for the major division "charities, hospitals, and corrections," and not for the functional divisions thereof.) It is not certain what the net effect of these two factors is; since they tend to offset one another at least to some extent, we shall use the $95 million in our consolidation of data for Quadrant III.

To estimate calendar-year expenditures for the fifth years, 1935 through 1950, in the absence of an annual series on a comparable basis, the unrevised series (available annually) was used to calculate the estimated percentage increase for the following year.[24] This percentage increase was then applied to the revised fifth-year figures to derive estimated revised expenditures in 1936, 1941, 1946, and 1951 (column 3 of Table 7-15). Calendar-year totals were estimated by averaging fiscal-year data.

[24] In the major revision of the social welfare expenditures series in 1958, no change was made in scope of the "other welfare services" category, but the estimates were refined and improved so that they differ from the unrevised series. The unrevised series first appeared annually in "Social Welfare in the United States, 1934–54," *Social Security Bulletin,* October 1955. In Table 7-15 the series appearing in *Historical Statistics* is used, since it represents a later estimate incorporating some revisions of data. Revised estimates of the institutional-care item largely account for the difference between the unrevised and revised series for 1940–50. In 1935, the revised total includes $26 million for child welfare, an item not included in the revised series for that year.

8 Social Insurance
and Public Housing

As noted in Chapter 5 and set forth in Table 5-1, the series developed
by Mrs. Merriam under the title "Social Welfare Expenditures Under
Civilian Programs" has been used here as a general guide or universe of
domestic public philanthropy. She grouped her many categories of these
expenditures into the following major classes: social insurance, public
aid, health and medical service, other welfare services, veterans' program, education, and public housing. This chapter will be devoted to the
eight items under social insurance and the one item of public housing.
The latter would not seem to require any particular discussion to warrant
placing it under public domestic philanthropy as the term is used herein.
It is part of the public sector of the American economy. On the other
hand, each of the eight items which she lists under social insurance will
be examined separately to determine whether the particular item con-
forms to our concept of public domestic philanthropy.

In order to examine the nine items quantitatively, the calendar-year
data for 1959 have been set forth in Table 8-1 in dollars and in percentages of GNP. (Following Mrs. Merriam's suggestion, the calendar-year
data for 1959 were developed by a moving average of the data for the two
fiscal years involved. Other source data for some of these separate items
are, in some instances, not quite as comprehensive as her fiscal-year
data.) The 1959 expenditures for the first item, OASDI, were $10,324

Table 8-1

Social Insurance and Public Housing Expenditures, 1959

Item	Million Dollars	Per Cent of GNP
1. Old-age, survivors, and disability insurance	10,324	2.139
2. Railroad retirement	852	.177
3. Public employee retirement	2,456	.509
4. Unemployment insurance and employment service	3,280	.680
5. Railroad unemployment insurance	208	.043
6. Railroad temporary disability insurance	63	.013
7. State temporary disability insurance, total	338	.070
8. Workmen's compensation, total	1,264	.262
Total social insurance	18,785	3.893
9. Public housing	166	.034
Grand total	18,951	3.927

Source: *Social Security Bulletin,* November 1962, Table 1, p. 4. Calendar-year data derived by moving average of fiscal-year data.

million, or 2.1 per cent of GNP. Thus the first item is by far the largest of the nine, which total $18,951 million, or 3.9 per cent of GNP. In turn, the grand total of all her items in 1959 was $50,766 million, or 10.5 per cent of GNP, and these nine items were 37.3 per cent thereof.

CLASSIFICATION OF TAX-WELFARE ITEMS

Some students of insurance and social insurance would not call all of Merriam's eight items types of social insurance. It means different things to different people. We are more concerned here with whether or not a particular item should be classified as public philanthropy. The following brief comments present our decision on excluding or including each of Merriam's social insurance items in public domestic philanthropy.

The first and largest item is old-age, survivors, and disability insurance. As will be shown later, we estimate that about 95 per cent of these expenditures, or transfer payments, should be classified as public domestic philanthropy during our period of study. Item 2, railroad retirement, is really a branch of OASI; 95 per cent of these expenditures are also classified in this quadrant.

Items 3, 5, 6, and 7 can be grouped together because they do not cover the public. But only item 3, public employee retirement, is excluded from the quadrant. State temporary disability insurance, item 7, operates in just four states. Items 5, 6, and 7 involve payments from public funds and are included here. A controlling factor in excluding public employee retirement is our attempt throughout this study to avoid discussion of pension plans and fringe benefits arranged for employees by their employers, with or without the process of collective bargaining, and the large windfall benefits that are involved in some of these programs. The employer-employee relationship may lead to programs which provide very substantial benefits. The actuarial deficit in the Federal Civil Service Retirement funds exceeded $30 billion in 1959. Just what will be done about this deficit in the future is problematical; it may increase. But to consider public employee retirement as a type of public domestic philanthropy or to consider it even as social insurance is, in our opinion, not careful classification.

Item 4 combines the costs of employment service and unemployment insurance, making a rather large total for 1959, $3,280 million and 0.68 per cent of GNP. The term "unemployment insurance" does not appear in the Social Security Act of 1935, as amended; rather the term is "unemployment compensation." Here again the term social insurance does not seem fitted to cover this item.

During the years preceding 1936, a large portion of the suffering and distress which brought forth the philanthropic activities, already described in Chapter 7, was certainly traceable to unemployment. It is not possible to separate out of the data the exact amounts of relief of many kinds which were occasioned by unemployment, but it certainly was a significant part of the total. The unemployed were fed, clothed, and housed and their daily wants were satisfied in whole or in part by means which were unquestionably philanthropic. The Social Security Act of 1935 produced a systematic program of providing certain benefits during unemployment. The employer paid the cost of these benefits through a new system of payroll taxes. This new system gradually displaced the older and traditional philanthropic activities on behalf of the unemployed. If the years 1929–36 were excluded from all parts of our study, the chain connecting the new system with the old would be largely severed. The fact that the new system gives the unemployed a legal right to monthly benefits is not a unique feature of public philanthropy, as old-age assistance also involves a legal right; and such public assistance is a part of a long tradition reaching back in time to the poor laws of England—an earlier form of public philanthropy.

Item 8, workmen's compensation, is a large item and important in the total. We would again raise the question in the first instance whether this should be called social insurance. Admittedly, workmen's compensation laws in some states do provide that the insurance must be carried in public funds. Nevertheless, this item should be excluded primarily for historical reasons. It would be pointless to review the long history of employers' liability preceding workmen's compensation laws which were widely established before 1929. These laws, of course, are subject to change as to benefits and coverage so that prior to the establishment of workmen's compensation acts in all of our states, and even after some of them were established, the need for philanthropic funds to supplement the family income has continued well into our period. Yet, on the whole, it seems that this new system was so well developed by 1929 and the costs were so widely recognized as a business charge, not a philanthropic one—and on industry rather than on the employees—that, in our judgment, this item is largely outside the scope of domestic public philanthropy.

Doubtless our reasoning will not meet with universal approval. It may seem to critics that we are using a very broad concept of philanthropy and applying it too narrowly. Nevertheless, workmen's compensation will be excluded, and $1,264 million, or 0.26 per cent of GNP, removed from the total of the nine items for 1959. This is the second large reduction in the totals for Table 8-1. The data for the entire period, 1929–59, could be reworked to include workmen's compensation by those who think it should not be excluded.

In summary, seven items in Table 8-1 will be included because they conform to our concept of public domestic philanthropy. Only public employee retirement (3) and workmen's compensation (8) are excluded —$2,456 and $1,264 million, or $3,720 million, which was 0.77 per cent of GNP in 1959.

WHY 95 PER CENT?

The evidence available indicates that at least 95 per cent of the OASI benefits during our period were public philanthropy receipts. To this extent, from the standpoint of the recipient, OASI resembles old-age assistance in the social security area.[1] While no specific study precisely states that an average of only 5 per cent of the benefits have been prepaid by the employer and the employee, there are published and unpublished studies and statements which provide very strong support for this figure.

The 95 per cent figure is based upon three solid sources.* The first is a staff report, entitled "Social Security after 18 years," made by Carl T. Curtis, Chairman of the Subcommittee on Social Security of the Committee on Ways and Means of the House of Representatives; it established a 96 per cent figure. The following quotation, taken from pages 69 and 70 of that report, explains the situation at the end of 1952:

As a group, today's aged on OASI will receive in benefits almost 50 times the amount they paid in OASI taxes.

As of December 31, 1952, there were 2,644,000 persons currently drawing OASI primary benefits. They themselves had paid $356,470,000 in OASI taxes. They already had drawn $3,665,400,000 in benefits—or more than 10 times the amount of their own tax contributions.

[1] Disability, the "D" in OASDI, has not been considered extensively in this study because it came so late in the period and was first applied only to persons 50 to 65 years of age. The amounts for disability, as distinguished from OASI, could have been separated for 1957–59. The use of 95 per cent as the non-prepaid portion is on the low side and is not specific enough to warrant the separation. It did not seem sufficiently important to try to determine a separate percentage of public philanthropy involved in this benefit.

* A fourth "solid source," which supports the above estimate, is "Studies on the Relationship of Contributions to Benefits in Old-Age Benefit Awards," by R. J. Myers and Bertram Oppal of the Division of the Actuary, Social Security Administration, *Actuarial Note No. 20,* June, 1965. [Footnote by Solomon Fabricant]

These same 2,644,000 primary beneficiaries can expect to receive, under existing law, an additional $13,500 million in benefits before they are removed from the rolls by death or for other reasons, according to actuarial estimates of the Bureau of Old-Age and Survivors Insurance. Thus, the total of past and future benefits for this group will be approximately $17,165 million—or a ratio of benefits as compared to taxes of 48 to 1.

If OASI taxes previously paid by employers on the past wages and salaries of the 2,644,000 primary beneficiaries at the end of 1952 are taken into account, the total OASI benefits ultimately payable to them will be equal to approximately 24 times the amount of taxes paid by and for them.

The second source is really summarized in several letters to the author from Robert J. Myers, Chief Actuary of the Social Security Administration. It is unfortunate that the Social Security Administration itself has never made a thorough study of the type reported to the House Ways and Means Committee, which describes the situation as it was in 1952. But Myers' letter of March 24, 1961, which follows, provides strong support for our use of 96 or 95 per cent.

In response to your letter of March 21, you are quite correct in the figures that you have developed as to the total OASDI benefit disbursements in 1959, namely, about $10.3 billion. You could readily apply a factor of 4% or 5% to this figure to indicate the proportion of this that was "purchased" by the contributions of the insured worker (and his employer) on whose earnings these benefits are based.

It would be very nice if we could make a full-fledged actuarial study of this matter but, as you may realize, the earlier study was based on very extensive nonroutine tabulations and could not be repeated without a considerable expenditure of money and time.[2]

[2] As Myers states, a full and complete actuarial analysis of the percentage of prepayment by employees and their employers—which we have approximated at 5 per cent for our period—would be most welcome. For example, it could examine the percentage of prepayment of benefits made by those who die before reaching retirement age. Their lives are, so to speak, cut short; also their OASDI taxes, along with their employers, are less. If they die without survivors, as the term is defined in the Social Security Act as amended, no survivorship benefits are paid. At the other extreme are the persons who pay taxes a relatively few years and leave a number of survivors who will draw large benefits. It is believed that the percentage of prepayment for survivorship benefits of persons who do not live to retirement age is considerably below 5 per cent. But students must wait and hope that the definitive actuarial study of the percentage of benefits prepaid will be forthcoming.

The results of an incomplete study by W. R. Williamson, who preceded Myers as the Social Security Actuary, was summarized in a letter dated November 1,

The third piece of evidence was published in 1964, a work manual by the Social Security Administration entitled *Work Book—Special Training for Technical Employees Office of Employment Development.* On page 45 of this manual the following sentences are pertinent:

> The benefits that a new entrant gets are not equal in value, over the long run, to the contributions that he and his employer pay. Present older employees and people now on the beneficiary rolls have paid far less in contributions—even including employer contributions paid on their behalf—than the value of the benefits that they will get. For those now on the rolls, it is likely that they would have paid, at most, for about 10% of the benefits actually payable to them.
>
> The fact is that people retiring today have by no means "purchased" their benefits. Accordingly, if the system is to pay far more to the present retirants and those coming up to retirement age in the next few decades than their contributions could buy, and if it is to be self-supporting from worker and employer contributions, then some people necessarily will be getting less than the value of the combined employer-employee contributions.

Congress is obviously free to select any terms in describing legislation. Congress chose words or terms (OASI and OASDI) which were thought to be more acceptable than alternative language which would correctly describe the system as a tax-welfare program. So the fact that we consider 95 per cent of these OASDI benefits as public charity or social charity or, more precisely, "private public" philanthropy is merely a question of classification. The point of language is of less importance than the concept of prepayment. OASI or OASDI has obviously involved what economists call transfer payments. In this case, the transfer payment is made by younger persons in many income classes to older persons in all income groups receiving benefits. Moreover, the survivorship benefits are not restricted to the poor.[3]

1965, as follows: "My study showed survivals of all years from 1940 onward in the granting of awards—but all of these very well justify your (and my) idea of 95% 'public philanthropy' for OASI—to date! I had long said 'dollars for nickels' even as early as the 1953 study. . . ."

[3] Elsewhere I have elaborated on these points and related matters concerning some of the peculiar features of what we commonly call "social security" but should more precisely call OASDI: (1) "The Social Security Principle," *Journal of Insurance,* December 1960, pp. 1–13. (2) This article was criticized by three actuaries—W. R. Williamson, the first Social Security Actuary; Robert G. Myers, the present Social Security Actuary; and Ray M. Peterson, Vice-President and Associate Actuary of the Equitable Life Assurance Society. These three comments

SOCIAL EVOLUTION AND SEMANTICS

Social evolution is a powerful but slow-moving force. He who tries to peer into the future must recognize that he cannot circumscribe completely the inventiveness of the future. Indeed, if one had the perspective of the entire twentieth century, he could look back from that vantage point over the thirty-one years covered in this study—the Great Depression, the great increase in the number of older persons, urbanization, and so on—and it is quite possible that he might think it was wise for federal officials and many private citizens to call OASI and OASDI by the high-sounding title of insurance; declare that the benefits had been prepaid by the individual and his employer and belong to the beneficiaries. Or he might take a milder point of view and refer to the windfall benefits of 95 per cent as "philsurance." [4] But the task in this study is to state the case as it actually appeared in the three decades covered, frankly admit that prophecy is still an exclusively divine gift, and that the final evaluation of a great social program must, for some purposes, await the verdict of history. In this study, therefore, OASDI must be considered as about 95 per cent public domestic philanthropy regardless of reappraisals made decades later.

TOTALS FOR SOCIAL INSURANCE

Each of the seven items included in public domestic philanthropy are shown in dollars and percentage of GNP (Table 8-2). The amounts for 1938 and 1939 for OASDI were small, so the important part of columns 1 and 2 really begins with 1940 and extends through 1959. The grand total through 1959 of 95 per cent of OASDI benefits was $50,747 million. The use of the heading OASDI implies that the last three years of the period involved the disability program. For the relevant years (1938–

and my rebuttal were published also in the *Journal of Insurance,* June 1961, pp. 111–127. (3) My statement before the Committee of Finance, United States Senate, 89th Congress, First Session, on H. R. 6675 (Social Security), pp. 1241–1248.

[4] See "Highlights of the Conference" in *Philanthropy and Public Policy,* Frank G. Dickinson, ed., New York, NBER, 1962.

Table 8-2
Social Insurance and Public Housing, 1937-59

Year	95 Per Cent of OASDI		95 Per Cent of Railroad Retirement		Unemployment Ins. and Employment Serv.		Railroad Unemployment Insurance	
	Million Dollars (1)	Per Cent of GNP (2)	Million Dollars (3)	Per Cent of GNP (4)	Million Dollars (5)	Per Cent of GNP (6)	Million Dollars (7)	Per Cent of GNP (8)
1937			40	.044	50	.055		
1938	9	.011	91	.107	286	.336		
1939	20	.022	107	.117	535	.587	10	.011
1940	57	.057	114	.113	530	.527	20	.020
1941	108	.086	123	.098	479	.381	16	.013
1942	149	.094	128	.080	366	.230	8	.005
1943	187	.097	130	.067	227	.118	4	.002
1944	230	.109	133	.063	195	.092	4	.002
1945	297	.139	142	.066	1,242	.582	14	.007
1946	392	.186	158	.075	2,374	1.127	38	.018
1947	487	.208	192	.082	2,047	.874	44	.019
1948	579	.223	242	.093	1,748	.674	43	.017
1949	686	.266	279	.108	2,038	.790	85	.033
1950	1,117	.392	297	.104	1,627	.572	74	.026
1951	1,727	.525	338	.103	1,126	.342	27	.008
1952	2,272	.655	407	.117	1,166	.336	42	.012
1953	2,888	.790	454	.124	1,508	.413	79	.022
1954	3,705	1.020	506	.139	1,976	.544	130	.036
1955	4,713	1.186	560	.141	1,852	.466	109	.027
1956	5,772	1.377	608	.145	1,733	.413	74	.018
1957	7,071	1.597	667	.151	2,572	.581	132	.030
1958	8,473	1.906	715	.161	3,517	.791	188	.042
1959	9,808	2.032	809	.168	3,280	.679	208	.043

Year	Railroad Temp. Disability Ins. Total		State Temp. Disability Ins. Total		Public Housing		Total Expenditures	
	Million Dollars (9)	Per Cent of GNP (10)	Million Dollars (11)	Per Cent of GNP (12)	Million Dollars (13)	Per Cent of GNP (14)	Million Dollars (15)	Per Cent of GNP (16)
1937					2	.002	90	.099
1938					4	.004	388	.455
1939							676	.742
1940					6	.006	727	.723
1941					12	.010	738	.587
1942					14	.009	665	.418
1943			3	.002	14	.007	565	.293
1944			5	.002	12	.006	579	.274
1945			5	.002	10	.005	1,710	.801
1946			11	.005	9	.004	2,982	1.415
1947			25	.011	8	.003	2,803	1.196
1948	30	.012	41	.016	6	.002	2,689	1.037
1949	32	.012	61	.024	9	.003	3,190	1.236
1950	30	.011	106	.037	22	.008	3,273	1.150
1951	28	.009	159	.048	33	.010	3,438	1.045
1952	37	.011	188	.054	40	.012	4,152	1.197
1953	46	.013	204	.056	56	.015	5,235	1.433
1954	50	.014	214	.059	77	.021	6,658	1.834
1955	53	.013	225	.057	100	.025	7,612	1.915
1956	52	.012	251	.060	115	.027	8,605	2.053
1957	53	.012	286	.065	127	.029	10,908	2.464
1958	56	.013	315	.071	145	.033	13,409	3.016
1959	63	.013	338	.070	166	.034	14,672	3.040
Total[a]	530	.012	2,437	.045	987	.016	95,764	1.568

Notes to Table 8-2

Note: Detail may not add to total because of rounding.

aSee note a, Table 2-1.

Source: Correspondence with Ida C. Merriam, Asst. Commissioner for Research and Statistics, Social Security Administration.

59), this grand total was 0.84 per cent of GNP; it rose from 0.06 per cent in 1940 to 2.03 per cent in 1959.

Expenditures for unemployment insurance and employment service, as Mrs. Merriam uses the term, totaled $32,474 million, or 0.53 per cent of GNP, for the years 1937–59; it rose from 0.06 per cent of GNP in 1937 to 0.68 per cent in 1959. This is the second largest of the three items of public domestic philanthropy treated in this chapter.

The grand totals for the seven items are presented for each year in Table 8-2, columns 15 and 16. The total for 1937–59 was $95,764 million, or 1.57 per cent of GNP. The percentage of GNP rose from 0.1 per cent in 1937 to 3.04 per cent in 1959.

9 Public
Foreign Philanthropy

In order to develop the emerging concept of civilian foreign aid as public philanthropy, it is necessary to start with a brief review of foreign aid during World War I, which ended a decade before the beginning of our period of study. The amount of public foreign aid between the two World War periods was less than $100 million. Hence the data presented here will be mostly for the period 1940–59.

WHAT IS FOREIGN AID AND PUBLIC PHILANTHROPY?

Governmental (public) foreign aid of substantial amounts had its beginnings in the United States with World War I. The timing was profoundly influenced by war or the threat of war. Historically it has also been in response to natural catastrophies. Today, however, in addition to these functions (and some would say superseding them), a new concept of foreign aid has evolved. It partakes of the humanitarianism which is evident in emergency relief, but it goes beyond the limited aims of relief and even rehabilitation in its traditional sense. Economic and technical assistance (as well as military support) is apparently a permanent feature of the United States federal government budget, however great may be the disagreements over the precise amount of aid in any given year. Many forms of technical assistance are similar to the non-preaching services rendered over many decades by our church missionaries in many countries.

Even as there are problems of definition of the term philanthropy, there are difficulties in circumscribing the concept of foreign aid and in determining what part of it is public foreign philanthropy. Instinctively one may regard foreign aid as funds and goods the United States government "gives away to foreign countries." This immediately raises the problem of loans or credits; is this "giving money away"? Assuredly, loans involve an obligation to repay, usually with interest. Theoretically, then, as Walther Lederer suggests, the aid component on loans "may be considered to be the difference between the actual interest rate charged by the government and the one which would have to be charged if the loans had to be made through commercial channels." [1] Though theoretically sound, this treatment is not practical for our purposes, since we do not know what interest rates would have prevailed on all the numerous loans if the rates had been set by market forces. Nevertheless, the omission from our data of the value to the borrower of the bargain rates of interest does understate the amount of public foreign philanthropy. This also leaves open the problem of defaulted (or permanent moratorium on) loans—the situation existing generally regarding loans of the World War I period. Such defaults are obviously not comparable to bad-debt losses of business enterprise, which are a cost of production.

Lederer also suggests a definition for foreign aid: "In theory, aid may be defined as a transfer of resources, either in goods and services or in money, without a commensurate retransfer either simultaneously or in the future." [2] There is no commensurate *quid pro quo*. The definition of foreign aid could be broadened not only to encompass government "unilateral transfers" to foreign countries but to include also government unilateral transfers to individuals abroad, e.g., pensions paid to Americans residing abroad, a portion of the expenditures for the support of our military forces abroad, and so on.

We have thought it undesirable or not especially worthwhile to devote the time and resources necessary to refine the data on government foreign philanthropy to fit theoretical concepts precisely; at any rate, such a

[1] Walther Lederer, "Foreign Aid and the United States Balance of Payments," *Social Science*, October 1954, p. 232.
[2] *Ibid.*, pp. 231–232.

procedure might not prove very meaningful because of the difficulties of valuation and, in some instances, simply lack of sufficiently detailed statistics.

The data here presented are those designated as "foreign aid" by the Office of Business Economics, United States Department of Commerce. Similarly, the division of grants into "military" and "other" (civilian) is that of the Office of Business Economics (with the exception of the World War II period, for which the OBE does not provide a breakdown and we made our own). The problem of classification into military and civilian is formidable; here again, however, it was felt that any extensive attempt to refine the OBE designations would be of relatively little worth. Moreover, there are some arguments for considering *all* foreign aid, military and civilian, as government philanthropy. We have chosen to exclude military aid from our concept of government philanthropy, although we realize there are many "gray" areas where military aid in fact may benefit mainly or indeed exclusively the civilian population. But the idea of calling, for example, guns and tanks "philanthropy" (love of mankind) is a bit difficult for us to consider. We have, however, presented the data for total foreign aid with its components clearly indicated.

As will be emphasized later in this chapter, public foreign philanthropy coincides with the concept of civilian but not military foreign aid. In order to develop annual data, nonmilitary grants and loans are treated separately. The new credits granted, principal repaid, and net credits are shown on an annual basis. From the standpoint of the United States and of the recipient nations, these credits may be regarded as aid in the year advanced; it is true that these are loans, not outright gifts, as are grants. (Soft-currency loans are, however, not expected to be paid in dollars; they have some of the characteristics of grants.) From a practical standpoint we have first accepted the OBE classification of credits as foreign aid; the data are shown both ways—including and excluding loans (credits).

WORLD WAR I

The United States government entered the field of foreign aid when it entered the war in April 1917. Prior to that time, foreign governments negotiated loans with private American citizens. As is well known, the

United States entered World War I as a debtor nation and emerged from the conflict as a net creditor nation. Private loans to the European governments are, of course, beyond the scope of the present study.

By the date of the armistice in November 1918, the United States government had loaned $7 billion to its allies in cash; after the armistice, also in cash, $2.5 billion, and credits extended for surplus property and relief supplies after the armistice, $0.7 billion. The major recipients were our principal European allies, Great Britain and France. It is impossible to separate the $7 billion loaned during World War I into military and civilian categories. The United States government naturally has no record of the disposition of these funds; undoubtedly the recipient countries did not segregate these funds in their accounts. Since these loans were made during the period of hostilities, it is reasonable to assume that the bulk of the funds was used for military purposes.

During the World War I period there were also loans devoted to relief and rehabilitation. These would include the $2,533 million advanced after the armistice and the $740 million credits extended for surplus property and relief supplies.[3] This is not to imply that the task of relief was limited to postwar activities. Indeed, perhaps the most dramatic relief mission was organized on the outbreak of the war. This was the Commission for the Relief of Belgium (C.R.B.).[4]

The C.R.B. was financed by a mingling of voluntary contributions and government loans or subsidies, not only from the United States but from many countries. (There was also an element of market activity.) In part this dual system of financing was deliberate; in part it was inevitable. The task which confronted the Commission was so enormous and so immediate that private philanthropy could not have shouldered the burden alone. In fact, only 6 per cent of the total funds of more than three-quarters of a billion dollars received by the Commission was from private philanthropy, and of this, two-thirds was from the United States. Yet, though the main underwriting of the Commission was by public philanthropy, the voluntary contributions were regarded as especially valuable in a qualitative sense. The Commission rejected a suggestion from the Belgian government that the American government subsidy be

[3] State Department Research Paper, *Hearings on Mutual Security Appropriation Act of 1957*, House Appropriations Committee, May 26, 1960, p. 953.

[4] Herbert Hoover detailed the Commission's work in the first volume of his *An American Epic*, Chicago, 1959.

increased to eliminate all charity appeals because it believed they were a "great source of moral strength." [5]

Government subsidies to the C.R.B. were in the form of loans, though Herbert Hoover, Chairman of the Commission, insists that this was a technicality: "Under the laws of Britain, France, and the United States, all advances from one country to another during the war were treated as 'loans.' Although this practice was maintained with regard to the advances for the Relief, neither we of the C.R.B. nor the high officials of the three governments considered them to be other than 'subsidies' and always referred to them as such in our discussions and negotiations." [6] But the United States government was insistent on the repayment, with interest, of the post-Armistice loans to Belgium, though they were mainly for relief.

Similarly, the World War I period loans were regarded by the United States as legal obligations and the interest was carefully calculated. The involved story of interallied debts, German reparations, the various plans that attempted to solve or relieve the debt situation in the twenties, and the political and economic conditions created thereby is beyond the scope of this study. Suffice it to say that the United States continued to regard the debts of its former allies as legitimate and indisputable international obligations; the principal was not reduced, though the terms of repayment were liberalized under various agreements. The Hoover Moratorium in 1931 marked the beginning of the end of payments on World War I debts. Finland has continued to make payments annually on the principal due; Great Britain made a single full payment in 1932 and a number of other countries made payments on the interest due in the thirties. The Allied debts of World War I are still carried on official United States records—at $18.5 billion in 1958; technically they have never been entirely canceled.[7] Of the $11.4 billion principal, less than 7 per cent has been repaid. In retrospect, some 93 per cent of the World War I loans may be regarded as *de facto* gifts or grants.

Prior to World War I, the United States government had extended virtually no aid to foreign countries. With the devastations wrought by

[5] *Ibid.*, p. 337.

[6] *Ibid.*, p. 421.

[7] "June 30, 1958 Supplement to Memorandum Covering the World War Indebtedness of Foreign Governments to the United States (1917–1921)," mimeographed from Senator Harry F. Byrd, November 19, 1959.

the war, the government entered the field of foreign relief and rehabilitation. Generally the financing was by means of loans for which the United States expected to be repaid after the immediate crisis. The government incurred no long-term foreign obligation.

Following the war and armistice the United States made a number of relatively small grants for emergency relief, for example, to Russia during the famine of 1921, to Japan after the earthquake in 1923. On a number of occasions in the 1930's the United States provided small-scale emergency aid on a rather informal basis for which no accurate value can be calculated. This aid was generally occasioned by a natural disaster—e.g., earthquake, hurricane, or flood. It usually took the form of transportation of people or supplies by United States military planes or vessels. Among the countries aided were the Dominican Republic in September 1930, Nicaragua in April 1931, and El Salvador in June 1934.

Another type of aid by the United States was occasioned by the Spanish Civil War. The American Red Cross purchased surplus flour and wheat from the government for relief of Spanish civilians. The Red Cross paid approximately $81,000 for this surplus, which originally cost the government $321,000. The amount of United States government aid to Spanish civilians in 1938–39 may be regarded as approximately $240,000, the difference between the original cost and the selling price.[8]

In the 1930's, through the Reconstruction Finance Corporation and Export-Import Bank, a number of loans were made which, in effect, gave important economic and financial assistance to foreign governments. For example, the R.F.C. made loans of $2.8 million to the Soviet Union in 1933 to finance sales of surplus cotton, of $20 million to China to finance cotton, wheat, and flour. These loans were subsequently repaid. The Export-Import Bank also extended loans to China and to Latin America. The late 1930's saw the beginnings of technical assistance to Latin America, nine countries receiving specialists from the United States government in fields such as agriculture, immigration, and police instruction. The United States paid approximately half the cost of each mission; the total cost of those programs to the United States in 1938 and 1939 was $64,000. The final major type of aid to Latin America in the interwar period was in connection with the Inter-American highway, for which the United States government appropriated a total of $1.2 million between 1929 and 1939. Latin America was also, of course, the recipi-

[8] State Department Research Paper *Hearings on Mutual Security Appropriation Act of 1957*, House Appropriations Committee, May 26, 1960, p. 953.

ent of emergency aid from the United States following hurricanes and earthquakes (as mentioned previously), but the provision of peacetime military assistance and the beginnings of technical and economic assistance foreshadowed the present-day type of foreign aid. The analogy can be carried one step further, for, following the Munich settlement in September 1938, assistance to Latin America was increased and in April 1939 President Roosevelt pledged economic support to any Latin American country threatened with military or economic aggression.

WORLD WAR II

Foreign aid extended by the United States in World War II differed from that in World War I in at least two important respects. First, the United States government undertook no aid prior to the official declaration of war in 1917; aid was begun, however, before the official United States entry into the war in December 1941. Second, World War I aid was via loans and credits or cash payments; financing of World War II aid was primarily through the institution of "lend-lease," whereby supplies were "loaned" to allies for the duration of the conflict without any financial commitment being incurred.

"An Act to Promote the Defense of the United States," the famous Lend-Lease Act, was passed on March 11, 1941. This marked a departure from earlier aid extended Britain and other friendly countries after September 1939 in that procurements were no longer on a cash-and-carry basis; it marked a departure also from the World War I policy of financing through credits. Britain, the main recipient of United States aid immediately prior to and during World War II, had virtually exhausted her ability to pay for goods by 1940; the disastrous political and economic consequences of the World War I loans made that method unpalatable.

Lend-lease was not described in official statements as merely a means of loaning money, nor as an act of charity. It was intended, as the title of the act makes evident, for the defense of the United States. Indeed, the bill probably would not have been passed except as a defense measure. Though the popular name of the program emphasized the lending and leasing aspects, the act was very broad; it provided authority to sell, transfer title to, exchange, lease, lend, or otherwise dispose of arms and other equipment, and to communicate any defense information.

In fact, the individual agreements with the Latin American countries specifically provided for payments in cash.

In general, of course, the United States "return" was not limited to the intangible one of greater common defense; the act laid down the principle of specific (direct or indirect) "benefits" to be extended to the United States. In fact, tangible "reverse lend-lease" and returns ultimately accounted for over 15 per cent of the gross aid extended by the United States under the lend-lease program. Assistance was mutual, not unilateral; this was underscored by the Mutual Aid Agreements and Reciprocal Aid Agreements concluded with Great Britain and other allied countries.

Lend-lease aid, which accounted for the overwhelming amount of United States government foreign aid during the war period, accounted for a relatively small share of the total defense effort, approximately 15 per cent.[9]

Lend-lease aid was of a very broad character. Services provided were one element, and, in addition to essentially military hardware such as ammunition and tanks, there was a considerable amount of agricultural and industrial goods—for example, meat and dairy products, petroleum, iron and steel. The "nonmilitary" goods helped to maintain and increase industrial war production and agricultural production in allied countries as well as to supply essential civilian needs. The primary emphasis in lend-lease aid was always on military considerations (although assuredly, in a situation of total war, "military considerations" are very broad). Although the amount of aid by country and the type and ultimate use of the aid by country are outside the scope of our study, we note in passing that the British Commonwealth countries received about three-fifths and the Soviet Union about one-fifth of total lend-lease commodities and services.

MILITARY AND CIVILIAN AID

Because of the shifts occurring in the official lend-lease reports to Congress we have taken our data for lend-lease and for the war period in

[9] *Foreign Aid by the United States Government, 1940–1951* (Supplement to *Survey of Current Business*), Office of Business Economics, U.S. Department of Commerce, Washington, 1952, p. 35.

general from *Foreign Aid by the United States Government, 1940–1951*. The total government foreign aid for the war period is shown in column 1 of Table 9-1. For our purposes, however, we need a breakdown of foreign aid into military and civilian, as it is our intention to exclude military aid during and after World War II from our totals for government foreign philanthropy.

Most of the programs are rather clear-cut, so there is no especial difficulty in making this distinction; e.g., civilian supplies distributed by the military forces, technical assistance, UNRRA, and the War Refugee Board are obviously nonmilitary programs. The $380 million granted under the Chinese stabilization and military aid program should be allocated partly to "civilian" to encompass the "stabilization" function; the aid was intended in part to assist in stabilizing the economy and halting inflation. We have no indication, however, what proportion of this sum should be so allocated and have designated all of it as military; it is a rather small part of the total foreign aid during the period.

Serious questions arise over the military-civilian division of lend-lease totals. It may be argued logically that all of lend-lease during the war period was essentially military (given the situation of total war), though specific commodities may not have been of 100 per cent military application. It is known, however, that some lend-lease aid did, in fact, benefit the civilian population. This would be true primarily of agricultural goods, and to a lesser extent of industrial goods; there are also instances of civilian philanthropy through military goods—e.g., jeeps abandoned by the military which were utilized by civilians. The government's accounting is not in terms of the ultimate recipient (i.e., whether military or civilian) but in terms of the type of commodity or service furnished. There are ten subdivisions or classifications: ordnance and ordnance stores; aircraft and aeronautical material; tanks and other vehicles; vessels and other watercraft; miscellaneous military equipment; facilities and equipment; agricultural, industrial and other commodities; testing, reconditioning, etc., of defense articles; services and expenses; and administrative expenses.

After examining the components of these major classifications, it was decided to make a rather conservative estimate by denoting as civilian only that proportion represented by three of the ten major groups: facilities and equipment for production; agricultural, industrial, and other commodities; and miscellaneous services and expenses. The percentage

Table 9-1

*World War II Government Foreign Aid, Military
and Civilian Category, Five War-Period Fiscal Years, 1941-45*
(millions of dollars)

	Total (1)	Military (2)	Civilian (3)
Gross foreign aid	49,224	30,520	18,704
Net foreign aid	40,971	22,689	18,282
Grants utilized	48,128	30,520	17,608
Lend-lease	46,728	30,140	16,588
Civilian supplies distributed by Army, Air Force, and Navy	813		813
Institute of Inter-American Affairs	50		50
Technical assistance	5		5
UNRRA	83		83
Chinese stabilization and military aid	380	380	
War Refugee Board	3		3
American Red Cross	62		62
Reconstruction Finance Corporation	2		2
Reverse grants and returns on grants	7,873	7,832	42
Reverse lend-lease	7,828	7,828	
Return of lend-lease ships			
Merchant	10		10
Navy	4	4	
War account cash settlements	32		32
Net grants	40,256	22,689	17,567
Credits utilized	1,096		1,096
Export-Import Bank	329		329
Lend-lease current credits and silver	349		349
R.F.C. and Institute Inter-Am Affairs	417		417
Principal collected on credits	380		380
Export-Import Bank	214		214
Lend-lease current credits	46		46
R.F.C. and Institute Inter-Am Affairs	120		120
Net credits	715		715

Note: Detail may not add to total because of rounding.

Source: *Foreign Aid Supplement, 1940-51,* pp. 81ff; division into military and civilian our own, described in text.

these three groups represented of total lend-lease through September 1, 1945—35.5 per cent of the grand total of aid—was applied to our entry for total lend-lease for the war period in Table 9-1 to derive the non-military portion.

The problem of treating reverse lend-lease also proves difficult. It would be possible to follow a procedure identical to that described above for lend-lease aid. The three categories classified as "civilian" accounted for about two-thirds of total reverse lend-lease. However, it is believed that a more reasonable procedure, in view of the fact that reverse lend-lease was overwhelmingly for the benefit of the military, is to enter all reverse lend-lease in the military category. This was the method followed.

The division into military and civilian for the war period, as thus derived, is shown in Table 9-1. The final column, "civilian," is what we have chosen to investigate and refine in order to determine the amount of government foreign philanthropy during the World War II period. Most of the aid extended was to relieve conditions imposed by the war; this group would include grants under lend-lease, civilian supplies distributed by the military, aid by UNRRA, the War Refugee Board, and the American Red Cross. The remaining grants (the Institute of Inter-American Affairs, $50 million; technical assistance, $5 million; and Reconstruction Finance Corporation, $2 million) total $57 million. These were to Latin American countries and may be regarded as a contribution of the prewar program of aid to this area. About 30 per cent of the total credits was utilized by Latin American countries; the British Commonwealth (especially the United Kingdom, India, and Canada) received the majority of the loans during this period. The Export-Import Bank and the Reconstruction Finance Corporation, the institutions which extended most of the loans during the war period, were both started in the 1930's.

We have no wholly consistent annual data during the war period. The fact that the lend-lease data presented above is through September 1, 1945, although reasonable from the point of view of lend-lease and a consideration of the war period, makes it difficult to compare to calendar- or even fiscal-year accounting. An indication of the annual magnitude of aid during the war by calendar years and by quarters for 1945 is presented in Table 9-2.

These annual data totaled $40,209 million net unilateral transfers for

Table 9-2
Government "Unilateral Transfers," Calendar Years, 1940-45
(millions of dollars)

Item	1940	1941	1942	1943	1944	1945				
						Total	Qtr.1	Qtr.2	Qtr.3	Qtr.4
To foreign countries										
Lend-lease		932	6,954	14,690	15,911	7,348	2,819	2,921	1,016	592
UNRRA					1	560	12	90	167	291
Aid to China			200	40	20	225		120	104	1
Civilian supplies dis-										
tributed by military					185	866	179	343	310	34
Other government transfers[a]	32	25	21	20	30	109	4	5	30	70
Total (gross)	32	957	7,175	14,750	16,147	9,108	3,014	3,479	1,627	988
From foreign countries										
Reverse lend-lease			640	1,997	2,287	2,444	1,010	960	456	18
Other government receipts[a]			322	95	75	100	19	24	25	32
Total			962	2,092	2,362	2,544	1,029	984	481	50
Net unilateral transfers	32	957	6,213	12,658	13,785	6,564	1,985	2,495	1,146	938

[a]Other government transfers and other government receipts are not coextensive with foreign aid; e.g., the entries for 1940 and 1941 in the transfer row represents largely refund of certain taxes on Philippine imports to the government of the Commonwealth.
Source: *International Transactions of the United States During the War, 1940-1945*, Economic Series No. 65, Office of Business Economics, Washington, 1948, pp. 218, 87.

the six calendar years, 1940–45. Net grants as shown in Table 9-1 for the World War II period of five fiscal years, 1941–45, totaled $40,256 million.

THE MASTER TABLE ON FOREIGN AID

Table 9-3 provides the summary of foreign aid during the period from the middle of 1940 through the end of 1959. The table is divided into four sections: military grants, nonmilitary grants and credits, net foreign aid, and net foreign aid as percentage of GNP. Both gross and net amounts are given. The latter are preferred because we are considering the American economy as an entity, a "person" in the corporate sense. Excluded from this table are certain amounts for other assistance in the nature of net short-term credits, which have been called temporary assistance. These amounts in millions of dollars are as follows: 1953, 8; 1954, 203; 1955, 330; 1956, 558; 1957, 619; 1958, 270; and 1959, 256. The total other assistance for the period was $2,245 million. These amounts are excluded because it seems much easier to dispose of them by merely assuming that they will be repaid soon and in full by the borrowers. Longer-term credits pose more difficult problems of classification.

The table is also divided into three time periods: the World War II period, 1941–45, without annual totals; the period from the middle of 1945 to the end of 1950, when civilian aid was much larger than military aid; and the "cold war" period, from 1951 through 1959. A subtotal is presented for the second and third periods. Separate data for the large post-World War II foreign aid programs, e.g., the Marshall Plan, Mutual Security, seem quite unnecessary.

The military grants are presented for the purpose of showing the complete record, although, as stated several times, we do not consider military grants during time of war or peace as public foreign philanthropy. They can be regarded as expenditures made by us to our allies in lieu of expenditures on our own military establishment. The fact that more than three-quarters of the funds spent on foreign aid during this period was spent in the United States is also irrelevant for the purposes at hand. When the money was spent here, the supplies acquired were shipped abroad. The gross military grants totaled $56,234 million during

Table 9-3

Public Foreign Aid Mid-1940 to 1959
(millions of dollars)

	Military Grants			Nonmilitary Grants			Nonmilitary Credits		
	Net (1)	Gross (2)	Reverse Grants & Returns (3)	Net (4)	Gross (5)	Reverse Grants & Returns (6)	Net (7)	Gross (new) (8)	Principal Collections (9)
Fiscal 1941-45[a]	22,688	30,520	7,832	17,567	17,608	41	716	1,096	380
7/1/45−1946	679	679		4,170	4,406	237	2,636	2,765	129
1947	47	47		1,887	2,125	239	3,781	4,086	305
1948	392	459	67	3,863	3,927	65	1,081	1,539	458
1949	213	213		4,983	5,226	243	454	694	240
1950	524	528	4	3,505	3,657	153	125	454	329
7/1/45−12/31/50[a]	1,854	1,925	71	18,410	19,346	936	8,076	9,537	1,461
1951	1,478	1,494	16	3,040	3,164	123	118	428	310
1952	2,664	2,730	66	1,980	2,065	85	400	825	425
1953	4,270	4,333	63	1,845	1,947	103	232	712	480
1954	3,192	3,201	8	1,662	1,726	65	-114	387	501
1955	2,408	2,417	9	1,904	1,964	60	-82	421	503
1956	2,646	2,662	16	1,733	1,792	59	-17	493	504
1957	2,499	2,512	12	1,616	1,683	67	351	986	635
1958	2,362	2,373	11	1,616	1,677	61	586	1,118	532
1959	2,046	2,067	21	1,633	1,667	34	6	998	993
1951-1959	23,565	23,789	222	17,029	17,685	657	1,480	6,368	4,888
7/1/45-1959[a]	25,419	25,714	293	35,439	37,031	1,593	9,556	15,905	6,349
7/10/40-1959	48,107	56,234	8,125	53,006	54,639	1,634	10,272	17,001	6,729

	Net Nonmilitary Grants & Credits (col. 4 + col. 7) (10)	Net Foreign Aid			Net Foreign Aid as Per Cent of GNP		
		Total (11)	Military (12)	Civilian (13)	Total (14)	Military (15)	Civilian (16)
Fiscal 1941-45[a]	18,283	40,971	22,688	18,283	4.843	2.682	2.161
7/1/45−1946	6,806	7,485	679	6,806	2.358	0.214	2.144
1947	5,668	5,715	47	5,668	2.439	0.020	2.419
1948	4,944	5,336	392	4,944	2.057	0.151	1.906
1949	5,437	5,650	213	5,437	2.189	0.083	2.107
1950	3,630	4,154	524	3,630	1.460	0.184	1.275
7/1/45−12/31/50[a]	26,487	28,341	1,854	26,487	2.093	0.137	1.956
1951	3,159	4,637	1,478	3,159	1.410	0.449	0.960
1952	2,379	5,043	2,664	2,379	1.453	0.768	0.686
1953	2,076	6,346	4,270	2,076	1.737	1.169	0.568
1954	1,548	4,740	3,192	1,548	1.305	0.879	0.426
1955	1,822	4,230	2,408	1,822	1.064	0.606	0.458
1956	1,716	4,363	2,646	1,716	1.041	0.631	0.409
1957	1,967	4,466	2,499	1,967	1.009	0.564	0.444
1958	2,202	4,564	2,362	2,202	1.027	0.531	0.495
1959	1,639	3,686	2,046	1,639	0.764	0.424	0.340
1951-1959	18,509	42,074	23,565	18,509	1.172	0.656	0.515
7/1/45-1959[a]	44,996	70,415	25,419	44,996	1.424	0.514	0.910
7/10/40-1959	63,279	111,386	48,107	63,279	1.923	0.831	1.093

Notes to Table 9-3

Notes: The data here presented are those designated as "foreign aid" by the Office of Business Economics, United States Department of Commerce, a grand total of $111 billion for the 18½ years through 1959. We have assigned 43 per cent, or $48 billion, to military items. The division of grants into "military" and "other" ("civilian") is also that of the OBE. Details may not add to totals because of rounding.

aSee note a, Table 2-1

Sources: 1941-45, (fiscal years) *Foreign Aid by the United States Government, 1940-1951* (Supplement to Survey of Current Business), Department of Commerce, 1952, p. 81 (see text on division of military and civilian); 1945/46-1950, *Balance of Payments,* Statistical Supplement, 1958, p. 120-123; 1951-57, *Semiannual Report of the National Advisory Council on International Monetary and Financial Problems,* 86th Congress, 1st Session, House Document No. 207, 1959, p. 46-47 (compilation does not include credits of $2,257 million representing settlements for postwar relief); 1958, 1959, *Foreign Grants and Credits by the United States Government,* December 1959 Quarter, OBE, Department of Commerce, p. S-7.

the period, of which $48,107 million was the net military grants; they are excluded entirely from Quadrant IV.

Grants and credits of a nonmilitary nature are summarized in columns 4 through 10 of Table 9-3. The total grants for the entire period was $54,639 million and the net grants were $53,006 million. The credits are shown in these columns on the accounting basis followed by the Export-Import Bank and other federal agencies. The loan or credit is regarded as a disbursement in the year made and as income in the year principal payments are received. This accounting procedure indicates a total of net credits outstanding at the end of the period of $10,272 million. New credits extended during the period totaled $17,001 million; collections totaled $6,729 million. Thus the net grants plus the net credits totaled $63,279 million for net civilian foreign aid. An alternative method of accounting is presented in Table 9-4 for the purpose of eliminating the loans entirely from the compilation.

"Net foreign aid," in Table 9-3 totaled $111,386 million, of which $48,107 million net was for military aid and is therefore excluded from our tabulation of public foreign philanthropy. The total net for civilian foreign aid, that is, public foreign philanthropy according to this accounting procedure, was $63,279 million.

In the last three columns, net foreign aid is expressed as a percentage of gross national product. For the entire period the total net foreign aid was 1.92 per cent of GNP, from which the military aid of 0.83 per cent of GNP is excluded by our concept of public philanthropy; civilian foreign aid amounted to 1.09 per cent of GNP. The total for the period of World War II, that is, civilian aid for fiscal 1941–45, was 2.16 per cent of GNP. Civilian foreign aid was highest in relation to GNP immediately after the war, reaching 2.42 per cent for 1947. For the middle period from 1945 through 1950, civilian foreign aid totaled 1.96 per cent of GNP. For the third division of our period of foreign aid, 1951–59, the total of civilian foreign aid was 0.52 per cent of GNP.

ACCOUNTING FOR LOANS

Particular attention is called to column 7 of Table 9-3, in which the net credits are recorded. In those years in which the principal collections exceeded new loans (1954–56), the entry is negative. The total of $10,272 million is, therefore, the amount of unpaid loans outstanding at the end of our period. This is not to say that this is the amount of loans due at the end of 1959 or in default. The accumulated loan total, however, includes "soft-currency loans," which are repayable in the currency of the borrower and available only to a very limited extent for expenditures of the government of the United States in the borrowing country. Walther Lederer estimated that soft-currency loans outstanding at the end of 1959 amounted to about $1,500 million (letter of August 9, 1961).

The form of accounting followed here in columns 7–9 of Table 9-3 assumes that the loans when made are to be considered as disbursements and the principal as income in the year received. Although this form of chronological accounting presents a simple flow-of-funds historical record, and is followed in many respects by the federal government, other forms of accounting might be employed. When loans are added to net grants, there is an implication that the accumulated amount of the loans outstanding at the end of any period of study one selects represents an amount that will not be repaid in the future; that is, the loans are somewhat similar to grants in this accounting.

We experimented with a number of assumptions regarding the outstanding loans of $10,272 million. One assumption was that all the loans made to the governments of Western Europe would be repaid in full, and one-half of the loans made to other parts of the world would also be repaid. But computation of reserves for bad debts is always hazardous, and especially so when the debtors are nations. No one knows what proportion of these loans will in fact be recovered. The collection experience with World War I loans cannot be applied. The exclusion of any value of the bargain rates of interest charged on these loans, as noted earlier in this chapter, would tend to offset, at least in part, the inclusion of all these loans as foreign aid. We finally decided to let the $10,272 million stand as credits outstanding at the end of our period, knowing that some unknown portion of these outstanding loans, including the soft-currency loans, will not be repaid. We cannot now estimate the amount that will be repaid, nor when, nor the additional value of the foreign aid given through these credits by charging rather modest rates of interest on the loans. When the losses on these loans are finally determined, ten, twenty, or more years hence, such losses should be prorated over our period and added to our estimates of public foreign philanthropy as additional "grants" for civilian aid.

In Table 9-4 the alternate system of accounting has been pursued. The net amounts of nonmilitary grants from column 4 of Table 9-3 are repeated as the first column of Table 9-4. These are what we estimate as public philanthropy. Table 9-4 presents a type of accounting for public foreign philanthropy in which all loans or credits are eliminated entirely from the accounts. As noted earlier, it is our intention to avoid an overstatement of the amount of philanthropy where there is some basic question as to the application of our broad definition or the applicable data—in this instance, the reduction of the total is due to our inability to forecast loan repayments. Thus the grand total of public foreign philanthropy for the entire period becomes only $53,006 million as compared with the $63,279 million shown as a grand total for net civilian foreign aid in Table 9-3. It seems wiser to clearly understate the amount of public foreign philanthropy rather than to risk overstating it because of the vagaries of federal government accounts, the problem of predicting the repayments on loans, and wide differences in attitude toward foreign aid in general. In effect, we assume that every dollar of all loans outstanding will be repaid. But it should be noted again that even if they are repaid in full, the absence of any estimate in this compilation of the real value of bargain rates of interest is also a factor in understating the amount of public foreign philanthropy during the nineteen-year period.

This alternate system of accounting also reduces the proportion of GNP being considered here as civilian foreign aid from 1.09 per cent for the entire period to 0.92 per cent; and to 2.07 per cent, 1.36 per cent, 0.47 per cent for the three subperiods. These are our *final* estimates for public foreign philanthropy.

Table 9-4

Public Foreign Philanthropy, 1940-59

| Year | Net Public Philanthropy | |
	Million Dollars (1)	Per Cent of GNP (2)
Fiscal 1941-45[a]	17,567	2.065
7/1/45−1946	4,170	1.324
1947	1,887	0.805
1948	3,863	1.489
1949	4,983	1.931
1950	3,505	1.232
7/1/45−12/31/50[a]	18,410	1.362
1951	3,040	0.924
1952	1,980	0.571
1953	1,845	0.505
1954	1,662	0.458
1955	1,904	0.479
1956	1,733	0.413
1957	1,616	0.365
1958	1,616	0.364
1959	1,633	0.338
1951-1959	17,029	0.474
7/1/45- 1959[a]	35,439	0.717
7/10/40-1959[a]	53,006	0.915

Note: Detail may not add to total because of rounding.

Source: Column 1 from column 4, Table 9-3. The percentages in column 2 are below those of column 16 in Table 9-3 because of the elimination of credits.

[a]See note a, Table 2-1.

THE VALUE OF CIVILIAN FOREIGN AID

Even these scaled-down totals for civilian foreign aid may be considered too large by those who claim that we, as a nation, have received an overriding *quid pro quo* for this money which we have given away. In the sense that Herbert Hoover spoke of the humanitarian gains from foreign aid in saving millions of people from starvation, our national culture and our national conscience have received some kind of *quid pro quo*. Against this type of consideration, however, there are other matters that would bear investigating if one were to attempt such a broad evaluation of foreign aid. How reliable is the gain in friendship for Uncle Sam? And when historical perspective on the last two decades of our period is clearer, there may also be doubt in the minds of many humanitarians that the pursuit of some of our objectives, although each was a worthy goal in itself, has, on balance, aided the peoples of the world. The population explosion which is considered such a great problem today, particularly in Asia and South America, has undoubtedly been augmented by our foreign aid both of the type considered in this chapter as public foreign philanthropy and in some forms of private philanthropy. These efforts have promoted public health measures throughout the world, which reduced the death rates; less has gone into trying to produce a new demographic balance in the direction of lowering the birth rates.

But these and similar questions about public policy in relation to foreign aid are largely outside the scope of this study. Suffice it to say, the final evaluation of the billions of dollars spent on civilian foreign aid in terms of *quid pro quo* can scarcely be made at the present time.

A reference to an alternate treatment, considered but rejected, may be helpful to those who are not in agreement with our concept of philanthropy or of public foreign philanthropy. This suggestion was to exclude both military and civilian aid during World War II, but include both military and civilian aid since 1945. The basic argument advanced by a colleague was that during World War II, a "total war," the distinctions between military and civilian aid were rather arbitrary and that peacetime military aid relieves the civilian budget of the recipient country. (Another variant of this chronological separation was to exclude also military aid since 1945.) However, providing for food, clothing, shelter, and sanitation, to mention a few worthy objectives, has been considered a philanthropic activity for many decades before our period of study, and we felt we could not depart from this view.

DIRECTOR'S COMMENT—Willard L. Thorp

With respect to this quadrant, Dickinson suggests a number of uncertainties in his discussion. For the war years, 1940–45, he decided to include as philanthropy the categories clearly civilian within the transfers under lend-lease. One can question their inclusion on the grounds that lend-lease shipments were the result of intergovernment negotiations allocating functions and resources. In fact, the European allies shifted capacity to the producing of military goods on the understanding that the United States would take over increased provision of civilian goods. In a real sense, it was a pooling of resources to win the war. One can question a little less strongly the inclusion of civilian supplies distributed by the military forces. As occupation forces, they were obligated by the Geneva Convention to do their best to prevent disease and unrest in former enemy territory, and these expenditures were so justified before Congress. Neither of these cases can be said to have stemmed from generosity. If one deducts them, it would reduce the $53 billion total attributed to this quadrant by $22.75 billion, of which $17.5 billion was in the 1940–45 period and $5.25 billion in the years immediately following.

On the other hand, it can be argued that certain other items should be added. The balance-of-payments entry, "Government pensions and other transfers," is not included and became significant after 1945. By the fifties, Veterans Administration payments were about $80 million per year while OASI payments were increasing rapidly. For the period 1945–59, this item was probably about $1.5 billion.

Another item which could well have been included is that of loans payable in local currency less any amounts planned for U.S. uses. These have usually been related to food aid and are called "grant-like contributions" and lumped with grants by the Development Assistance Committee in its tabulations. Such loans, totaling $2.46 billion, all fall in the period 1953–59.

The largest item not included received Dickinson's approval but was ruled out as not possible to calculate, namely, the grant element in loans made on concessionary terms. Since 1959, a number of estimates have been made by the method of calculating the discounted present value of the future payments. This can be done by comparison with the costs of money to the government, in which case the grant element has been estimated at about 20 per cent for the United States. The more usual procedure is to compare the concessionary rates with the cost to the economy, i.e., the estimated net return on capital. In the latter case, the grant element is about 60 per cent of the loans for the years for which it has been calculated. Since the total in the economic loan category since 1940 is given by Dickinson as $17 billion, the grant element would thus be about $10 billion.

Finally, Dickinson uses a net figure, considering the American economy as a single entity. However, it does not operate that way. Congressional and executive action are in terms of gross flows and they are the better measure of American intentions. If gross were used instead of net, the total would be increased by about $1.6 billion.

These various suggested modifications would reduce the over-all total for the period in this quadrant by about $7 billion. Since the reductions are all related to World War II and the additions cover the entire period, the annual figures since 1947 would all be higher.

10 Conclusions:
The Comprehensive Estimates
of Philanthropic Giving

As has been stated repeatedly, economists who investigate philanthropy are faced with the obvious fact that it does not involve buying and selling; it is not a marketplace operation. Fixing the boundaries of economic activities covered by the term has been among the most difficult parts of this investigation. Hence, in evaluating the final estimates, attention should again be called to some of the problems of definition and concepts which have plagued the author. Throughout this volume, however, there has been an attempt to arrange the data so that critics who regard a particular economic activity as not falling within the domain of philanthropy would have little trouble removing the item by merely striking out a whole column of figures.

Before stating the conclusions, the concept of philanthropy should be briefly restated. My concept is: Giving away money (or its equivalent) to persons outside the family and to institutions without a definite or immediate *quid pro quo* for purposes traditionally considered philanthropic.

In the most general terms the conclusion of this study is that 5.1 per cent of GNP in 1929 was devoted to purposes falling within the concept of philanthropy used in this study—1.8 per cent for private domestic

Table 10-1

Philanthropic Giving, Quadrant Totals, 1929-59
(millions of dollars)

Year	Private Domestic (1)	Private Foreign (2)	Public Domestic (3)	Public Foreign (4)	All Public (3)+(4) (5)	Total Philanthropy (6)
1929	1,878	343	3,112		3,112	5,333
1930	1,817	306	3,167		3,167	5,290
1931	1,590	279	3,333		3,333	5,202
1932	1,498	217	3,580		3,580	5,295
1933	1,327	191	3,865		3,865	5,383
1934	1,559	162	4,436		4,436	6,157
1935	1,599	162	4,897		4,897	6,658
1936	1,865	176	3,897		3,897	5,938
1937	2,019	175	4,338		4,338	6,532
1938	2,012	153	4,957		4,957	7,122
1939	2,245	151	5,389		5,389	7,785
1940	2,316	178	5,535			9,786[a]
1941	2,755	179	5,667			12,114[a]
1942	3,434	123	5,720	17,567[a]	46,340[a]	12,790[a]
1943	4,110	249	5,775			13,647[a]
1944	4,339	357	6,076			14,285[a]

1945	4,570	473	8,346	4,170[b]	25,289[b]	16,536[a][b]
1946	4,788	650	12,773	1,887	17,248	20,991[b]
1947	5,527	669	15,361	3,863	20,463	23,444
1948	6,114	683	16,600	4,983	23,432	27,260
1949	6,313	521	18,449			30,266
1950	7,125	444	19,005	3,505	22,510	30,079
1951	8,360	386	18,928	3,040	21,968	30,714
1952	9,156	417	19,742	1,980	21,722	31,295
1953	10,029	476	21,409	1,845	23,254	33,759
1954	10,219	486	23,993	1,662	25,655	36,360
1955	11,332	444	26,432	1,904	28,336	40,112
1956	12,200	503	29,352	1,733	31,084	43,788
1957	12,962	535	33,967	1,616	35,583	49,080
1958	13,498	525	38,821	1,616	40,437	54,460
1959	14,367	563	42,221	1,633	43,854	58,784
1929-59[c]	172,923	11,176	419,143	53,006[d]	472,149	656,248

Notes to Table 10-1

Note: Detail may not add to total because of rounding.

[a]Total for fiscal 1941-45. Data were not available to break down this five-year total. In order to estimate separate calendar-year figures for inclusion in column 5, the fiscal 1941-45 total was arbitrarily broken down as follows: 1940, 1,757; 1941, 3,513; 1942, 3,513; 1943, 3,513; 1945, 1,757.

[b]Total for mid-1945 through 1946; arbitrary breakdown for inclusion in column 5: 1945, 1,390; 1946, 2,780.

[c]See note a, Table 2-1.

[d]Total for mid-1940 through 1959. GNP over this period, the denominator of the ratio in Table 10-2, equaled $5,790 billion.

Source: Columns 1 and 2: Table 2-1; column 3: Table 5-3; column 4: Table 9-4. Over 10 per cent of the figures in this table involve estimation, interpolation, or extrapolation (see earlier chapters).

plus 0.3 per cent for private foreign plus 3.0 per cent for public domestic, but, of course, none for public foreign, as this form of aid was negligible between the two world wars. The percentage for all types combined rose rapidly to 9.6 in 1933 (when GNP was low), declined to 6.8 in 1944, and did not exceed 9.6 until 1946. The peak percentage was 12.3 in 1958. Stated briefly, the percentage had risen from the 5 per cent figure for 1929 quickly to 10 per cent during the depression, then irregularly to 12 per cent in 1959—the end of our period.

The amounts in millions of dollars and percentages of GNP for each of the quadrants, and for all quadrants combined are set forth in Tables 10-1 and 10-2.

The second over-all conclusion is that the public sector accounted for most of the increase from 5 to 12 per cent of GNP between 1929 and 1959. The private sector, which was less than the public sector in every year—even in 1929—increased from 2.1 to 3.1 per cent. The public sector increased from 3.0 to 9.1 per cent of GNP.

There has been no attempt to develop diagrams or deflate the figures and establish trend lines in this study. The basic reasons for these omissions lie in the data themselves. There is no really adequate information on the changes in prices associated with expenditures on philanthropic activities, though the Consumer Price Index or GNP deflater could be used for some purposes. But deflation is not essential in the present case because we place our emphasis on percentages of GNP rather than on the millions of dollars expended. In the second place, not all of these philanthropic activities existed throughout the entire thirty-year period;

for example, the foreign aid between World War I and World War II was so small that no attempt was made to record it.

It is hoped that the tables themselves—in dollars and, particularly, percentages of GNP—and the descriptive discussions of the data will be sufficient to set forth the procedures and the findings of this study.

Finally, in an attempt to make these final conclusions brief enough to silhouette the major findings, the author has omitted details. The reader should refer to the numerous tables in earlier chapters for data on particular types and kinds of philanthropy. The author is very much aware of the brevity of his conclusions.

This volume covers a part of the social history of the American people during three decades when there were many changes, particularly the increasing role of the public sector in philanthropic activities as defined herein. It seems to the author that the basic finding of this study is this: During these three decades the American people have become more generous. Moreover, in our type of pluralistic economy, this greatly increased generosity has been manifested very largely in what I have designated as public philanthropy. But private philanthropy has also increased. The mainspring of this expanding generosity remains the basic philanthropic attitudes of our people, revealed before 1929 and revealed even today in the impressive volume of private philanthropy.

Table 10-2

Philanthropic Giving, Totals, as Percentage of Gross National Product, 1929-59

Year	Private Domestic (1)	Private Foreign (2)	Public Domestic (3)	Public Foreign (4)	All Public (3)+(4) (5)	Total Philanthropy (6)
1929	1.798	0.328	2.980		2.980	5.106
1930	1.994	0.336	3.476		3.476	5.806
1931	2.085	0.366	4.370		4.370	6.820
1932	2.562	0.371	6.123		6.123	9.057
1933	2.371	0.341	6.906		6.906	9.619
1934	2.399	0.249	6.827		6.827	9.476
1935	2.205	0.223	6.754		6.754	9.183
1936	2.254	0.213	4.710		4.710	7.176
1937	2.224	0.193	4.779		4.779	7.195
1938	2.361	0.180	5.816		5.816	8.357
1939	2.464	0.166	5.916		5.916	8.545
1940	2.302	0.177	5.501			9.726[a]
1941	2.190	0.142	4.504			9.628[a]
1942	2.158	0.077	3.594			8.037[a]
1943	2.135	0.129	3.000	2.065[a]	21.538[a]	7.089[a]
1944	2.052	0.169	2.874			6.758[a]

Year						
1945	2.140	0.221	3.908 ⎫	1.324[b]	11.295[b]	7.743[a][b] ⎫
1946	2.273	0.309	6.063 ⎬	.805	7.361	9.964[b] ⎬
1947	2.359	0.286	6.556	1.489	7.888	10.006
1948	2.357	0.263	6.399	1.931	9.080	10.508
1949	2.446	0.202	7.149			11.729
1950	2.504	0.156	6.678	1.232	7.910	10.569
1951	2.541	0.117	5.754	.924	6.678	9.336
1952	2.639	0.120	5.689	.571	6.260	9.018
1953	2.745	0.130	5.859	.505	6.364	9.239
1954	2.814	0.134	6.608	.458	7.066	10.013
1955	2.851	0.112	6.650	.479	7.129	10.092
1956	2.910	0.120	7.002	.413	7.415	10.446
1957	2.927	0.121	7.671	.365	8.036	11.085
1958	3.036	0.118	8.733	.364	9.097	12.251
1959	2.976	0.117	8.747	.338	9.085	12.178
1929-59[c]	2.575	0.166	6.242	.915[d]	7.031	9.773

See Table 10-1 for Source and Notes.

Index

76 D